Swiss Foreign Policy, 1945–2002

Swiss Foreign Policy, 1945–2002

Jürg Martin Gabriel
Professor of Political Science
Swiss Federal Institute of Technology
Zurich

and

Thomas Fischer
Research Assistant
Swiss Federal Institute of Technology
Zurich

palgrave
macmillan

First published 2003 by
PALGRAVE MACMILLAN
Houndmills, Basingstoke, Hampshire RG21 6XS and
175 Fifth Avenue, New York, N.Y. 10010
Companies and representatives throughout the world

PALGRAVE MACMILLAN is the global academic imprint of the Palgrave Macmillan division of St. Martin's Press, LLC and of Palgrave Macmillan Ltd. Macmillan® is a registered trademark in the United States, United Kingdom and other countries. Palgrave is a registered trademark in the European Union and other countries.

ISBN 1–4039–1275–0

This book is printed on paper suitable for recycling and made from fully managed and sustained forest sources.

A catalogue record for this book is available from the British Library.

Library of Congress Cataloging-in-Publication Data
Swiss foreign policy, 1945–2002 / Jürg Martin Gabriel & Thomas Fischer [editors].
p. cm.
Includes bibliographical references and index.
ISBN 1–4039–1275–0 (cloth)
1. Switzerland—Foreign relations—1945– 2. Internal security—Switzerland—History—20th century. 3. Human rights—Switzerland—History—20th century.
4. Neutrality—Switzerland—History—20th century. 5. Switzerland—Foreign economic relations. I. Gabriel, Jürg Martin, 1940– II. Fischer, Thomas, 1971–

DQ75.S85 2003
327.494'09'045—dc21

2003045182

10 9 8 7 6 5 4 3 2 1
12 11 10 09 08 07 06 05 04 03

Printed and bound in Great Britain by
Antony Rowe Ltd, Chippenham and Eastbourne

Contents

List of Tables

Foreword

Under the influence of ever more rapid change in its strategic environment, the foreign policy of neutral Switzerland has undergone some remarkable adaptations since the collapse of the Berlin Wall. This book succeeds in explaining, for the first time to English speaking readers, the mindset of Swiss policy makers and public opinion in the aftermath of the Second World War, their further evolution under the political constraints of the Cold War, which did not hinder Switzerland's integration into a rapidly globalising world economy, and, finally, the gradual shift towards a policy of 'security through co-operation'. The policy, without any formal departure from neutrality, consisted of small and pragmatic steps opening Switzerland to the new realities of an increasingly interdependent world. While the individual steps did not seem spectacular at the time, they nevertheless added up to a major re-orientation of Swiss foreign policy.

It is the special merit of the eight authors contributing to this volume that they make this development transparent and understandable to a foreign public mostly unaware of the realities of Swiss referendum democracy, its institutions and practices. The value added is considerable, as most past publications in English concentrated on the time before the end of the Second World War. In this study, however, the Cold War period is covered fully, thereby showing the background against which to set off the changes of the 1990s.

The subjects of the contributions are well chosen, as each stands for a traditional field of activity or a classical feature of Swiss foreign policy. They all relate to the same central theme of Switzerland's coming to terms with the end of the Cold War: the (in)adequacy of maintaining an already high profile in international economic, developmental and legal affairs, whilst remaining aloof from political co-operation proper in a peacefully uniting Europe and a functioning world-wide collective security system.

It is to be hoped that Swiss readers will also take note of this work because it raises pertinent questions about unresolved issues that need further public debate and call for political decisions. The question of autonomy versus integration is of particular importance, since it dominates Swiss relations with the outside world.

Brussels, January 2003

ANTON THALMANN
Ambassador of Switzerland to Belgium
and Head of the Swiss Mission to NATO

Preface

There are only a few studies on Swiss foreign policy available in English, and there is no publication at all providing a general overview of the subject. This book represents an attempt to fill this void, at least in part.

Anyone familiar with the subject knows that it is impossible to examine all the topics in one volume; a selection has to be made. We opted to cover mainly, but not exclusively, those issues that have been researched by present or former members of the Center for International Studies at the Swiss Federal Institute of Technology Zurich (ETH). We also decided to give the study a historical as well as a thematic perspective. The book, by covering the period since 1945, argues that since the end of the Cold War, Swiss foreign policy has been undergoing a slow but fundamental change. Given the extraordinary stability of Swiss politics, this change – although for many of us *too* slow – is of historical proportions.

Obviously, the book omits a number of topics. They include such important issues as development assistance, migration, international finance and a number of regional matters relating mainly to the changes taking place in Europe. The primary focus of this volume is on the global level. European integration is the most pressing issue facing the Swiss, but it comprises a vast range of questions that need to be handled in a separate volume.

Our gratitude goes to all the contributors and also to the Swiss Federal Institute of Technology Zurich (ETH), whose generous financial contribution made the publication of this study possible. Special thanks go to Ellen Russon on Cape Cod in Massachusetts. She not only handled the proofreading of the final manuscript, but also did a solid job translating some of the articles from German into English.

Zurich, January 2003

Jürg Martin Gabriel
Thomas Fischer

Notes on Contributors

Jon A. Fanzun is a research assistant at the Center for International Studies (CIS), Swiss Federal Institute of Technology, Zurich and a PhD candidate at the University of St Gallen, Switzerland. He is co-author of *Die Schweiz und die Welt: Aussen- und sicherheitspolitische Beiträge der Schweiz zu Frieden, Sicherheit und Stabilität, 1945–2000* (2000), a monograph on Swiss foreign and security policy since 1945. His dissertation is on Swiss human rights policy.

Thomas Fischer is a research assistant at the Center for International Studies (CIS), Swiss Federal Institute of Technology, Zurich and holds a PhD in Political Science from the University of Zurich, Switzerland. His doctoral thesis is on the Swiss UN- and CSCE-policy during the 1970s and 80s. He has published several articles on Swiss foreign policy in the Cold War, with special reference to the topic of good offices.

Jürg Martin Gabriel is Professor of Political Science at the Swiss Federal Institute of Technology, Zurich. At present he is serving as Director of the Mediterranean Academy of Diplomatic Studies at the University of Malta. Jürg Martin Gabriel has published several books including *Worldviews and Theories of International Relations* (1994) and *The American Conception of Neutrality After 1941* (2002).

Hans-Peter Gasser is a former delegate and a former senior legal advisor with the International Committee of the Red Cross (ICRC), Geneva. He has published extensively on general and legal issues related to international humanitarian law and the activities of the ICRC. He is now retired but he continues to lecture and publish on topics of humanitarian concern.

Andrea E. Heinzer works for the export control policy and sanctions division of the Swiss ministry of economics, where she is responsible for the regimes against biological and chemical weapons. Before joining federal administration she was a research assistant at the Center for International Studies (CIS), Swiss Federal Institute of Technology, Zurich where she worked on a research project about Swiss Arms Control and Disarmament Policy. She is a PhD candidate at the University of Zurich, Switzerland.

Daniel Möckli is a research assistant at the Center for Security Studies, Swiss Federal Institute of Technology, Zurich and a PhD candidate at the Department of Political Science, University of Zurich, Switzerland. He is the author of *Neutralität, Solidarität, Sonderfall* (2000), a monograph on the Swiss foreign policy concept of the post-War era. He has published articles on Swiss relations with the UN and the European Union as well as on post-Cold War international security issues. In his dissertation he analyses the origins of European Political Cooperation between 1967 and 1974.

Richard Senti is Professor Emeritus of the Center for Economic Research at the Swiss Federal Institute of Technology, Zurich. He is the author of *WTO, System und Funktionsweise der Welthandelsordnung* (2000), *Das Abkommen Schweiz-EG* in the Handbook 'Bilaterale Verträge Schweiz-EG' (2002) and *Der Schweizer Binnenmarkt* in '10 Jahre EU-Binnenmarkt' (2002).

Andreas Wenger is Professor of International and Swiss Security Policy and Director of the Center for Security Studies at the Swiss Federal Institute of Technology, Zurich. He has published numerous articles on Swiss security policy and is co-author of *Schweizer Sicherheitspolitik seit 1945* (2001) and co-editor of the annual *Bulletin zur schweizerischen Sicherheitspolitik* and of the annual *Sicherheit: Aussen-, sicherheits- und verteidigungspolitische Meinungsbildung im Trend.*

List of Abbreviations

ABB	Asea Brown Boveri
AUNS	Action for an Independent and Neutral Switzerland
BBl	Official Bulletin of the Swiss Government
BTWC	Convention on the Prohibition of the Development, Production and Stockpiling of Bacteriological and Toxin Weapons and on their Destruction
BWC	Biological Weapons Convention
CD	Geneva Conference on Disarmament
CDE	Conference on Confidence- and Security-Building Measures and Disarmament in Europe
CFE	Treaty on Conventional Armed Forces in Europe
Cocom	Coordinating Committee for Multilateral Export Controls
CoE	Council of Europe
CSBMs	Negotiations on Confidence- and Security-Building Measures
CSCE	Conference on Security and Cooperation in Europe
CTBT	Comprehensive Test Ban Treaty
CWC	Chemical Weapons Convention
EAC	East African Community
ECHR	European Convention on Human Rights
EDA	Federal Department of Foreign Affairs, FDFA (formerly Department of Political Affairs, EPD)
EEA	European Economic Area
EEC	European Economic Community
EFTA	European Free Trade Area
ELN	Ejército de Liberación Nacional
ERG	Export Risk Guarantee
ESDP	European Security and Defense Policy
ETH	Swiss Federal Institute of Technology Zurich
EU	European Union
FARC	Fuerzas Armadas Revolucionarias de Colombia
FDFA	Federal Department of Foreign Affairs
FDoD	Federal Department of Defense, Civil Protection and Sports
FISSBAN	Fissile Material Production Ban
FLN	Algerian National Liberation Front
FSC	Forum for Security Cooperation
GATS	General Agreement on Trade in Services
GATT	General Agreement on Tariffs and Trades
GDP	Gross Domestic Product
GSP	Generalized System of Preferences

IAEA	International Atomic Energy Agency
ICC	International Criminal Court
ICRC	International Committee of the Red Cross
INF	Intermediate Range Nuclear Forces
LTBT	Limited Test Ban Treaty
MINURSO	Mission des Nations Unies pour le référendum au Sahara occidental
MTCR	Missile Technology Control Regime
N+N	Neutral and Non-aligned States
NATO	North Atlantic Treaty Organization
NEAT	Swiss Network of North–South Railroad Tunnels
NGO	Non-governmental organisation
NNSC	Neutral Nations Supervisory Commission
NNRC	Neutral Nations Repatriation Commission
NPT	Nuclear Non-Proliferation Treaty
NSG	Nuclear Suppliers Group
NZZ	Neue Zürcher Zeitung
OECD	Organisation of Economic Cooperation and Development
OEEC	Organisation of European Economic Cooperation
ONUC	Opérations des Nations Unies au Congo
OPBW	Organization for the Prohibition of Biological Weapons
OPCW	Organization for the Prohibition of Chemical Weapons
OSCE	Organisation on Security and Cooperation in Europe
OSEC	Swiss Office for Trade Promotion
OSGA	Office of the UN Secretary-General in Afghanistan
PfP	Partnership for Peace
POW	Prisoner of war
SALT	Strategic Arms Limitation Talks
Seco	State Secretariat for Economic Affairs
SFr.	Swiss francs
SPLA	Sudan People's Liberation Army
SPP	Swiss People's Party
START	Strategic Arms Reduction Talks
UN	United Nations
UNCTAD	United Nations Conference on Trade and Development
UNEF	United Nations Emergency Force for the Middle East
UNHCR	United Nations High Commissioner for Refugees
UNIMOG	United Nations Observer Mission in Georgia
UNSCOM	United Nations Special Commission on Iraq
UNTAG	United Nations Transition Assistance Group to Namibia
VBS	Federal Department of Defence, Civil Protection and Sports, FDoD (formerly Military Department, EMD)
WEOG	Western European and Other States Group
WHO	World Health Organization
WTO	World Trade Organization

1

The Price of Political Uniqueness: Swiss Foreign Policy in a Changing World

Jürg Martin Gabriel

Introduction

On 3 March 2002, the Swiss voted in favour of joining the United Nations. Less than a year earlier, on 10 June 2001, they had approved a government bill permitting regular units of the Swiss Armed Forces to participate in operations abroad. Although in both cases the voting results were extremely narrow, they are an indication of change. Switzerland is overcoming its traditional reluctance to participate actively in international politics and to join the necessary organisations.[1] However, there is still a long way to go. Switzerland is not a member of the European Union, and neither is it part of the European Economic Area (EEA), the Union's antechamber. Needless to say, the country is not a member of the North Atlantic Treaty Organization (NATO), although it has begun to participate in a number of activities related to NATO's Partnership for Peace (PfP). As is well known, Switzerland is hesitant to join certain international organisations.[2]

In fact, Switzerland suffers from an interesting *dualism*: Economically, scientifically and culturally the country is extremely *interdependent* internationally, while at the same time it places extraordinary emphasis on maintaining its *independence*. The dualism can also be seen as a case of *asymmetry*: When it comes to promoting the 'low politics' of well being, the Swiss are internationalist; when matters of 'high politics' or security are involved, their preferences are national.[3] Put in more modern terms, the Swiss are excellent globalisers and free traders in some areas, but perfect isolationists and protectionists in others.[4] This explains why they have joined most of the United Nations' specialised organisations, including the World Trade Organization (WTO) and the Bretton Woods Institutions (International Monetary Fund and World Bank), long before becoming a full UN member. It must be added, however, that they joined these economic organisations much later than comparable countries.

Up to a point, contradictions like these are part of any country's foreign policy, but in the case of Switzerland they are extreme. This is a puzzle that needs explaining. I will try to shed some light on the matter by isolating a set of *political institutions* that amount to what is often called a *Sonderfall*, a term connoting 'political uniqueness'. It is a very useful concept, because the Swiss are convinced that their domestic and foreign politics are markedly different from those of other countries.[5]

It is the purpose of this introductory chapter to characterise 'political uniqueness' and to trace its origins, its development and changing nature. In so doing, it also introduces the eight contributions contained in this book. As the reader will discover, uniqueness is a theme that all the contributors touch upon. It surfaces in the areas of national defence, international trade and integration, but it also affects arms control, human rights and the provision of good offices. Uniqueness even played a part in the recent controversy over the restitution of Jewish assets.

The essay has three main parts. It begins with *domestic politics*, because that is where uniqueness is most clearly visible. Switzerland is a pluralistic country with a political system that is not only strongly federalist in nature, but exhibits a number of special features, some of which have foreign policy ramifications. The second part of the article will focus on the main Swiss *foreign policy* components – sovereignty and neutrality. The latter concept is especially important in explaining the feeling of uniqueness and, as I will point out, neutrality has a number of ramifications that are directly tied to domestic politics. In fact, it is the tight link between domestic and foreign politics that to a large extent explains the difficulty Switzerland exhibits in adjusting to change in the international arena.[6]

In the third part, I want to show how much the *international setting* has changed. Switzerland was born into the classical European balance of power system. This system self-destructed in two world wars and, under American leadership, was reorganised after 1945. The 'American century', as some have called it, was characterised by a combination of *multilateralism* and *hegemony*. Most Western Europeans accommodated to the emerging pattern and played by the new rules. Switzerland was different. It had difficulty with both the multilateralist and the hegemonic aspects of the new system and would have preferred to play by the old rules. In the long run, that proved to be impossible, and the country, however reluctant, had to adjust.

The essay concludes with remarks about the situation today and the developments to be expected in the near future. As indicated at the outset, a turn of sorts has been achieved, but the really big hurdles are still ahead – and they lie in Europe. NATO has survived the demise of the Soviet Empire; it proved useful in getting the wars in the Balkans under control and is expanding eastward. The European Union, too, is integrating rather than disintegrating. Many Swiss expected the opposite to occur, and some saw a bright future for neutrality.[7] They were proven wrong, but such scepticism has a price.

As I will point out, non-membership in the Union is costly. Some of the costs are economic and financial, but most of them are more directly political. By not participating in European decisions that affect our future, the credibility of Swiss sovereignty and of its political institutions is suffering.

1.1 Domestic 'uniqueness'

Politically, culturally and religiously Switzerland is highly *heterogeneous*. No one religion, language, or ethnic affinity holds the country together.[8] In that sense Switzerland is typical of Europe as a whole and is a miniature version of the European Union. But Switzerland was never a typical European *nation*, and so it was largely immune to nationalism of the cruder sort. In 1848 it became a federation of 25 (later 26)[9] cantons, many of which had a history of internal division. The Canton of Grisons, to name just one example, was itself a federated republic (*Frei Rätien*) before it joined the Confederation, and to this day it is made up of Catholics and Protestants speaking German, Italian and Romanish. There is much that separates and divides the Swiss people. What unites them is a strong will towards self-governance along republican and democratic lines. Switzerland is what in German is called a *Willensnation*.

The history of Swiss unity – like that of European unity – is one of overcoming divisions, fragility and internal conflict.[10] Even when it entered the First World War, the country was divided. The German Swiss sympathised with the Kaiser and the French Swiss with the Associated Powers. Joining one of the two sides would have led to internal disruption. The country was split along social lines as well. In 1918 Switzerland witnessed its only general strike, organised by the Social Democrats in 1918 and put down ruthlessly by federal troops. It was not until the advent of German fascism that the country began to truly unify. The contrast was considerable: while the First World War saw a divided nation, the Second World War brought unprecedented unity.[11]

In retrospect, this new sense of unity turned out to be extremely important. It had a profound impact on the Swiss mentality as well as on political institutions, and it was accompanied by a feeling of success. In contrast to their neighbours, Switzerland had miraculously survived a terrible inferno. The Swiss saw this as an expression of their own efforts and virtues.[12] For them the miracle was a consequence of their uniqueness, of a set of specific political institutions on the inside and the practice of armed neutrality towards the outside.

Swiss political institutions are both ancient and modern. In part they date back to medieval times, and, since Switzerland never experienced absolutism and centralisation, they have survived to this day. For the same reason Swiss domestic politics are strongly local. However, Switzerland is also a modern polity with institutions established in 1848. At that time, and for many years thereafter, it was the only working democracy on the European continent. While the revolutions of 1848 failed in most other countries, in Switzerland the renewal succeeded. Ever since, the country has for many of its citizens been a model republic, blending the traditional with the modern.[13] The change in 1848 was so important, because it brought the drafting of a modern constitution, a strong emphasis on the rule of law, and the introduction of economic liberalism. Let us look at the results more closely.[14]

1.1.1 Federalism, collegiality and concordance

Given the heterogeneity of the country, it is no surprise that *federalism* is highly developed in Switzerland. Although the cantons abandoned some of their sovereignty in 1848, the federal government was consciously kept weak. In the meantime there has been a trend towards centralisation, but the cantons still guard their autonomy jealously. Federalism is also reflected in the bicameral shape of the national *legislature*, which is roughly a copy of the American system. In order to accommodate the cantons, there is not merely a chamber representing the people numerically (the 'National Council'), but also a 'Council of States' in which each full canton has equal weight.[15]

The shape of the *executive*, however, is not inspired by the American model. There is no publicly elected president. In fact there is no real president at all, since the executive consists of seven members (Federal Council) elected by the two chambers meeting jointly.[16] The shape of the Federal Council is truly one of a kind. Elected for four years, and in fact for life, its seven members have equal rights. They are meant to speak with one voice and to practice *collegiality*. The council's chairmanship (called President of the Confederation) rotates annually among the seven. The system precludes the emergence of a leading figure. It actually discourages prominence by any one leader and punishes those who try. Switzerland has ministers, but no Prime Minister. They are meant to govern jointly and in a collegial spirit, but there are times when the executive is divided and decision-making is slow.[17]

Since the members of the executive are not elected publicly, there are no persons 'running' for office on a given foreign policy platform. In contrast to the United States, Great Britain, Germany or France, there are no national elections with personalities linked to specific foreign policy goals. In the public eye, the government's main function is to administer the country and not to pull it in one direction or the other. That is the job of the people. This has serious foreign policy implications.

The executive is extremely stable, but stability must not be equated with strength. Unlike the British Cabinet, the Federal Council has no automatic majority in parliament and has to fight for each bill in two separate chambers, which are dominated by a multitude of parties.[18]

Federalism, collegiality and the dual legislature are formal institutions set out in the constitution, but there are informal arrangements as well. The most important is *concordance*, which refers to the distribution of chairs among the seven members of the government. After 1848 it was the Liberals that occupied all seats for almost half a century. As other political parties began to form on the right and on the left, and as the Liberals themselves turned more conservative, the seven seats were shared with other parties proportional to their parliamentary strength. Today the government includes two Liberals, two Social Democrats, two Christian Democrats and one member of the People's Party. Of course, the linguistic minorities are also accommodated.[19]

The bicameral legislature and collegiality, tied to concordance, emphasise unity in diversity and have certainly succeeded in integrating the country. Almost everyone, so it seems, is represented in the government, and there is no real opposition. In fact, the Swiss dislike the idea of an organised opposition and of alternating governments. They prefer low-key politics to boisterous election campaigns and to divisions typical of other democracies. While it is entertaining to watch televised debates of the German Bundestag or the French National Assembly, the brilliance of confrontations does not accord with Swiss collegiality, concordance and soberness.

1.1.2 Direct democracy and smallness

Nonetheless, there are moments of political tension. They occur not when the Swiss elect, but when they *vote*.[20] It is *direct democracy* that divides the public, polarises and is often accompanied by populist rhetoric. Although direct popular participation in politics has ancient roots, the 1848 constitution did not overly emphasise its practice. At the federal level, direct democracy developed largely after 1848, and to this day there are tendencies for more rather than for less public participation. The Swiss vote on all levels and on almost everything through referendums and initiatives. The direct involvement of citizens in political decisions is all-important. In foreign affairs, many public votes have hindered rather than promoted the shaping of progressive policies. Direct democracy is the single most important factor explaining Switzerland's foreign policy dualism.

Another trait of Swiss political culture is *smallness*, or what in German is referred to as *Kleinstaatlichkeit*. The Swiss are extremely aware of being a small polity, and it is something that they like. It is no coincidence that the only Swiss political philosopher of renown is Jean-Jacques Rousseau, the Genevan famous for his advocacy of small, directly ruled republics. Like most Swiss, Rousseau was sceptical of large political units. In many of his publications he depicted the evils of large and centrally governed kingdoms.

The weakness of a small country became particularly glaring when Napoleon occupied Switzerland and turned it into a French satellite. Later the Swiss watched the growth and decline of the Second and Third German Reich, and they also witnessed the expansion and the collapse of the Soviet Empire. To this day many Swiss are convinced that large political entities and *Grossräume* are inherently unstable. From this perspective, the European Union is seen as bound to fail. Although the United States has turned out to be both large and successful, it is its size and power that bother the Swiss at times. As I will show in greater detail later on, in Switzerland it is easy to mobilise sentiments against the American superpower.[21]

The combination of these institutions – of federalism, collegiality, condordance, direct democracy and smallness – constitute a political system that the Swiss identify with strongly, consider to be unique and want to preserve. The Swiss are reluctant to change these institutions, and they are extremely sensitive when they come under foreign pressure to do so. Political change 'imposed' from abroad is generally resisted, irrespective of its origin. The Swiss are ready to defend their 'uniqueness' against authoritarian neighbours, democratic superpowers or international organisations. Actually, foreign policy is largely seen as an instrument useful to defend the Swiss political system against such incursions from abroad.

1.2 Foreign uniqueness

1.2.1 Sovereignty and neutrality

The institutions most commonly associated with Swiss foreign policy are seen to be equally unique as those characterising domestic politics. This holds for the Swiss conception of *sovereignty* and of *neutrality*. Both are central to an understanding of Swiss foreign policy and, in addition, both are tied intimately to domestic institutions. It is necessary, therefore, to look at them more closely. I will emphasise neutrality particularly, not only because it has been the most dominant but also because it is linked to three other factors – to a specific conception of *national defence*, to the notion of a *militia army* and to a belief that Switzerland is particularly suited to offer international *good offices*.

Over the centuries, and especially as a result of fascism, the Swiss have become sensitive about anything that might diminish their *sovereignty*. Instead of seeing sovereignty as an instrument to preserve more basic values, such as individual freedoms, security and economic well-being, there is a tendency to regard it as an end in itself and to equate it with a maximum of political *independence*.[22] Any diminution of sovereignty is seen as prejudicial and as a loss of 'national freedom'. The idea of sharing sovereignty with others, a notion common in today's Europe, is alien to most Swiss. They make no distinction, therefore, between a voluntary and an involuntary transfer of sovereignty.

Neutrality, like sovereignty, is held in equally high esteem. In part this can be explained by domestic politics, since entering into alliances might have torn the country apart. As I mentioned earlier with reference to the First World War, to remain neutral was at times tantamount to preserving the country's unity and its domestic institutions. At such moments direct democracy, federalism, collegiality, concordance, sovereignty and neutrality all became one.

However, neutrality also has an *international* dimension. Seen from this angle the concept is relatively flexible. It is a policy designed for situations when *others* are at war – but once a neutral *itself* is attacked, it is free to join alliances. It is an *instrumental* concept meant to serve a country's security. This conception squares with international law, is in line with the Swiss constitution and is also the official position of the federal government. Unfortunately, it is not the view held by the public at large. Like sovereignty, neutrality is seen by many to be an end in itself. Let us take a closer look at the Swiss neutrality conception.[23]

The international law of neutrality was codified in the Hague Conventions of 1907. When war breaks out among sovereign states, these conventions make it legal for states wishing to stay apart to declare neutrality, a status involving certain rights and duties. Among other things, a neutral has to declare its neutrality publicly, must prevent the misuse of its territory by the warring parties and has the right to carry on free trade with all sides. Because this body of rights and duties can be claimed by any state when war breaks out, it is identified as *occasional* neutrality. For the Swiss this was not enough. It has been their aim to practice *permanent* neutrality. What exactly does this mean?

In 1815, at the Congress of Vienna, Switzerland was recognised as a permanent (perpetual or everlasting) neutral. This meant that Switzerland, in case of war, would not declare neutrality at the last minute. In contrast to other countries, it was ready to transcend occasional neutrality and to declare its abstention from war *in times of peace*. For the Swiss, therefore, neutrality had a *political dimension* preceding the outbreak of war, and a *legal dimension* taking effect with the occurrence of war. It was the political dimension to which the government paid special attention, and it became characteristic of Swiss neutrality. It consisted of a certain number of *voluntary measures* intended to preserve Swiss credibility when war breaks out. Put generally, the country should not enter into any obligation that might jeopardise its abstention from a war. As the Swiss like to say, *neutral politics* have the function of protecting the credibility of *neutral law*.[24]

Over the years the government distinguished a certain number of self-imposed obligations meant to strengthen credibility. Some were *military* in nature, others *economic*: Switzerland would refuse to enter into any military arrangement that could be interpreted as an alliance, and it would not participate in economic sanctions of any kind. Both principles looked good on paper but, as it turned out, were difficult to practice. Let me concentrate on alliances first.

Alliances were an integral part of classical European politics and meant to preserve the balance of power. As the Swiss experienced, the alliance mechanism failed repeatedly during the time of Napoleon, yet the old system was restored at the Congress of Vienna. Based on the act mentioned above, Switzerland declared itself part of the newly recreated balance and, as a permanent neutral, promised not to enter into *preventive alliances*. Once attacked, however, the Swiss were free to choose any ally. In that sense, and in no other, Switzerland's neutrality was recognised internationally. As indicated, it was permanent only until violated.[25]

Based on this arrangement, Swiss decision-makers were faced with the difficult question of determining when an alliance was *reactive* and in accordance with the rules and when it was *preventive* and in violation of the rules. From a military perspective it all depended on the *threat perception*. If the threat to Swiss sovereignty was minor, there was no problem; if the threat were perceived to be grave, however, then caution would dictate the planning of a preventive alliance and the establishing of first (and secret) contacts. The Swiss did just that in two world wars – a highly controversial move, of course.[26]

One cannot blame the government for not publicising its attempts to form preventive alliances. It is less understandable, however, why it never communicated the fact that *once attacked*, Switzerland would enter into an alliance. On the contrary, the idea of permanent neutrality was communicated in such a way as to exclude any type of military co-operation. The language used publicly clashed fundamentally with the actual policy. In private the federal government was ready to practise two types of policies – one being valid *while* neutral, the other *after* neutrality had been abandoned.[27] However, by not discussing openly both the dimensions of Swiss security policy, most Swiss began to think that dying as a neutral was more honourable than surviving as an ally. Small wonder that neutrality was perceived as an end in itself rather than as an instrument. The mistaken perception prevailed during the Second World War, and it was carried into the Cold War.[28]

The communication gap had yet another dimension. When speaking about neutrality the government failed to draw a distinction between *bilateral* and *multilateral* alliances or, more precisely, between classical ad hoc alliances belonging to the balance of power system and permanent alliances as part of collective security. Throughout the twentieth century the impression was maintained that neutrality was incompatible with *any type of alliance*. Today, both of these communication gaps have to be overcome.[29]

Let me turn to *economic sanctions* next. As mentioned earlier, under the Hague Conventions neutrals have the right to trade freely in times of war. During the limited wars of the nineteenth century this right was realistic, but as wars grew total in character – and as economic warfare grew in importance – the practice of neutral free trade became impossible. The idea suffered yet another blow when economic sanctions were made part of the League of Nations and of the United Nations. In the twentieth century, therefore, the Swiss government was confronted with an increasing number of trade restrictions, the origins of which were either abroad or at home.

Given their neutrality conception, the Swiss were especially sensitive to *foreign* restrictions, to those imposed by international organisations or, worse, by large actors such as the United States and the European Union.[30] I will deal with this issue in more detail later on, but it is quite obvious that Swiss sensitivities were particularly acute in the grey zone between economic and military goods. As Andrea Heinzer points out in her essay, the Federal Council has traditionally pursued an extremely cautious policy in the area of export controls involving 'strategic goods'. In today's world this is an important foreign policy area with direct links to arms proliferation, arms control and various international non-proliferation regimes. As Andrea Heinzer demonstrates, the Swiss government has in the past – officially at least – not participated in such efforts. This has changed, but it meant that the government had to alter its conception of neutrality.

1.2.2 Armed neutrality and good offices

As mentioned earlier, a neutral state has the obligation to prevent the warring countries from misusing its territory for the conduct of their military campaigns, be this at sea, on land or in the air. In order to fulfil this duty, a neutral is expected to maintain armed forces adequate for the purpose. However, there is no obligation to maintain a massive military establishment in order to win a war autonomously. Yet, as Andreas Wenger shows in his contribution to this volume, *autonomous* self-defence (or national defence) stands at the core of traditional Swiss foreign and security policy, and it is explicitly equated with *armed neutrality*. Although from a legal perspective the link is wrong, that is not the public perception. For most Swiss, neutrality and autonomous defence are identical. This, too, is a conception cemented during the Second World War.[31]

National defence and armed neutrality are tied to a third concept held dear by the Swiss – to the idea of a *militia army*. Seen historically this is surprising, because for centuries the Swiss had served as professional mercenaries in foreign wars. However, this did not prevent them from raising a militia to fight foreign invaders. As a result Switzerland knows both the traditions, but with the increased emphasis on national sovereignty and on neutrality, professionalism went into oblivion. The militia principle became the corner-stone of the Swiss military system.

The idea of the citizen-in-arms became so completely part of Swiss life that until a few years ago, it was often said that Switzerland did not *possess* but *was* an army.[32] Every male citizen became a soldier, thousands of university graduates were officers, and many prominent politicians were high-ranking commanders. Today this tradition is changing, but during the twentieth century it was another feature of Swiss uniqueness. During the Second World War, the identity of neutrality and of the militia army was (almost) total. Armed neutrality, intimately tied to sovereign independence and the preservation of domestic political institutions, was the core of Swiss political identity.[33]

As an 'island of peace' in the middle of a Europe at war, neutral Switzerland was willing to provide *good offices*. This instrument of diplomacy, as Thomas Fischer's contribution to this volume shows, also became part of Swiss foreign policy. Especially during the Second World War, when many countries broke off diplomatic relations, Switzerland assumed 'protecting mandates' over abandoned embassies and, in case of need, served as a channel of communication among enemies. Furthermore, the city of Geneva became an important site for diplomatic conferences.

The number of protecting mandates held by the Swiss during the Second World War was impressive. It was at that time that in the eyes of the public the country acquired the image of a uniquely qualified provider of good offices. It must be emphasised, however, that such good offices were of a purely *technical* character and excluded mediation. In fact, in all of their history the Swiss have been involved in very few mediation efforts. Some of them failed so badly that the Federal Council became extremely cautious in this regard. Furthermore, the number of protecting mandates has decreased continually.[34]

Protecting mandates are strictly *bilateral*, which fit well with the Swiss preference for quiet diplomacy. The public, preoccupied with the absorbing nature of direct democracy, was happiest when foreign policy did not intrude. It was often said with pride that, in the public mind at least, neutrality stood for the absence of foreign policy. It was thus not surprising that foreign policy was handled by a small group of people in Bern, who had a strong preference for personal and private bilateralism of the classical sort. Multilateralism, especially of the kind practised on Swiss soil in the era of the League, was not to their taste. When it was resumed within the United Nations system, the Swiss were not unhappy to stand aside.

From a Swiss perspective, good offices also have a *humanitarian* dimension. The International Committee of the Red Cross, a wholly Swiss institution, has the function of protecting the military and civilian victims of war.[35] As Hans-Peter Gasser's contribution to this volume shows, the links between the ICRC and the government are multiple and relatively close. ICRC presidents are often former senior officers of the federal government, and Bern finances a portion of the institution's budget.[36] Furthermore, neutrality is one of the ICRC's operating principles, which, in the eyes of many, is additional reason for considering it to be an expression of Swiss 'uniqueness'. However, the intimacy between the ICRC and the federal government has its downside as well. As Jon Fanzun argues in his contribution, the Federal Council has found it useful to use its ICRC support as an excuse for not developing a comprehensive and modern human rights policy.

To sum up, Swiss 'political uniqueness' has an inward and an outward face, and for a long time this formula proved successful. The Swiss political culture managed to integrate the divided people, gave the country internal and external peace and created a valuable framework for scientific, technical and economic modernisation. However, success can also have a blinding effect. The Swiss were slow to realise that their international environment no longer conformed to the standards of the nineteenth century.[37] Of course, they were not alone in this. Politicians like Winston Churchill, Charles de Gaulle and Lady Thatcher also tried to deny and even resist the changes taking place and to continue along familiar national patterns. But they failed in due course and were superseded by politicians who steered a different course. The Swiss, given the nature of their political system, take much longer to catch on.

1.3 The changing international setting after 1945

The year 1945 was a watershed in world affairs. In Europe, at least, the age of the classical nation-state and of balance of power politics came to an end. So did the era of traditional bilateral interstate relations. From now on, and with strong American backing, there was a trend toward *multilateralism* and *supranational* integration. The change was symbolised by the birth of international bodies like the Organisation of European Economic Cooperation (OEEC, now OECD), the Council of Europe, NATO, the European Coal and Steel Community, the European Community (now the European Union) and the European Free Trade Area (EFTA), to mention only the more important ones. In Europe, the *age of independence* is giving way to the *age of interdependence* and of supranational integration.

Multilateralism had yet another purpose: it helped to *legitimise American leadership* or, as some would say, American *hegemony*. That, too, is largely a story of success. Multilateralism made the 'American century' more bearable for second-rank powers. Unlike the fascist and Soviet hegemonies, American preponderance was combined with a measure of self-restraint and the ability of dependent states to participate in the making of important decisions. Of course, as a typical hegemon the United States also practised unilateral power politics, but in its relations with Europe that trait was not dominant.[38]

The Swiss experienced both trends of the 'American century'. They began to sense the irresistible dynamics of multilateralism and of integration, but they also had several direct encounters with the American hegemon. Both tendencies clashed head on with the traditional Swiss worldview. To put it mildly, Switzerland had problems with both multilateralism and American leadership. Let me begin with some remarks about Swiss–American relations and then turn to the issues of multilateralism and integration.

1.3.1 American hegemony

As Richard Senti points out in this book, Switzerland had no great difficulty identifying with American initiated trade liberalisation after 1945. Except for the field of agriculture, where protectionism had the upper hand, Swiss foreign economic policy favoured the removal of trade barriers. As a small and landlocked country with no natural resources except ample water supply, Switzerland is strongly dependent on international trade. In this sense the 'American century' was to their liking, and they profited handsomely from its advantages.

As already indicated, matters were different at the intersection of economics and security. From 1945 to the present, there have been four major clashes between the United States and Switzerland in this area. In each case the central issue was *neutral free trade*. Over this matter the Swiss quarrelled regularly with the United States, and although the problem is less acute today, it has bedevilled Swiss–American relations until recently. A first clash occurred toward the end of the Second World War, followed by two more conflicts during the Cold War. A fourth clash happened after the end of the Cold War and, ironically, had a direct link to the first encounter of 1944–6.

During the *Second World War* the United States conducted an intensive campaign of economic warfare directed both at the fascist powers and the neutrals. Among other things, America froze all neutral assets on its own soil, a measure hitherto unknown. Then, in 1943, it began to put pressure on all neutrals to stop 'trading with the enemy'. The neutrals were expected to end their commercial and financial transactions with Germany. As a matter of principle, and based in the main on their classical interpretation of sovereignty and of neutral law, the Swiss refused steadfastly to sever their economic ties to the fascist powers.[39]

At the end of the war, however, American pressure was so intense that the Swiss had no choice but to conform and to sign the Washington Agreement of 1946, which dealt mainly with the restitution of monetary gold and private German assets. The Swiss were outraged and saw it as an exercise of raw power: David had been blackmailed ruthlessly by Goliath. In the area of neutral trade Switzerland was experiencing more trouble with the United States than it had with Nazi Germany. When engaged in economic warfare, the Americans were no longer willing to respect traditional international law.[40]

American and Swiss positions did not change during the Cold War, and it was not surprising, therefore, that a second confrontation occurred during the *Korean War*. The United States, now on behalf of the Paris-based Coordinating Committee for Multilateral Export Controls (Cocom), pressured Switzerland into signing what historians have termed the Hotz-Linder Agreement of July 1951. Although the Swiss again resisted, they ultimately conformed to Cocom rules. This meant adopting Cocom's three control lists and a reduction of certain categories of 'strategic' exports. In contrast to 1946, the arrangement was kept secret and became public knowledge only towards the end of the Cold War.[41]

The third confrontation between the United States and Switzerland occurred during the *Reagan Administration*, when economic sanctions, which the Nixon Administration had loosened, were once more tightened. Since neither the American nor the Swiss documents on this matter have been published, it is difficult to be precise. It is a fact, however, that a young

Swiss diplomat by the name of David de Pury was stationed in Washington during those years in order to 'co-ordinate' East–West trade. His major counterpart in the Department of Defense was Richard Perle, and there are speculations that there may have been another (if informal) Hotz-Linder Agreement.

As indicated, the fourth confrontation came after the end of the Cold War and had its roots in the events of the Second World War. In the foreground, stood the issue of restituting *Jewish assets* 'dormant' in Swiss bank accounts. However, in the background loomed the familiar question of neutral economics in times of war. Formally speaking, the problem of Jewish assets dates back to the Washington Agreement of 1946 and arose in connection with German assets (or so-called 'flight capital') transferred to Switzerland during the war. The United States, together with France and Great Britain, demanded the transfer of these assets to the Allied Control Council. At that time, the issue of Jewish assets was not central, but it became so later. The main reason for the resurfacing of the matter after so many decades was the extremely restrictive handling of individual Jewish claims by Swiss banks, for which – unfortunately – they had the government's tacit approval.[42]

The fact that the issue had a link to neutrality became evident once the confrontation over restitution started. The introduction to the Eizenstat Report, issued by the US Department of State in 1997, made explicit reference to neutrality. It also questioned the morality of Swiss financial (and gold) transactions, with particular emphasis on the final phase of the Second World War.[43] Predictably, many Swiss felt outraged and agreed with the editorial opinion of the *Neue Zürcher Zeitung* that the Americans 'do not understand neutrality'.[44] Once again the United States and Switzerland had clashing conceptions of the international rules of the game in general and of neutrality in particular. As so often – the hegemon won.

1.3.2 Multilateralism and integration

Let me now turn to the second dimension of the post-1945 system – the new *multilateralism* and the European trend toward *integration*. These developments also meant a change of international rules that, depending on the concrete circumstances, was bound to create difficulties for the Swiss. The new developments occurred at three different levels: the global, the Euro–Atlantic and the Western European.

At the *global* level multilateralism is chiefly embodied in the United Nations system. As already mentioned, Switzerland was reluctant to adjust. As part of its dualistic policy of distinguishing between international organisations engaged in 'low' and 'high' politics, the country joined the major functional organisations but, for a long time, refused to join the United Nations itself. Daniel Möckli's contribution shows vividly that the process of joining the 'political' core of the UN system was excruciatingly difficult and that the government's argumentation often lacked coherence. It was only at the end of the Cold War and with the publication of the 1993 Foreign Policy Report that some of the old concepts were brought in line with the logic of multilateralism in general and collective security in particular.

As Jon Fanzun points out, the 1993 Report also elevated *human rights* to the level of an official objective, thus establishing the issue as a serious foreign policy concern. Pressure to do so had come from a number of sources at home and abroad. Domestically it was mainly the Social Democratic party that demanded a serious commitment to human rights. In doing so it ran up against the more traditional groups on the political right that considered ICRC support to be the only human rights commitment compatible with neutrality. The argument was also used to oppose UN membership. ICRC neutrality and effectiveness, so the reasoning, would suffer from a Switzerland belonging to an organisation committed to collective security. Fortunately, a majority of Swiss were not convinced.

Adjusting to the developments at the *Euro–Atlantic level* turns out to be more difficult, the main reason being the Swiss attitude toward alliances. At its core NATO is a preventive (or defensive) alliance and, as outlined above, a permanent neutral can join alliances only reactively. Had the Soviets invaded Western Europe during the Cold War, it was to be expected that Switzerland would, at some point, end up on the side of NATO. How extensively the military prepared for such an eventuality is uncertain. Historical studies seem to suggest that, in contrast to the two world wars, there was no secret agreement.[45] One thing is clear, however: membership in a preventive alliance ends permanent neutrality. If the Swiss were to sign the NATO treaty as it stands today, it would mean the end of a long tradition.

For the time being, NATO membership is not the most pressing Swiss foreign policy issue. The real challenge lies at the level of *European integration*. Although Switzerland joined the OEEC right after the Second World War and adhered to the Council of Europe in 1963, it has exhibited difficulty with coming to terms with integration. When the European Economic Community was founded in 1958, Switzerland, together with Great Britain, was instrumental in setting up EFTA.[46] However, the British joined the EEC in the early 1970s, and given the reduced importance of EFTA, the Swiss were forced to negotiate a bilateral free trade agreement with the EEC. It was superseded only in 2002 by the bilateral package agreement mentioned earlier. As I have pointed out already, an attempt to find a multilateral arrangement with the EU failed when the Swiss, in a public vote, refused to join the EEA in 1992.[47]

Let me conclude by once more emphasising that the classical European system no longer exists. Switzerland would have preferred to play by the old rules but had to realise that this was impossible.[48] Classical neutrality is in decline. It had been on the rise in the eighteenth and nineteenth centuries, and, ironically, the United States in those days contributed in an important way to the development of the law of neutrality. After 1917, however, and particularly as a major power, the United States changed course on neutrality. Especially in the area of economic neutrality, the United States contributed to its decline.[49]

Conclusions and outlook

More than ever, the United States dominates international politics and is capable of influencing and, if necessary, enforcing the rules of the game. Furthermore, the forces of interdependence and globalisation, which are at the root of multilateralism and integration, are difficult to resist. The Swiss government is aware of these realities but, as the narrow results of recent public decisions indicate, the process of adjustment continues to be difficult. Many Swiss still adhere to the asymmetrical worldview mentioned at the outset of this chapter: globalism in the area of 'low politics', national solutions in matters of 'high politics'.

In the light of this dilemma the Federal Council's 1993 Foreign Policy Report was a useful step towards redefining basic concepts. The maintenance of sovereign independence, formerly the only goal of Swiss foreign policy, is no longer a top priority. It has been replaced by a cluster of five different goals, paving the way for more flexibility and realism. The goals include peace and security, economic well-being, democracy and human rights, social justice and ecological balance. As already mentioned, the importance of neutrality has been reduced.[50]

Major challenges lie ahead, however. Although the Cold War is over, matters pertaining to the interface of economics and security can still become an issue between the United States and Switzerland. After the events of 11 September 2001, Washington has pressured Switzerland in the area of banking. Although for the United States terrorism is a matter of 'high politics', the Swiss government considers it to be an issue not of inter-state war but of international crime, thereby isolating terrorism from neutrality. Yet it is conceivable that new security threats will assume larger proportions and transatlantic pressures increase. In such a case a renewed encounter with the US hegemon over 'free trade in war' (or the banking secret) is entirely possible.

The main challenge to Swiss foreign policy, however, is the growing dynamism of the *European Union*. Since that organisation is supranational in character, the Swiss will not only have to alter their conception of sovereignty but also to refashion their domestic institutions. There is no doubt that, once a member of the Union, direct democracy will be reduced and that the collegial form of government will have to undergo some alterations.[51] It is to be expected that these institutional issues will become more important than neutrality.

In the meantime, the new package of bilateral agreements will have to be implemented. It consists of seven parts covering, among other things, the free flow of labour, transportation, agriculture and science. The Federal

Council has already announced that it intends to negotiate another package. As it appears at present, Brussels will insist that several sensitive issues be part of the deal or, worse, it might make them a precondition for entering into negotiations. The main issues are banking regulations (or tax evasion) and closer co-operation in matters of justice, police and refugees (Schengen and Dublin accord, and the like). North–South transit, although partly covered by the first agreement, is also becoming an ever-growing problem.

Major changes also lie ahead in the *security* field. At present, the Defence Ministry is busy with a reorganisation of the Swiss Armed Forces. The changes envisaged are massive and, as Andreas Wenger indicates, many will touch such core values as the militia principle, autonomous defence and armed neutrality. It is true that important first steps have been undertaken. Under the auspices of the OSCE an unarmed contingent of the Swiss army was involved in Bosnia, and there is now an armed military unit stationed in Kosovo under NATO command.[52]

These are giant steps by Swiss standards, and there are bound to be more commitments of this kind in the future. The Swiss army will therefore require a more highly developed professional component. Up to now, the only professional soldiers have been full-time militia instructors. This is changing rapidly; there simply are not enough young militia officers, and professionals increasingly have to take their place. For the moment, the supply of soldiers is adequate, and there is no resistance against compulsory military service among the young. Yet empirical studies indicate that various socio-economic trends work in favour of abolishing mandatory service. A voluntary and much smaller militia is in sight.[53]

Conservative and nationalist groups oppose these developments, and they will again succeed in retarding the process. Since NATO is their favourite object of hostility, they will undertake special efforts to resist more intensive Swiss involvement within the Partnership for Peace. Fortunately, in this field the government is largely autonomous; it is therefore to be expected that there will soon be further steps toward more intensive PfP participation. Furthermore, the General Staff is keeping a close watch on the development of the European Union's security policy, which – in the long run – constitutes the most important challenge to the Swiss Armed Forces.[54]

As the UN vote shows, the traditionalists are no longer as successful as they once were. In 1986 they set up an organisation called 'Action for a Neutral and Independent Switzerland' (AUNS). It was instrumental in defeating the government's first attempt to join the United Nations. Since then, the group has been taken over by the People's Party, headed by Chrisoph Blocher, a wealthy Swiss industrialist. For the last fifteen years, Blocher has been the undisputed leader of a strongly traditionalist movement. Although Blocher made his personal fortune by selling chemical technology around the globe, he is staunchly nationalist. His success in business is for many voters solid evidence that the traditional Swiss dualism of combining internationalist 'low politics' with nationalist 'high politics' still works.

With his populist style, Blocher appeals to many of the disgruntled voters and, in the last national elections, managed to absorb practically all small parties of the extreme right wing of the political spectrum. In terms of seats won in legislative election, the People's Party continues to grow. Although Blocher and his followers pretend to be 'the people's voice', they have lost on many issues put to public vote. It is one thing for a Swiss party to gain seats in local and national legislatures; it is quite another thing to win majority in public votes. The People's Party may well continue to grow in size, but it has lost some of its appeal on specific issues.

Christoph Blocher will continue to emphasise 'political uniqueness', and he will no doubt succeed in retarding the process of EU membership. Such procrastination will come at a *price* that is both economic and political. OECD studies show that the Swiss economy, relative to that of EU member states, has been stagnating. But the price to pay lies chiefly in the *public* domain; it is basically political and has a budgetary side. Let me explain.

EU membership is not free; the Union has a budget, and Switzerland, when joining, will be a net contributor. However, non-membership also has its costs. Still thinking largely in national terms, Switzerland has a tendency to embark on expensive projects said to be of 'national' importance. The recent salvaging of our 'national' airline – Swissair – is a good example. The cost to taxpayers is 2 billion Swiss francs. It was also a question of pride to hold the 6th Swiss 'national' exhibition in the year 2002, a celebration that placed a heavy burden on the public till.

The most expensive venture said to be in the 'national' interest is the network of North–South railroad tunnels that the Swiss are now building (NEAT). The project serves the European Union more than Switzerland. If Switzerland were a member of the Union, there is a possibility that such infrastructural undertakings would (at least in part) be financed by all Europeans. The same applies to the construction of additional North–South automobile tunnels. They, too, are financed by the Swiss taxpayers but used largely by citizens of the Union. The Swiss do not even levy a toll. National pride has its price in budgetary terms.

Less measurable, but nonetheless real, is the purely political price Switzerland is paying. Many of the decisions taken in Brussels affect our daily lives, and it has become almost routine for the Swiss to implement what others decide – while pretending to be sovereign. If Switzerland were a member of the European Union, the loss of domestic sovereignty would be made up for by sovereignty gains at the European level. In the absence of such compensation, the Swiss political culture is weakened. To believe the opposite is an illusion. In the long run, therefore, it makes political sense for Switzerland to join the Union and to alter its sense of political 'uniqueness'.

Notes

1 Although 55 per cent of the voters favoured UN membership, the cantonal majority – which was also required – was only 12 to 11! The armed forces decision was won by merely a few thousand votes.
2 For a brief summary of important Swiss foreign policy facts, see Jürg Martin Gabriel and Sandra Hedinger, 'Aussen- und Sicherheitspolitik', in Ulrich Klöti *et al.* (eds), *Handbuch der Schweizer Politik* (Zürich: NZZ Verlag, 1999), pp. 694–723.
3 For decades after the Second World War, the Swiss government distinguished between 'technical' and 'political' international organisations and argued that adhering to the latter was incompatible with neutrality. Membership in 'technical' organisations like the Council of Europe or WTO (formerly GATT), so the government argued, was in the national Swiss interest. Although the unfortunate distinction was formally abandoned some time ago, it is still engrained in the public mind. The United Nations, the European Union, and NATO are still considered to be highly 'political'. See Jürg Martin Gabriel and Manuel Rybach, 'Die Schweiz in der Welt', in Klöti *et al.*, *Handbuch der Schweizer Politik*, pp. 35–51; see also Urs Altermatt, 'Die Schweiz auf dem Weg von der Isolation zur Kooperation', in Roman Berger *et al.* (eds), *Für den Uno Beitritt der Schweiz* (Basel: Friedrich Reinhard Verlag, 1982), pp. 102–11.
4 Klaus Armingeon, 'Integriert und isoliert: Die Schweiz im Prozess der Globalisierung', in Klaus Armingeon (ed.), *Der Nationalstaat am Ende des 20. Jahrhunderts – die Schweiz im Prozess der Globalisierung* (Bern: Paul Haupt Verlag, 1996), pp. 7–20.
5 Kris W. Kobach, *The Referendum: Direct Democracy in Switzerland* (Aldershot: Dartmouth Publishing, 1993).
6 For more details on how the Swiss see their role in foreign policy and on the link between domestic and foreign policy, see Laurent Goetschel, Magdalena Bernath, Daniel Schwarz, *Schweizerische Aussenpolitik: Grundlagen und Möglichkeiten* (Zürich: Verlag Neue Zürcher Zeitung, 2002), pp. 39–82.
7 The government's 1990 Security Report is based on strategic 'uncertainty' and a return to the old balance of power politics; see *Schweizerische Sicherheitspolitik im Wandel: Bericht 90 des Bundesrates an die Bundesversammlung über die Sicherheitspolitik der Schweiz vom 1. Oktober 1990*; see also Alois Riklin, 'Die Neutralität der Schweiz', in Alois Riklin, Hans Haug and Raymond Probst (eds), *Neues Handbuch der schweizerischen Aussenpolitik* (Bern: Paul Haupt Verlag, 1992), pp. 206–7. See also John Mearsheimer, 'Back to the Future: Instability in Europe after the Cold War', *International Security*, 15/1 (Spring, 1990), pp. 5–56.
8 The four official languages are German, French, Italian and Romanish. Catholics make up 47 per cent of the population and Protestants 45 per cent.
9 To be exact, the federation now consists of 20 full cantons and 6 half cantons. For voting purposes, and for the determination of a cantonal majority, the number is 23 cantons, and the absolute majority is 12.
10 Division also characterised the 1848 revolution. The creation of the new Confederation was opposed by the conservatives and most of the Catholic cantons. They seceded in 1847, took to arms, fought a short civil war – and lost. The victors were the largely Protestant and liberal cantons that, for the following half century, ruled the federation almost single-handedly. It was only in 1891 that the first Catholic-Conservatives joined the Federal government.
11 It was not the Federal Council, however, that symbolised unity but rather General Henri Guisan from the French part of Switzerland. The seven men constituting

the federal executive were divided among themselves, and, in terms of anti-fascist patriotism, most of them could not compete with the general.

12 Altermatt, 'Die Schweiz auf dem Weg von der Isolation zur Kooperation', pp. 94–6.

13 For a general discussion of the 'Swiss Model', see Georg Kreis, 'Nach der schweizerischen jetzt die europäische Integration: Zur Idee der schweizerischen Modellhaftigkeit', in Thomas Cottier and Alwin R. Kopse (eds), *Der Beitritt der Schweiz zur Europäischen Union: Brennpunkte und Auswirkungen* (Zürich: Schulthess Polygraphischer Verlag, 1998), pp. 189–212.

14 For a general discussion of the Swiss political system, see Wolf Linder, *Swiss Democracy: Possible Solutions to Conflict in Multicultural Societies* (Basingstoke: Macmillan, 1994); Jan-Erik Lane (ed.), *The Swiss Labyrinth: Institutions, Outcomes and Redesign* (London: Frank Cass, 2001); Hanspeter Kriesi, *Le système politique suisse* (Paris: Economia, 1998).

15 There are six half-cantons counting together as three full ones.

16 Adrian Vatter, 'Föderalismus', in Klöti *et al.*, *Handbuch der Schweizer Politik*, pp. 77–108; Ruth Lüthi, 'Parlament', in Klöti *et al.*, *Handbuch der Schweizer Politik*, pp. 131–58; Ulrich Klöti, 'Regierung', in Klöti *et al.*, *Handbuch der Schweizer Politik*, pp. 159–86.

17 For more details on decision-making in Swiss foreign policy, see Goetschel *et al.*, *Schweizerische Aussenpolitik: Grundlagen und Möglichkeiten*, pp. 83–103; see also Ulrich Klöti *et al.*, *Handbuch der Schweizer Politik*, pp. 511–689.

18 Pascal Sciarini, 'La formulation de la décision', in Klöti *et al.*, *Handbuch der Schweizer Politik*, pp. 589–650.

19 The careful balancing is said to be represent a 'magic formula' further stabilising the political system. It was an especially symbolic event when the first seat was turned over to the opposition Social Democrats in 1943. More than any other event, it shows how strongly that the Second World War integrated the country.

20 Jürg Martin Gabriel, 'Wahlen statt Abstimmungen', in Silvio Borner and Hans Rentsch (eds), *Wieviel direkte Demokratie verträgt die Schweiz?* (Chur: Verlag Rüegger, 1997), pp. 243–57; for a discussion of the impact on voting on foreign policy, see Raimund E. Germann, 'Der Verfassungsentwurf von 1995 und die aussenpolitische Handlungsfähigkeit', in Borner and Rentsch (eds), *Wieviel direkte Demokratie verträgt die Schweiz?*, pp. 155–65.

21 Jürg Martin Gabriel, 'Kleinstaatlichkeit und Identität – oder das Problem der Kontextlosigkeit', in Wolf Linder *et al.* (eds), *Schweizer Eigenart – eigenartige Schweiz* (Bern: Paul Haupt Verlag, 1995), pp. 215–30.

22 For a constitutional point of view, see Dietrich Schindler, 'Der Weg vom "geschlossenen" zum "offenen" Verfassungsstaat', in Bernhard Ehrenzeller *et al.* (eds), *Der Verfassungsstaat vor neuen Herausforderungen* (St. Gallen: Dike Verlag AG, 1998), pp. 1027–41.

23 For a brief history of Swiss neutrality, see Edgar Bonjour, *Schweizerische Neutralität: Kurzfassung der Geschichte in einem Band* (Basel: Helbing & Lichtenhahn, 1978).

24 For a general discussion of Swiss neutrality, both legal and political, see Hanspeter Brunner, *Neutralität und Unabhängigkeit der Schweiz im ausgehenden 20. Jahrhundert – Bestandesaufnahme und Ausblick* (Zürich: Schulthess Polygraphischer Verlag, 1989).

25 Since the Hague Conventions do not mention permanent neutrality, this concept is not considered to be part of neutral law but only of neutral politics. For a detailed discussion of the distinction, see Jürg Martin Gabriel, *Sackgasse Neutralität* (Federal Institute of Technology Zurich: vdf Hochschulverlag AG, 1997), pp. 18–27; for a short English language version, see Jürg Martin Gabriel,

The American Conception of Neutrality After 1941 – Updated and Revised Edition (London: Palgrave/Macmillan, 2002), pp. 9–16.

26 Daniel Sprecher, *Generalstabschef Theophil Sprecher von Bernegg* (Zürich: NZZ Verlag, 2000); Georg Kreis, *Auf den Spuren von 'La Charité'* (Basel: Helbing & Lichtenhahn 1976).

27 Gabriel, *Sackgasse Neutralität*, pp. 19–27, 75–92, 129–58.

28 The Federal Council did nothing to dispel the myth. Until the end of the Cold War, 'general defence' exercises were conducted in which large portions of the military and civilian elite participated actively for an entire week. As a rule Europe would find itself in a general state of war in the exercise, with the Russians using nuclear devices and coming right up to the Swiss frontier. At this point the exercise was usually terminated. The scenario beyond neutrality was never acted out in public. It would have made headlines in the Swiss press, and the voters would have been outraged. No wonder neutrality was perceived as an end in itself – which it was never meant to be. It was only with the report on national security of the year 2000 that the government for the first time discussed the issue openly and explicitly. See *Sicherheit durch Kooperation: Bericht des Bundesrats an die Bundesversammlung über die Sicherheitspolitik der Schweiz vom 7. Juni 1999.*

29 Gabriel, *Sackgasse Neutralität*, pp. 129–58.

30 Jürg Martin Gabriel, 'Switzerland and Economic Sanctions: The Dilemma of a Neutral', in Marko Milivojevic and Pierre Maurer (eds), *Switzerland's Defense and Foreign Policy* (Oxford/New York: Berg, 1989), pp. 232–45; Jürg Martin Gabriel, 'Die Stellung der Schweiz zu Wirtschaftssanktionen', in Alois Riklin *et al.* (eds), *Neues Handbuch der schweizerischen Aussenpolitik*, pp. 919–28. Until recently it has been difficult to find a written document containing the official Swiss position on export controls and economic sanctions. The best one had was a paper written in 1954 by the Foreign Ministry's legal advisor, Prof. R. Bindschelder of Geneva. For the actual document, see Dietrich Schindler (ed.), *Dokumente zur schweizerischen Neutralität seit 1945* (Bern: Paul Haupt Verlag, 1984), pp. 15–19.

31 For a general account of Swiss defence policy since the Second World War, see Kurt R. Spillmann *et al.*, *Schweizer Sicherheitspolitik seit 1945* (Zürich: Verlag Neue Zürcher Zeitung, 2001); see also Marko Milivojevic and Pierre Maurer (eds), *Swiss Neutrality and Security: Armed Forces, National Defense and Foreign Policy* (Oxford/New York: Berg, 1990).

32 The militia principle also prevails in politics. The members of the federal legislature, for instance, serve on a militia basis, and the same is true for most cantonal and local politicians. The militia principle, therefore, has some affinity with republicanism and with the ideas expressed by such philosophers as Jean-Jacques Rousseau. For highly interesting discussion of this link, see Jan Metzger, *Die Milizarmee im klassischen Republikanismus* (Bern: Paul Haupt Verlag, 1999). See also John McPhee, *La Place de la Concorde Suisse* (New York: Farrar, Strauss & Giroux, 1984).

33 During all of the twentieth century the army did much to tie the nation together and to promote a tightly knit elite. Some groups were left out, however. In contrast to Israel, where the militia principle is also at the heart of the defence system, Swiss women are not subject to military service. The Social Democrats were also marginalised, although during the Cold War some of them made their way into the officer corps.

34 Altermatt, 'Die Schweiz auf dem Weg von der Isolation zur Kooperation', pp. 94–111.

35 Hans Haug, *Humanity for all: The International Red Cross and Red Crescent Movement* (Geneva: Henry Dunant Insitute, 1993).

36 During the Second World War the link between the Federal Council and the ICRC was particularly intimate and also problematic, especially regarding the issue of holocaust information. See Jean-Claude Favez, *Une mission impossible? Le CICR, les déportations et les camps de concentration nazis* (Lausanne: Librarie Payot, 1988).

37 Altermatt, 'Die Schweiz auf dem Weg von der Isolation zur Kooperation', pp. 96–102. As Altermatt shows, success was coupled with a feeling of superiority. To this day the Swiss have a tendency to not only look down on their 'less democratic' neighbours but also on such 'lesser neutrals' as Sweden, Finland and Austria. The neighbouring republic of Austria in particular constituted a clear case of 'inferiority' suffering from a triple handicap: it lacked a tradition of democracy, was an opportunistic neutral and possessed a weak army, thereby constituting a veritable 'transit zone' for a Soviet march on Switzerland.

38 For a general discussion of the concept of American hegemony, see Bernd W. Kubbig, 'Introduction: The US Hegemon in the "American century". The State of the Art and the German Contributions', *Amerikastudien/American Studies*, 2001/46, pp. 495–524.

39 Heinz K. Meier, *Friendship Under Stress: US-Swiss Relations 1900–1950* (Bern: Verlag Herbert Lang & Co., 1970); Gabriel, *The American Conception of Neutrality After 1941*, pp. 42–65.

40 Gabriel, *The American Conception of Neutrality After 1941*, pp. 54–65.

41 André Schaller, *Schweizer Neutralität im West-Ost-Handel: Das Hotz-Linder-Agreement vom 23. Juli 1951* (Bern: Verlag Paul Haupt, 1987).

42 Schlussbericht der Unabhängigen Expertenkommission Schweiz-Zweiter Weltkrieg (Bergier-Kommission), *Die Schweiz, der Nationalsozialismus und der Zweite Weltkrieg* (Zürich: Pendo Verlag, 2002), pp. 181–515; Unabhängige Expertenkommission Schweiz-Zweiter Weltkrieg, *Die Schweiz und die Goldtransaktionen im Zweiten Weltkrieg* (Bern: EDMZ, 1998).

43 United States Department of State, 'US and Allied Efforts to Recover and Restore Gold and Other Assets Stolen or Hidden by Germany During the Second World War', Foreword by Stuart E. Eizenstat, Under Secretary of Commerce for International Trade, Special Envoy of the Department of State on Property Restitution in Central and Eastern Europe, Washington, DC, May 1997.

44 'Kein Verständnis für die Neutralität', editorial, *Neue Zürcher Zeitung*, 9 May 1997, p. 11.

45 Mauro Mantovani, *Schweizerische Sicherheitspolitik im Kalten Krieg 1947–1963* (Zürich: Orell Füssli, 1999).

46 Roland Maurhofer, *Die schweizerische Europapolitik vom Marshallplan zur EFTA 1947 bis 1960: Zwischen Kooperation und Integration* (Bamberg: Difo-Druck GmbH, 2001).

47 For a detailed study of the process – and its failure – see Ralf Langejürgen, *Die Eidgenossenschaft zwischen Rütli und EWR* (Chur: Verlag Rüegger, 1993); see also Raimund E. Germann, 'Die bilateralen Verhandlungen mit der EU und die Steuerung der direkten Demokratie', *Schweizerische Zeitschrift für Politische Wissenschaft*, Vol. 1, Issue 2–3 (1995), pp. 35–60.

48 Neutral Sweden adjusted more quickly and more gracefully. It, too, was not invited to San Francisco but joined the United Nations as early as 1946. From the beginning it declared that it would not be neutral in cases where collective security functioned. Should the Security Council be paralysed, however, the country would

pursue its traditional neutrality. This two-track policy implied an adjustment to the new rules of international politics and turned out to be entirely realistic.

49 Gabriel, *The American Conception of Neutrality After 1941*, pp. 1–5.

50 *Bericht über die Aussenpolitik der Schweiz in den 90er Jahren vom 29. November 1993.* See also Jürg Martin Gabriel, 'Neutralität für den Notfall: Der Bericht des Bundesrats zur Aussenpolitik der Schweiz in den 90er Jahren', in Gabriel, *Sackgasse Neutralität*, pp.129–58.

51 For a detailed discussion of the possible impact of EU membership on Swiss political institutions, see various articles in Cottier and Kopse (ed.), *Der Beitritt der Schweiz zur Europäischen Union: Brennpunkte und Auswirkungen*, pp. 273–569.

52 Jürg Martin Gabriel (ed.), *Schweizerische Aussenpolitik im Kosovo-Krieg* (Zürich: Orell Füssli Verlag AG, 2000).

53 Karl W. Haltiner, Andreas Wenger, Jonathan Bennet and Tibor Szvirczev (eds), *Sicherheit 2000: Aussen-, Sicherheits- und Verteidigungspolitische Meinungsbildung im Trend* (Zürich: Forschungsstelle für Sicherheitspolitik und Konfliktanalyse der ETH Zürich und Militärische Führungsschule an der ETHZ, 2000).

54 Heiko Borchert and Jürg Martin Gabriel, 'Die Schweizer Armee und die europäische Sicherheitsordnung: Herausforderungen und Aufträge', in Cottier and Kopse (eds), *Der Beitritt der Schweiz zur Europäischen Union: Brennpunkte und Auswirkungen*, pp. 609–36; Heiko Borchert and René Eggenberger, 'Selbstblockade oder Aufbruch? Die Gemeinsame Sicherheits- und Verteidigungspolitik der EU als Herausforderung für die Schweizer Armee', *Österreichische Militärische Zeitschrift*, Nr 1/40 (Jan./Feb. 2002), pp. 1–19.

2

Swiss Security Policy: From Autonomy to Co-operation

Andreas Wenger

Introduction

Swiss security policy is currently undergoing a radical change, moving away from the paradigm of autonomy and towards that of co-operation. In the last decade we have witnessed the end of the Cold War and the historic events of the period from 1989 to 1991 – revolutions in Eastern Europe, the collapse of the Soviet Union, the dissolution of the Warsaw Pact and German reunification. These events have fundamentally changed both the internal and external factors that shape Swiss security policy. Until the late 1980s, Swiss strategy was driven by the twin principles of neutrality and autonomous national defence. However, the federal government and parliament have recently placed greater emphasis on international co-operation and involvement.[1]

The new focus follows a general international trend. Only through co-operation can some of the risks that have recently emerged be countered. Terrorism, the proliferation of weapons of mass destruction, and large-scale waves of migration are thought of. The primary strategic task in the Euro–Atlantic region is no longer to deter and contain a clearly defined military opponent, but to make concerted efforts to stabilise a series of crises occurring on the fringes of Europe and to manage global security issues.[2]

What sets Switzerland apart is the fact that the process of adaptation is taking longer than in other European countries. It has also been accompanied by a serious polarisation of public opinion.[3] The desired consensus on national values – values that the population considers worthy of defending with force, if necessary – depends on normative, institutional and historical factors. Neutrality has shaped Swiss national identity strongly and has affected the country's foreign and security policy. As Jürg Martin Gabriel argues in the introductory chapter of this book, neutrality is also tied to a set of 'special' domestic institutions that – all considered – result in what the Swiss consider 'political uniqueness'. Actually, neutrality changed from being a pragmatic tool meant to serve national security to an all-encompassing dogma of a utopian republic situated between opposing blocs, well integrated domestically and admired around the world as the model of democratic statehood.

Defence policy is an area where the 'special case' is particularly visible because, as part of their direct form of democracy, the Swiss make it a habit to vote on military matters.[4] They recently decided twice on the issue of abolishing the armed forces. Both times, in 1989 and again in 2001, around two thirds of the voters decided to maintain their army, but as a consequence of these plebiscites there is an intensive discussion about the role the armed forces should play. Controversy centres on issues such as armaments policy, the cost of national defence and the deployment of Swiss troops abroad. In the summer of 2001, Swiss voters narrowly approved an amendment permitting the deployment of armed units in peace support operations, provided there is a UN or an OSCE mandate.[5]

Switzerland is experiencing great difficulty in adapting its security policy to the changes taking place in its international environment. It is the purpose of this chapter to outline the typical problems involved. I will begin by tracing their origins in the Second World War and will then show the evolution of the debate during and after the Cold War. As the reader will discover, for many years the emphasis was on continuity rather than on change. Simply put, Swiss security policy rested on the concept of *armed neutrality* that, when looked at more closely, meant *national* (or autonomous) *military defence*.[6] This is changing. Armed neutrality, in all of its dimensions, is undergoing a complete reinterpretation.

This chapter consists of three parts, beginning with an overview of the development of Swiss security policy. Its origins can be traced to the Second World War and the challenges resulting in Switzerland's post-War isolation immediately after 1945. The full 'uniqueness' of Switzerland's security policy emerged gradually at the beginning of the Cold War. In the mid-1950s, neutrality and autonomous national defence had become clearly defined security pillars. However, the habit of separating 'low' from 'high politics', of seeking international economic co-operation while preferring military isolation, began to restrict Switzerland's security options. Given the extensive nuclearisation of the European theatre of war, the political and financial limits of an autonomous defence became apparent.

The second part of the chapter deals with the long struggle to achieve what was called a 'comprehensive security strategy', a struggle that developed parallel to the gradual relaxation of tensions between the East and the West in the 1960s and 1970s. At the conceptual level, the Federal Council's 1973 Security Report combined a proactive and outward-looking component with a purely defensive component. On the one hand it envisaged the political participation in international security organisations such as the CSCE, on the other hand it stated the armed forces' exclusive assignment to protect Swiss territory. However, the two components were applied unevenly in the

1970s and 1980s. While much effort went into military security, the international dimension existed mostly on paper. Furthermore, there was a shift in public values entailing a gradual decay of the defence consensus. Faced with increasing criticism about the army as the most important security instrument, the authorities' reaction was confined to an insistence on traditional principles. The result was an increased polarisation, as shown in the surprisingly high number of votes – 35.6 per cent – in favour of the 1989 popular initiative to abolish the army.

The third part of the chapter investigates the ongoing process of reorienting Swiss security policy, a process that began at the end of the Cold War. The Federal Council's 1990 Security Report contained initial conceptual changes, yet the new strategy was no more than transitional. Within a very short period, therefore, a more comprehensive report became necessary. The importance of what became known as Security Report 2000 is obvious: it commits Switzerland to co-operate with other countries and expects the army to make a serious effort towards promoting international stability.

The chapter concludes by showing that Switzerland has gradually expanded its security policy commitment within Europe, albeit within the limits of that which has been domestically possible. In the short term it is important for Switzerland to deal both with the reforms implied by what is called 'Army XXI' and to generally modernise the armed forces. In the medium term it is evident that there must be re-examination of the compatibility of a consistent strategy of co-operation with neutrality and an aloofness from the security institutions in the Euro–Atlantic region – the EU and NATO. The path toward partial integration that Switzerland has taken in the past decade must be continued and expanded: from increased and deeper co-operation under the Partnership for Peace, to occasional engagements in peace support operations, to the final goal of full EU membership.

2.1 The Second World War legacy: becoming a 'special case'

The foundation of traditional Swiss security policy was laid at the start of the Cold War. The experiences of the Second World War – particularly the general feeling of the population that Switzerland was an island of safety while battle raged around it throughout Europe – dominated security thinking in the post-War years. The League of Nations, established in line with the concept proposed by US President Woodrow Wilson at the end of the First World War, had proved powerless to prevent the rise of Adolf Hitler, the unexpected collapse of France after the onslaught of the German army and the dramatic demise of the British Empire. As Europe set about clearing the rubble left by war, Switzerland saw confirmation of the correctness of its security policy of combining neutrality and autonomous defence in the fact that its state, economy and society had been spared the impact of the war.

Large sections of the population took it for granted that Switzerland's self-perception, which had become more clearly defined during the war years, and its policy of remaining neutral and on the sidelines should continue unchanged into the Cold War era. However, as Switzerland became politically isolated after 1945, the national government had serious problems deciding what position to adopt, as the struggle to establish a post-War order commenced. The war years had strengthened the country's domestic unity, but Switzerland's relations with the most influential new powers – the United States and the Soviet Union – were barely developed. In addition, with the establishment of the United Nations and the renunciation of force enshrined in the UN charter, the concept of neutrality came under increasing pressure, not just on moral grounds but also in terms of its legal justification. In an environment where in the future the world would judge what was a just war and what was an unjust war, a policy of neutral passivity was seen as generally incompatible with the idea of collective security. Not surprisingly, the Swiss Federal Council decided in 1946 that Switzerland could not join the UN.[7]

As the front between East and West hardened, Switzerland's isolation diminished by degrees up to the mid-1950s. The beginning of the Cold War allowed Switzerland to consolidate its position as a special case. As early as 1946, the national government succeeded in normalising bilateral relations with the United States and the Soviet Union. The fact that Switzerland was not a member of the political institutions at the UN did not make an unduly negative impression, thanks to the growing rivalry between the super powers that soon obstructed the system of collective security. The division of the world into two antagonistic power blocs gave renewed respectability to Switzerland's 'good offices' and to the role of the neutral state as intermediary.[8]

A parallel development can be seen in the move towards European integration. Alongside economic ideals, the idea of a unified Europe had always incorporated a strong security component: the political finality of the integration process was primarily geared towards incorporating, and thus controlling, the forces that for the second time in the twentieth century had drawn Europe, and indeed the world, into armed conflict. However, with the division of Europe along the Iron Curtain, the vision of a comprehensive union had to be forgotten for the time being. The problem of Germany's insecure position as the central power was resolved by the incorporation of one of the two German states into each of the two blocs that emerged. As none of the other neutral states in Europe had joined the new North Atlantic Alliance, when NATO was founded in 1949, the pressure on Switzerland to join a European defence association diminished. As a group, the neutral states found themselves assuming certain balancing roles in a Europe that was split into two, such as, for example, during the Conference on Security and Cooperation in Europe (CSCE) process in the early 1970s.[9]

By the mid-1950s, the immediate danger of war was reduced by the consolidation of the two military blocs in Europe, the Warsaw Pact and NATO. This, in turn, reduced the pressure on Swiss decision makers to reconsider the repercussions on Switzerland's security policy and on the practicalities of going it alone. NATO membership was never an option, due to the legal and political ramifications of Switzerland's neutrality. However, as Switzerland was clearly positioned as a Western state, both economically and in terms of its political principles, it actually benefited from the nuclear umbrella that NATO and the United States provided. Foreign policy and security strategies had been firmly established in internal politics, and the greater the balance between the two blocs the less pressing was the need to initiate public debate on such matters.[10]

2.1.1 Neutrality restrictions on security

In the light of these developments, it is not surprising that the guidelines for the implementation of the key principle of Swiss foreign and security policy during the Cold War, namely continuing armed neutrality, were codified in the 'Bindschedler Doctrine'. The guidelines outlined the following: for neutrality reasons, Switzerland should not become a member of any political or military organisation; however, for reasons of solidarity, it should play an active role in economic, humanitarian and technical organisations. This extremely narrow definition of a neutrality policy paved the way towards the country's special case status.[11]

Switzerland made determined use of external economic co-operation to overcome its international isolation, since such co-operation was important for a small, export-oriented state. The political guidelines on neutrality allowed for an active bilateral and multilateral external economic policy – at least as long as economic integration remained only loosely connected to political integration. Switzerland, therefore, reacted nervously to the formation of the European Economic Community (EEC) in the Treaties of Rome in 1957, whose political goals could no longer be overlooked. Switzerland's efforts not to be left behind in the move towards economic integration resulted, in 1961, in its joining the European Free Trade Association (EFTA), an organisation whose goals were restricted to economic co-operation between member states. In 1963, when French President Charles de Gaulle imposed his veto for the first time on British entry to the EEC, it was clear that EFTA's position was secure for some years to come. Seen from this perspective, the economic and political divisions of the major European powers encouraged a policy of wait-and-see on Switzerland's part. As Martin Senti shows in his contribution on foreign economic policy, Switzerland played an active role in the General Agreement on Tariffs and Trades (GATT).[12]

Yet as far back as the 1950s, it proved very difficult in practice to draw a clear distinction between the economic and the political strands of the neutrality policy. During the rapidly accelerating arms race, the United

States made every effort to oblige NATO and the Western bloc states to impose strict controls on exports to Eastern bloc countries. In 1951, Switzerland bowed to the enormous pressure of the US sanctions policy and partially applied the trade embargo on 'strategic goods' imposed by Cocom. As Jürg Martin Gabriel and Andrea Heinzer show in their respective contributions to this volume, the Swiss Federal Council unilaterally reduced the normal average number of trade transactions, which meant a complete stop to trade in certain goods with the East. Switzerland thus participated in the Western economic blockade of the East bloc, departing from the neutrality policy it had formulated – without making this a topic for domestic discussion.[13]

Although the separation between economic co-operation and political integration allowed Switzerland to preserve its external economic interests, in the long run the Bindschedler Doctrine reduced Switzerland's room for manoeuvre on security matters. The use of the political neutrality formula by the Federal Council, as the basis for deciding whether or not Switzerland should become involved internationally, resulted over the years in a restriction of Switzerland's involvement in peacekeeping operations to the mere provision of logistical and technical services. The problems of accepting mandates with a political character had already been illustrated in the 1950s, in connection with the Korean War and the Suez crisis.[14]

Switzerland was involved in the ceasefire agreement in the Korean War in 1953 through two international commissions, but with Sweden it adopted a clear position as a 'neutral Western state', as opposed to the 'neutral Eastern states', that is, Czechoslovakia and Poland. This alignment was a fundamental contradiction to the neutrality position espoused by the national government and was therefore viewed at home with considerable scepticism. Subsequently, the Federal Council therefore declined any further mandates involving political obligations.[15]

The Suez crisis, in turn, illustrated the limitations of the extent to which a small neutral state could engage in diplomatic mediation on the global political stage. Towards the end of 1956, considering the crisis in the Middle East and at the same time the suppression of the Hungarian revolution by Soviet tanks, the Federal Council believed that there was a direct threat to world peace and launched an extraordinary peace initiative. This occurred on precisely the same date that Britain and France were forced to suspend their operations on the Suez Canal, following enormous pressure from their ally, the United States, which had been taken by surprise by the turn of events. Consequently, the Swiss initiative won the approval only of the Soviet Union, a fact registered largely with disapproval at home, whereas the crisis in Hungary was a subject of much greater interest to the population. The Federal Council had clearly overestimated the mediation role that could be assumed by a small neutral state that was excluded from the international flow of information.[16]

Until the end of the Cold War, Swiss peace promotion involving the army was restricted to relatively modest active support activities that followed what could be called a 'niche policy'. This included the provision of individual delegates and medical and logistics units. Switzerland's independent defence strategy meant that its army was excluded from any progressive build-up of military co-operation in training and peacekeeping.

Switzerland's reduced ability to act on security matters resulting from the separation between economics and politics was reflected by a gradual segregation of foreign trade policy from defence and military policy. In the 1950s, the structures in the management and administration apparatus at the departmental and sector level were not conducive to the development of a systematic security policy. While the Swiss Department of Foreign Affairs (then called Department of Political Affairs, EPD) concentrated on matters of foreign trade policy, the federal military department focused primarily on military matters. Matters relating to higher-level security strategy and organisational problems relating to the co-ordination of all military and civil resources involved in general defence were generally handled without the involvement of foreign policy or the EPD. As a result, the Federal Council's strategic leadership focused primarily on military crisis management in exceptional situations.

2.1.2 The limits of autonomous defence in the nuclear age

The Swiss army's ability to defend Swiss territory – that is, Switzerland's credible autonomous defence system – played a significant role in the traditional system of European power balances in the nineteenth and early twentieth centuries. However, with the outbreak of the Cold War and the division of Europe along the Iron Curtain, Switzerland was suddenly removed from the flashpoint between the major powers. As early as 1947 the Federal Council recognised that this would diminish Switzerland's strategic military importance. The main concern in analyses of the military situation was no longer the possible threat of a direct attack aimed at incorporating the country into a power bloc, but rather the risk of Switzerland being completely surrounded by one or the other of the two power blocs.[17]

In the early 1950s, given this new analysis of the situation, it was clear that the army needed to move away from its 'réduit' approach – the strategy of withdrawing into the alpine heartland of Switzerland in a military crisis – towards a more flexible defence strategy. However, the question of exactly how this could be achieved provoked a fierce debate within military circles. The dispute between those who favoured a policy of 'mobile defence' and the proponents of an 'area defence' strategy was conducted amidst growing concerns about the increasing nuclearisation of the European continent. The supporters of mobile defence believed that the introduction of tactical nuclear weapons in Europe called for greater army mobility and firepower. Their intention was to ensure that the enemy had no fixed targets to attack while assuring that counterattacks could be made against the enemy. This point of view led to demands for a major upgrade of the mobility and mechanisation of the armed forces, including the air force.[18]

Yet those in favour of retaining the traditional military response insisted that the principle of defence autonomy was part of the agenda. The proponents of static defence warned that the mobile defence strategy was not feasible, given the geographic and financial circumstances of a state as small as Switzerland. In addition, they argued that the mobile defence concept could raise the suspicion that Switzerland was preparing to join forces with one of the power blocs, since mobile units are much easier to integrate into a military coalition. Many of the ideas of the supporters of mobile defence were incorporated into Troop Ordinance 61, which led the German magazine *Der Spiegel* to conclude that Switzerland was well on the way to creating an army that conformed to NATO requirements.[19]

The principle of independent defence demanded that in the nuclear age the option of equipping the Swiss army with nuclear weapons be carefully examined. The public debate was initiated in July 1958 by a policy statement from the Federal Council about the possibility of Switzerland procuring atomic weapons. The government stated that the army must be provided with the most effective means to preserve independence and neutrality, and that therefore the option of nuclear weapons could not be automatically excluded. In response, in the first extra-parliamentary opposition movement, the Swiss Social Democratic party and the Swiss Movement against Atomic Armaments launched two popular initiatives that would make any decision on acquiring nuclear arms subject to a national referendum.[20]

Although both initiatives were rejected in 1962, the broader public debate demonstrated that the issue of nuclear weapons was discussed as a matter of political self-perception and not as an issue of military policy. The discussion centred on whether there was any moral justification at all for Switzerland to possess, threaten to use or even use nuclear weapons. Further, the issue was a thorny one for parliament and the public alike, because the extremely high costs involved in procuring nuclear weapons meant that any decision on the procurement of such weapons would also involve major economic and financial considerations. In fact, as far as Swiss defence doctrine went, nuclear weapons were discussed only in specialist committees.[21]

The Mirage affair in 1964 focused public attention on unresolved military and political debates and demonstrated to all the political and economic limitations of an independent defence strategy. Errors in planning and information by the Federal Military Department (EMD) during the purchase of the first batch of what was to be a total of 100 Mirage fighter aircraft resulted in a serious loss of confidence in the department and in the national defence policy by parliament and public alike. As a result, parliament rejected the supplementary credit requested by the Federal Council, and only 57 fighters were ultimately purchased. The reduction in the number of authorised aircraft was a serious blow to the mobile defence concept, because the available aircraft could not guarantee the mobile troop units effective protection from the air. In the aftermath of the Mirage affair, the Federal Council also decided not to request an increase in the number of combat tanks, also necessary for the mobile defence program. After this, there could be no question of procuring nuclear weapons.

The subsequent review of the role of the army resulted in the national military defence plan of 1966. This scheme called for a combat approach in which infantry forces in a specific area worked together with mechanised units, air force units and air defence units. The fighting power of the attacker was to be channelled and absorbed by a compact defence system. This approach re-established consensus on matters of defence policy, so that there would be no major changes to the engagement policy of the Swiss army until the end of the Cold War. In its essence, however, this deterrent was similar to the scorched earth policy used in the Second World War.[22]

In the light of these developments, upgrades to the army after 1973 generally had an air of déjà vu about them. The EMD's efforts remained focused on expanding conventional defence systems. Apart from increases in the amount of mechanised artillery, tank defences, the air force and air defence forces, the purchase of the German Leopard II combat tank stands out. In the second half of the 1980s, in the course of this armaments deal, Swiss defence spending reached its highest level of the Cold War era. In terms of numbers, Switzerland now had one of the largest armies in Europe, comprising over 500 000 troops. However, it was an army with a developmental strategy and doctrine that had remained unchanged since the 1960s.

2.2 Long struggle for comprehensive security

In the 1950s, the security debate in Switzerland was dominated by military questions. This situation changed at the start of the following decade, as the system of European security stabilised in the wake of the two most serious crises of the Cold War – the Berlin crisis (1958–62) and the Cuban missile crisis (1962) – became based on a territorial and nuclear status quo. The threat of nuclear war, hanging like the sword of Damocles, made it clear to everyone, not only to those states with nuclear weapons, that national interests needed to be pursued with non-military methods. Japan and US allies in Europe had developed into major economic powers. They now demanded greater consultation rights and called for serious efforts to be made to achieve détente between East and West. A contributing factor here was the ever-deepening entanglement of the leading Western power in the Vietnam War at this time. The conditions for rapprochement between Moscow and Washington also appeared to have improved, since the deep ideological and political rift between the Soviet Union and China had become obvious by the mid-1960s.

In a world of diffused power, the emphasis on the range of security choices shifted increasingly from the military sphere to the political and economic spheres. The forces in favour of global détente proposed a move away from the traditional systems of national defence and military policy towards a comprehensive security policy supported by an integrated and interdisciplinary approach. Even in Switzerland, there were first signs of a move towards a new strategic stance. The process of shaping the strategy for a comprehensive security policy lasted well into the 1970s, eventually coming to a temporary resolution with the 1973 Security Report.[23]

However, it should be noted that the great debates on military policy and organisational reform of the 1950s were concluded long before the first systematic security policy concept for Switzerland was produced in 1973. Thus, due to the practical reality of the situation, traditional concepts were favoured, and most of these concepts were to remain in place until the end of the Cold War. The national defence plan of 1966 re-established a consensus on matters of military doctrine. Circumstances also led to the fact that plans by the Swiss army to acquire nuclear weapons were shelved around the same time. The federal law of 1968 on organisational structures and the comprehensive defence council solved, for the moment, any organisational problems in general defence. In the subsequent course of the Cold War, the principle of general defence became firmly established, both horizontally at the federal administration level and vertically, from the federal government to the police forces of each canton. By the end of the Cold War, it had been institutionalised almost perfectly.[24]

2.2.1 The 1973 security report: between theory and practice

The 1973 Security Report combined these schemes into a two-part strategy. One component was external and proactive, and the other was defensive and geared to protection only. However, Swiss security policy was still concerned only with dangers emanating from surrounding countries that might be prepared to use force against Switzerland. The main goals of the security strategy were the preservation of territorial integrity, basic values, institutions and the independence of the state. This illustrates the extent to which the military aspect was still the dominant influence, taking the form of a deterrent – and understood as 'the prevention of war through a willingness to defend the country'. As to the defensive component in Swiss security policy, the goal was to maintain as great a degree of independence as possible, with the results already described.

The 1973 Report recognised the need to integrate preventive and internationally effective elements into the strategic range of tools, but it was generally content to confine these to carrying out the traditional good offices abroad. If the defensive element was supported by the rhetoric of a centuries-old tradition of armed neutrality, the proactive component had to counter the reverse of this same neutrality ideology, which would have Switzerland abstain from any foreign involvement. The national government realised that the military dimension to international security in the 1970s and 1980s was being increasingly eclipsed by economic and other non-military risks, and by factors such as the accelerated integration of increasing numbers of policy areas into multilateral bodies. The consequence was a gradual decrease of the importance of neutrality. However, the practical implementation of this realisation was achieved only partially.[25]

Although the army was systematically expanded and improved, the process of developing the proactive elements in Swiss security policy was extremely slow. It is true that at the start of the 1970s, Swiss diplomats became more involved in areas that were relevant to security as part of a general policy of greater Swiss foreign policy activity. A major component of this was the initiative to create a European system for settling disputes peacefully, which was Switzerland's most valuable contribution to the CSCE process. In practice, however, the increase in activity as part of the CSCE process and the support provided to UN missions were still restricted to continued provision of the traditional good offices, to promoting international humanitarian law, co-operation on development work and providing personnel and material assistance for peacekeeping operations.[26] Only occasionally did Swiss contributions to the stabilisation of international affairs show evidence of a genuinely comprehensive Swiss strategy. As the period of détente between the two military alliances came to an end in the late 1970s, Switzerland again found it had less room for manoeuvre on foreign policy and security matters. As a result, the Federal Council once again focused on expanding the defensive elements in the twin security strategy.

2.2.2 Conceptual stagnation and social change: polarised opinions

In the 1960s, as radical social changes occurred, more and more sectors of the population began to have doubts about the ability of a small state to defend itself in the nuclear age. In the 1970s, the question was also raised in Switzerland about whether investing large sums in independent national defence as the central platform of Swiss security policy, really made the best use of the country's limited financial resources, particularly in view of the process of détente that had now begun. This opinion shift, which was particularly pronounced in the younger generation, was influenced by the Vietnam War and by the 1968 student unrest in the United States and in many western European countries. The generally recognised leading model that formed Swiss national identity in the 1950s was anti-communism, yet many young people saw the greatest danger not in the Soviet Union but in the instruments of power within their own society. The police and the army, in particular, were seen by these groups as instruments for maintaining discipline and suppressing liberal ideas.[27]

In the field of security, the shift in perspective was reflected by a sharp increase in the number of people refusing to do military service and in numerous 'soldier committees', which demanded the democratisation of how the armed services were run. A commission set up by the Federal Council in 1970 found signs of changing awareness in the post-War generation: The younger generation no longer felt obliged to follow the hero cult of the Swiss founding fathers, had more liberal attitudes and were prepared to revisit the concept of independence. In the young people's eyes, the concept of war as a continuation of politics by other means was increasingly losing credibility, particularly in an environment where nuclear weapons were commonplace, making the pursuit of war seem pointless.[28]

The existing consensus on Swiss security policy was severely damaged. Instead of feeling a sense of shared solidarity with the national defence strategy, as people had during the Second World War and, generally speaking, during the early part of the Cold War, people now tended to adopt one of the two diametrically opposed positions. On the one hand, there were those who had fundamental doubts about the effectiveness of traditional means of defence, in particular about the army. In the 1989 popular initiative to abolish the army, which was rejected, the surprisingly high 35.6 per cent vote in favour showed that this was more than an insignificant fringe group. On the other hand, in the opposition camp were those who clung tightly to traditional models and attempted to preserve the status quo by rejecting alternative ideas out of hand.[29]

A key reason for the polarisation of opinions on security was not least due to the fact that Swiss security policy had been essentially reduced to issues relating to military and defence policy. There were no alternatives to the principle of independent defence due to the self-limitations imposed by neutrality. There was no question of increased military co-operation, let alone integration, or of developing and expanding the army contribution as part of a proactive security policy. In the face of this gradual process of erosion of the credibility of national military defence, the Federal Council would have required a high degree of management and communication skills. As Daniel Möckli shows in his contribution to this volume, the Federal Council petitioned parliament at the end of 1981 to join the UN. However, this plan was destroyed when in 1986 voters and cantons rejected UN membership by a resounding majority. Once again, the form of government based on the principle of collegiality, with no presidential department or strong federal president, had come out in opposition to any centralisation of authority. The Swiss political and social system, designed to ensure a diffusion of power, had taken the neutrality principle so much to heart that any change in the security strategy would be difficult to accomplish.

2.3 Post-Cold War dilemma: foreign needs and domestic realities

With the 1989 popular initiative to abolish the army, the high number of votes in favour left no doubt in anyone's mind that the national consensus that had existed until then on security policy was beginning to fragment. It was evident that over the years an enormous pressure to engage in reform had built up. In the watershed years of world politics between 1989 and 1991, the crisis of identity regarding people's relationship to the state spread throughout many sections of the population. Domestic policy consisted of a series of reluctant exercises in introspection; national security policy was brought into disrepute by the uncovering of a scandal involving a large-scale file system on voters; and, a parliamentary commission of enquiry was set up to examine the discovery of a secret resistance organisation (P-26) and a clandestine intelligence service (P-27). In the wake of such scandals, celebrations to mark 700 years of the Confederation and events to commemorate the general mobilisation in 1939 were muted accordingly.

As had been the case in other Western industrial states, an increasing number of technological and environmental catastrophes resulted in a greater awareness of the vulnerability of modern societies. Increasing awareness of the risks involved brought about an expansion of the concept of security. Among large sections of the population, greater importance was now attached to the political, economic, social and ecological dimensions of security than to matters of military security. As the fear of war receded, attempts to achieve military security would increasingly be perceived as standing in direct competition with social welfare and environmental safety. Whereas on the one hand the calls grew louder for a pay-off for the fact that there was now peace, the perception that no single state would be able to cope with the new security risks also gained ground. Perspectives for national security in isolation seemed to promise less and less chance of success, and the new challenges increasingly demanded joint solutions.

In the midst of the dramatic changes on the international stage around Switzerland, the federal authorities produced a new document on security policy – the 1990 Report on Security Policy in Transition. If one considers the startling pace of change in the foreign landscape, the federal government reacted extremely quickly in publishing the new security policy position in October 1990. The Soviet Union was still in the process of disintegration when the Federal Council published its first decisions on a new strategic policy direction. The early timing of the publication, however, should also be seen as influenced by the domestic pressure for reform. In addition, the Federal Council was able to fall back on the preparatory work already carried out to reformulate Swiss security policy. Another consequence of the timing of the publication, however, appearing as it was in the midst of the strategic upheaval in Europe, was that the 1990 security policy could only be a strategy for transition.

2.3.1 Transition: security policy in the 1990s

The 1990 Report by the Federal Council heralded a change in direction away from an independent to a co-operative security policy, which a decade later would lead to the strategic guidelines on 'Security through Cooperation' and the Security Report 2000. The 1990 Report took as its starting point the increased importance of non-power-political risks and threats, such as ecology, ethnic conflicts, racism, migration and drugs and arms trafficking, and anchored security policy in the context of a general policy to safeguard the existence of the state. The intention was that this would allow all kinds of risks that threatened the survival of the population or the state to be assessed continuously in terms of all their inter-relationships and complexities. The real object of security policy, however, remained the sphere of power-political threats, with the instruments of security policy made available to counter the other fundamental risks – an approach that, in retrospect, could convince no one.[30]

The crucial conceptual change in policy planning was to specify the proactive components in relation to security policy goals. The 1990 Report, for the first time, called for a 'contribution to international stability, particularly in Europe'. By contributing to general peacekeeping operations, crisis management and the removal of the root causes of conflict, Switzerland could also increase its own national security. The 1990 Report heralded an increase in the importance of foreign policy as an instrument of security policy, in particular, in terms of the institutional preservation of a new European peace structure. There was also provision for various international peacekeeping roles for the army: participation in UN missions, deployment of observers, a consultancy role in the field of defence doctrine and the deployment of military experts for verification duties.[31]

The 1990 Report symbolised the beginning of a new attitude towards security policy in Switzerland. After 1990, security policy involved much more than simply defence and military policy. Nevertheless, the actual implementation of the policy requirements continued to occur against a background of disagreement over active co-operation in European security organisations and over the traditional adherence to neutrality. It was no surprise, therefore, that the process of implementing initial steps on security policy over subsequent years was undertaken with caution and did not proceed without difficulties, such as, for example, the voters' rejection in 1994 of a proposal to establish a UN peacekeeping battalion.

In terms of the proactive elements in Swiss security policy – those elements that were implemented so cautiously during the Cold War era – the national government pursued a much more active policy in the 1990s to try to influence Switzerland's international environment, particularly in Europe. Yet, individual decisions in this area were generally accompanied by a prolonged struggle to achieve domestic political consensus. On the international level, Switzerland attracted much attention when it chaired the OSCE in 1996. Its presiding role in the OSCE – the former CSCE – represented a special challenge for Swiss diplomacy. For a start, the organisation was in the midst of a fundamental reform process. In addition, it had been entrusted, at the end of 1995, with the civil implementation of important sections of the Dayton peace agreement for Bosnia and, in particular, with the responsibility for holding elections and monitoring human rights. Switzerland committed a sizeable level of personnel and financial support to the operation, thus making a substantial contribution to the success of the OSCE mission in Bosnia.[32]

Following a protracted decision-making process, Switzerland decided at the end of 1996 to participate in the NATO Partnership for Peace initiative. Implicitly conceding to domestic popular opinion, Swiss involvement focused primarily on non-military areas, such as the democratic control of the armed forces, civil–military co-operation, various security policy training programmes and the promotion of free flow of information, such as, for example, through the International Relations and Security Network. The Swiss programmes are viewed as valuable contributions, although they are somewhat modest, compared to the activities of other small states. Switzerland contributed with an uncharacteristic level of involvement to bringing about a comprehensive treaty banning anti-personnel mines. By stages, Switzerland increasingly set the pace of the 'Ottawa Process'. The treaty prohibits not only the use, but also the stockpiling, production and transfer of anti-personnel mines.[33]

However, the government had greater difficulty implementing the new security policy approach in the military sphere. In the course of the 1990s, as the Federal Council progressively expanded international involvement in foreign policy security areas, it could bring about only a very limited expansion of the armed forces' contribution to peacekeeping operations. The 1995 army reform had begun in the final phase of the Cold War with the twin goals of rationalisation and improved efficiency. This 'bottom-up' reform of the 1966 army scheme was hardly the result of a careful strategic analysis of the new international trends. On the contrary, it was influenced to a considerable degree by financial, demographic and domestic political constraints imposed by the neutrality doctrine and the militia system. In fact, the target size of the army was reduced from 550 000 to 400 000 troops. However, the guidelines on defence engagement under the strategy of dynamic territorial defence, were fundamentally the same as the operational doctrine of the past.[34]

The new scheme still focused mainly on large and relatively static infantry units. The central role of the infantry was in keeping with the country's military traditions and with the federalist army structures. The army contribution to international peacekeeping operations, with deployment of a few hundred specialists, still looked extremely modest. The army of 1995 was in no position to counter the population's loss of confidence in it, nor could it dispel the growing scepticism in business and industry regarding the value of military training. It soon transpired that the need for reforms in the area of national military defence had not been satisfied. In this context, the full importance of the Security Report 2000 becomes apparent. This document represents a milestone in the shift from independent national defence to a co-operative security policy for Switzerland.

2.3.2 The Security Report 2000 and 'Army XXI'

The Report 2000 on Swiss security policy describes Switzerland's immediate European environment as stable. At the same time, it points out that crises on the outskirts of Europe and on the international stage can have direct repercussions for Switzerland. The focus is especially on new threats such as terrorism, which, although not primarily directed against the territory of Switzerland, can nevertheless have an effect on internal security and the order of the state.[35]

Report 2000, based on the change in the risk situation and recognising Switzerland's limited financial and technical options, documents the limits of the country's ability to maintain security independently in the twenty-first century. Security policy goals can no longer be achieved through the pursuit of small-state niche strategies. Participation, rather than neutrality or an independent national defence strategy, will safeguard the government's freedom of action in today's political environment, which is characterised by transnational problems. The report points out that the new co-operative security policy strategy is not just a concession to the notion of solidarity, but represents, primarily, a security policy dictated by national interests.

The Federal Council plans to utilise the improved opportunities for promoting international peace through active Swiss participation in efforts to stabilise the environment beyond Switzerland's borders, where national security might be compromised. Thus, the Report 2000 extends the role of the army in peacekeeping and crisis management, underlining the conviction that a successful policy of stabilisation requires the army to play a substantial role. Given the narrow limits of the 1995 army reform, this also indicates that the current army reform, Army XXI, is the key factor in the new policy framework.

The planning, currently under way for implementing Army XXI, shows that the process is revolutionary for Switzerland. There will be a further drastic cut in the number of troops to 120 000 active soldiers, 20 000 recruits and a reserve of 80 000. At the same time, the professional section will be expanded to a degree that is domestically acceptable. In essence, the Swiss military is in the process of changing from an organisation geared towards training to one geared towards rapid deployment, including all the necessary changes regarding its policy, structure and operations. A policy is being pursued to enhance the army's ability to co-operate on a national and international level with military and civilian partners. This affects all three of the army's key roles (peacekeeping and crisis management; protecting Swiss territory and defence; and secondary deployment for the prevention and containment of large non-military risks). Interoperability is listed as a horizontal function affecting the army as a whole. Adapted specifically to Swiss domestic circumstances, the Army XXI reform follows the international trend in which the range of duties of armed forces today has shifted from the defence of territory to crisis response and crisis prevention.[36]

While the Swiss Defence Ministry, now called Department of Defence, Civil Protection and Sports (VBS in German) was preparing the concept for reform, specific elements of the reform project gave rise to heated public debate. At the end of 2000, the redistribution initiative, which called for a reduction in defence spending within ten years to half of the 1987 level, was firmly rejected by over 60 per cent of voters. The voters accepted the savings already implemented in the military sector and were willing to allow the government an annual budget of around 4.3 billion Swiss francs to create a modern, well-equipped army. Thus, for the near future the financial framework for implementing Army XXI appears to be set.

In contrast, the margin by which the referendum on military law was accepted in the summer of 2001 was much closer, with 51 per cent of voters in favour. The new legal provisions simplify co-operation on military training and allow full contingents of troops to be armed on peace support operations abroad, provided there is a UN or OSCE mandate. The new law will thus allow Switzerland to gradually reach normal levels and types of military contributions for promoting stability. The legal, financial and strategic bases are now established for Switzerland to start modernising its army through the Army XXI reform. However, initiatives submitted by representatives of political parties, cantons, militia associations and special interest groups in parliament and in the public arena are likely to complicate the implementation of the reform project.[37]

The Army XXI reform will not be the end of the modernisation process for the Swiss army. The army will also need to become more flexible, so that it is able to continually adapt to the rapid changes in national and international circumstances. The development process of the military from a territorial defence device to a crisis response force is not yet complete. The plan to establish a large battalion for peace support operations is relatively modest by international standards. Issues related to the increasing inequity in the drafting of recruits and questions surrounding the long-term justification for having a militia, as opposed to a professional army, will also become increasingly important factors. Finally, there remains a contradiction between the desire for as great a degree of independence in defence as possible and the need to retain the option of co-operating with other countries, should defence become necessary.

Conclusions and outlook

Although significant military changes are already on the Swiss short-term agenda, it must be assumed that, at a more political level and in the long run, the question of ensuring security without integration (an issue not addressed by the Report 2000) will become relevant. Given the current status of Swiss security policy, the country is able to make specific, targeted contributions abroad. However, Switzerland still has no means to influence European and international security policy. In view of the increasing globalisation of security matters, a tendency highlighted by the terrorist attacks on New York and Washington, this inability becomes a growing matter of concern.

As Daniel Möckli shows in his contribution to this volume, the Swiss were most reluctant to join the United Nations. It will be more difficult yet to convince them of the need for EU or NATO membership. NATO is still seen as a classical alliance and the European Union is primarily perceived as an economic and monetary entity. Accordingly, Swiss discussions of EU membership tend to focus on economic repercussions, on the transfer of sovereignty and on the need for institutional reforms. However, the EU has accomplished economic and monetary union and is now moving towards a union in the area of security policy. The level of progress on matters of internal security and migration is one example of this process. At present, Switzerland is attempting to compensate for the disadvantages of not being part of the Schengen and Dublin agreements by negotiating bilateral agreements with the EU. In the long term this is no satisfactory alternative to membership. It should also be noted that the pace of development of a European Security and Defense Policy (ESDP) has accelerated sharply over the past two years. The Union has become a major player in matters of security, and it is expanding its civil and military capability for crisis management. In conjunction with NATO, it will play an important role in defining European security structures.[38]

In 2002, the EU will establish a rapid reaction force to carry out the so-called Petersberg missions – humanitarian and peacekeeping tasks, crisis management for combat forces, including peace enforcement operations to be carried out with or without a UN or OSCE mandate. The first such involvement may take place in Macedonia and EU members must adapt their operational capabilities. Yet, the planning for Switzerland's Army XXI indicates that in terms of numbers any contribution to the European crisis response force would be far smaller than that pledged by European states of a similar size. Even with the amended military legislation, Switzerland has less legal room for manoeuvre than is required to carry out Petersberg missions.

As a member of the EU, Switzerland could participate as an equal partner in civil and military operations. Since these are intergovernmental in nature, no loss of national sovereignty is involved. Most importantly, EU membership would ensure that Switzerland is involved in the decision-making process for the future development of ESDP. However, Switzerland would still lack security guarantees, since collective defence remains a NATO responsibility. Unfortunately, the Security Report 2000 does not discuss alliances, although the same document confirms the impossibility of independent defence against an enemy in possession of modern weapons.

Neutrality, which lies at the core of such reluctance, has been retained in view of the emotional nature of the subject. In the medium- to long-term, Switzerland will be obliged to decide whether neutrality is a useful instrument for providing effective national security in the twenty-first century. There can be no doubt that in the past neutrality has helped to preserve independence. Given the success of European integration, Switzerland is no longer placed on the dividing line between its neighbours' clashing geopolitical interests. Even at the fringes of Europe, challenges have shifted from inter-state to internal conflicts, a fact that renders neutrality all the more obsolete. Even the provision of good offices is no longer the preserve of neutral states.

All this goes to demonstrate that neutrality has lost most of its usefulness as an effective security strategy, thereby making the institutional shortcomings in Swiss foreign and security policy particularly serious. The path that has been taken towards partial integration must be pursued systematically. In addition, the country needs a continuing public discussion on foreign and security policy. The idea of Swiss 'uniqueness' – the image of a Utopian republic at the heart of Europe, well integrated domestically and admired by the world as the model of statehood – needs to be rewritten as we move into the twenty-first century.

Acknowledgements

The author would like to thank Michael Brunner, Jürg Martin Gabriel, Christoph Münger and Michelle Norgate for their comments on and help with the manuscript.

Notes

1 For a history of Swiss security policy since 1945, see Kurt R. Spillmann, Andreas Wenger, Christoph Breitenmoser, Marcel Gerber, *Schweizer Sicherheitspolitik seit 1945: Zwischen Autonomie und Kooperation* (Zürich: Verlag Neue Zürcher Zeitung, 2001).

2 On strategic change since the end of the Cold War, see Kurt R. Spillmann, Andreas Wenger (eds), *Towards the 21st Century: Trends in Post-Cold War International Security Policy*, Studies in Contemporary History and Security Policy 4 (Berne: Lang Verlag, 1999).

3 Karl W. Haltiner, Kurt R. Spillmann, Andreas Wenger (eds), *Sicherheit 2001: Aussen-, Sicherheits- und Verteidigungspolitische Meinungsbildung im Trend* (Zürich: Forschungsstelle für Sicherheitspolitik und Konfliktanalyse der ETH Zürich und Militärische Führungsschule an der ETHZ, 2001).

4 In 1992 Switzerland voted to introduce civil service as an alternative for conscientious objectors; in 1993 it voted on the popular initiative '40 military bases are enough – The military's responsibility to protect the environment' and 'For a Switzerland without new combat aircraft'; in 1994 on the referendum on the federal law on deploying Swiss troops in peace support operations; and in 1997 on the popular initiative 'For a prohibition of the export of war materials'. Finally, the popular initiative 'Reducing the cost of the military and national defense – Towards more peace and future-oriented jobs' and the federal law on the army and military administration (co-operation in training/armaments) were put to the vote in 2000 and in summer 2001, respectively.

5 Previously, Swiss military units had not been allowed to carry arms when deployed abroad.

6 See Andreas Wenger, Christoph Breitenmoser, Marcel Gerber, 'Vermächtnisse des Kalten Krieges – Sechs Thesen zum schwierigen Wandel der schweizerischen Sicherheitspolitik', in *Bulletin 2000 zur schweizerischen Sicherheitspolitik* (Zürich: Forschungsstelle für Sicherheitspolitik und Konfliktanalyse der ETH Zürich, 2000), pp. 109–28.

7 On Switzerland's policy towards the UN, see the chapter by Daniel Möckli in this volume; Cf. Antoine Fleury, 'La Suisse et le défi du multilatéralisme', in Georg Kreis (ed.), *Die Schweiz im internationalen System der Nachkriegszeit 1943–1950: Referate des Historiker-Tages 1995*, Itinera 18 (Basel: Schwabe, 1996), pp. 68–83; Peter Hug, 'Verhinderte oder verpasste Chancen? Die Schweiz und die Vereinten Nationen, 1943–1947', in Georg Kreis (ed.), *Die Schweiz im internationalen System der Nachkriegszeit 1943–1950: Referate des Historiker-Tages 1995*, Itinera 18 (Basel: Schwabe, 1996), pp. 84–97.

8 On Switzerland's 'good offices', see the chapter by Thomas Fischer in this volume; Cf. Raymond Probst, *Good Offices in the Light of Swiss International Practice and Experience* (Dordrecht/Boston/London: Nijhoff, 1989); Reto Borsani, *La Suisse et les bons offices* (Geneva: IUHEI, 1994).

9 On Switzerland and the European integration process, see Pierre du Bois, *Die Schweiz und die europäische Herausforderung 1945–1992* (Zürich: Verlag Neue Zürcher Zeitung, 1990); Hans Ulrich Jost, *Europa und die Schweiz 1945–1950: Europarat, Supranationalität und schweizerische Unabhängigkeit*, Schweizer Beiträge zur internationalen Geschichte 2 (Zürich: Chronos, 1999); Rudolf Wyder, *Die Schweiz und der Europarat 1949–1971: Annäherung und zehn Jahre Mitarbeit in der Parlamentarischen Versammlung*, Schriftenreihe der Schweizerischen Gesellschaft für Aussenpolitik 10 (Bern/Stuttgart: Paul Haupt, 1984).

10 On Swiss security policy during the early Cold War, see Mauro Mantovani, *Schweizerische Sicherheitspolitik im Kalten Krieg (1947–1963): Zwischen angelsächsischem Containment und Neutralitäts-Doktrin* (Zürich: Orell Füssli, 1999).

11 The 'Bindschedler Doctrine' is reprinted in Dietrich Schindler (ed.), *Dokumente zur schweizerischen Neutralität seit 1945: Berichte und Stellungnahmen der schweizerischen Bundesbehörden zu Fragen der Neutralität 1945–1983*, Schriftenreihe der Schweizerischen Gesellschaft für Aussenpolitik 9 (Bern/Stuttgart: Paul Haupt, 1984), pp. 15–19. On Switzerland's neutrality policy in the early Cold War, see Daniel Trachsler, *'Les conditions de la neutralité n'existent plus aujourd'hui': Infragestellung und Konsolidierung der schweizerischen Neutralitätspolitik durch den Beginn des Kalten Krieges (1947–1952)*, Zürcher Beiträge zur Sicherheitspolitik und Konfliktforschung 63 (Zürich: Forschungsstelle für Sicherheitspolitik und Konfliktanalyse der ETH Zürich, 2001); Daniel Möckli, *Neutralität, Solidarität, Sonderfall: Die Konzeptionierung der schweizerischen Aussenpolitik der Nachkriegszeit, 1943–1947*, Zürcher Beiträge zur

Sicherheitspolitik und Konfliktforschung 55 (Zürich: Forschungsstelle für Sicherheitspolitik und Konfliktanalyse der ETH Zürich, 2000).

12 On Switzerland's foreign economic policy, see Peter Hug and Martin Kloter (eds), *Aufstieg und Niedergang des Bilateralismus – Schweizerische Aussen- und Aussenwirtschaftspolitik 1930–1960: Rahmenbedingungen, Entscheidungsstrukturen, Fallstudien*, Schweizer Beiträge zur internationalen Geschichte 1 (Zürich: Chronos, 1999); Jakob Tanner, 'Die Schweiz und Europa im 20. Jahrhundert: Wirtschaftliche Integration ohne politische Partizipation', in Paul Bairoch and Martin Körner (eds), *Die Schweiz in der Weltwirtschaft (15.–20. Jahrhundert)* (Zürich: Chronos, 1990), pp. 409–28; Roland Maurhofer, *Die schweizerische Europapolitik vom Marshallplan zur EFTA 1947–1960: Zwischen Integration und Kooperation* (Bamberg: Difo-Druck GmbH, 2001).

13 See André Schaller, *Schweizer Neutralität im Ost-West-Handel: Das Hotz-Linder-Agreement vom 23. Juli 1951*, St. Galler Studien zur Politikwissenschaft 12 (Bern: Paul Haupt, 1987).

14 On Switzerland's peacekeeping activities, see Robert Diethelm, *Die Schweiz und friedenserhaltende Operationen 1920–1995* (Bern/Stuttgart/Vienna: Paul Haupt, 1997).

15 On Switzerland's mission in Korea, see Archiv für Zeitgeschichte (ed.), *Dreissig Jahre Schweizerische Korea-Mission 1953–1983* (Zürich: Institut für Geschichte ETHZ, 1983); Marius Schwarb, *Die Mission der Schweiz in Korea: Ein Beitrag zur Geschichte der schweizerischen Aussenpolitik im Kalten Krieg*, Geist und Werk der Zeiten 72 (Bern/Frankfurt a.M/New York: Lang Verlag, 1986); Urs Alfred Müller-Lhotska, *Schweizer Korea-Mission im Wandel der Zeit, 1953–1997* (Zürich: Transslawia Verlag, 1997).

16 See Andreas Boesiger, *Die Doppelkrise Suez/Ungarn 1956 und ihre Rezeption in der Schweiz* (Bern: MA thesis, 1991).

17 See Henri Guisan, *Rapport à l'Assemblée fédérale sur le service actif 1939–1945* (Bern, 1946); *Bericht des Bundesrates an die Bundesversammlung zum Bericht des Generals über den Aktivdienst 1939–1945 vom 7. Januar 1947*, in BBl 1947 I 473.

18 On the development of the Swiss army, see Alfred Ernst, *Die Konzeption der Schweizerischen Landesverteidigung 1815 bis 1966* (Frauenfeld: Huber, 1971); Hans Rudolf Kurz, *Geschichte der Schweizer Armee* (Frauenfeld: Huber, 1985).

19 See *Botschaft des Bundesrates an die Bundesversammlung betreffend die Organisation des Heeres (Truppenordnung) vom 30. Juni 1960*, in BBl 1960 II 321; *Der Spiegel*, 7 September 1960.

20 On Switzerland and nuclear weapons, see Dominique Metzler, *Die Option einer Nuklearbewaffnung für die Schweizer Armee (1945–1969)* (Basel: MA thesis, 1995); Jürg Stüssi-Lauterburg, *Historischer Abriss zur Frage einer Schweizer Nuklearbewaffnung* (Zürich: 1995); Heinrich Buchbinder, *Landesverteidigung im Atomzeitalter* (ed.) Schweizerische Bewegung gegen atomare Aufrüstung (Zürich: 1966); Gustav Däniker, *Strategie des Kleinstaats: Politisch-militärische Möglichkeiten schweizerischer Selbstbehauptung im Atomzeitalter* (Frauenfeld: Huber, 1966); Markus Heiniger, *Die schweizerische Antiatombewegung 1958–1963: Eine Analyse der politischen Kultur* (Zürich: MA thesis, 1980); Peter Hug, *Geschichte der Atomenergieentwicklung in der Schweiz* (Bern: MA thesis, 1987).

21 See Gustav Däniker, 'Zurück zur Strategie', in *Si vis pacem: Militärische Betrachtungen von Schweizern. Festschrift für Georg Züblin zum 60. Geburtstag* (Frauenfeld: Huber, 1964), pp. 84–101.

22 See *Bericht des Bundesrates an die Bundesversammlung über die Konzeption der militärischen Landesverteidigung vom 6. Juni 1966*, in BBl 1966 I 853; Beat Näf, 'Anfang und erste Entwicklung einer schweizerischen Strategie (Sicherheitspolitik)

1969–1973', *Sams-Informationen*, Vol. 1 (1984), pp. 51–146; Hans Senn, *Friede in Unabhängigkeit: Von der Totalen Landesverteidigung zur Sicherheitspolitik* (Frauenfeld: Huber, 1983).

23 On Switzerland's struggle for a comprehensive security policy during the 1960s, see Christoph Breitenmoser, *Strategie ohne Aussenpolitik: Zur Entwicklung der schweizerischen Sicherheitspolitik im Kalten Krieg* (Bern: Lang Verlag, 2002).

24 See *Botschaft des Bundesrates an die Bundesversammlung zum Bundesgesetz über die Leitungsorganisation und den Rat für Gesamtverteidigung vom 30. Oktober 1968*, in BBl 1968 II 641.

25 See *Bericht des Bundesrates an die Bundesversammlung über die Sicherheitspolitik der Schweiz (Konzeption der Gesamtverteidigung) vom 27. Juni 1973*, in BBl 1973 II 112; for an analysis, see Thomas Köppel, *Auf dem Weg zur Doppelstrategie: Die Entstehung der schweizerischen Sicherheitspolitik 1945–1973* (Zürich: MA thesis, 1994); Elisabeth Glas, *Aufbruch der Schweiz in die multilaterale Welt: Die schweizerische Aussenpolitik 1965–1977* (Zürich: MA thesis, 1999).

26 On Switzerland and the CSCE process, see Christoph Breitenmoser, *Sicherheit für Europa: Die KSZE-Politik der Schweiz bis zur Unterzeichnung der Helsinki-Schlussakte zwischen Skepsis und aktivem Engagement*, Zürcher Beiträge zur Sicherheitspolitik und Konfliktforschung 40 (Zürich: Forschungsstelle für Sicherheitspolitik und Konfliktanalyse der ETH Zürich, 1996); Hans-Jörg Renk, *Der Weg der Schweiz nach Helsinki: Der Beitrag der schweizerischen Diplomatie zum Zustandekommen der Konferenz über Sicherheit und Zusammenarbeit in Europa (KSZE), 1972–1975* (Bern/Stuttgart/Vienna: Paul Haupt, 1996).

27 See also Kurt Imhof, Heinz Kleger, Gaetano Romano (eds), *Vom Kalten Krieg zur Kulturrevolution: Analyse von Medienereignissen in der Schweiz der 50er und 60er Jahre*, Krise und sozialer Wandel 3 (Zürich: Seismo, 1999); Kurt Imhof *et al.*, *Die Schweiz in der Welt – die Welt in der Schweiz: Eine vergleichende Studie zu Bedrohungsaufbau und Bedrohungsverlust als Koordinaten der schweizerischen Aussenpolitik, 1944–1998* (in publication).

28 See *Bericht der Kommission für Fragen der militärischen Erziehung und Ausbildung der Armee (Kommission Oswald)* (Bern Eidgenössisches Militärdepartement, 1970), pp. 26–9. For an assessment of the effects of the report, see Heinrich Oswald, 'Geschichte des "Oswald-Berichtes"', *Allgemeine Schweizerische Militärzeitschrift*, Vol. 11 (1995), p. 18f.; Stephan Zurfluh, *Turn around in der Milizarmee: Verkannt – erkannt – vollzogen* (Zürich: Thesis-Verlag, 1999).

29 On social change and public perception of the army, see Karl W. Haltiner, *Milizarmee: Bürgerleitbild oder angeschlagenes Ideal? Eine soziologische Untersuchung über die Auswirkungen des Wertewandels auf das Verhältnis Gesellschaft – Armee in der Schweiz* (Frauenfeld: Huber, 1985).

30 See *Bericht des Bundesrates an die Bundesversammlung über die Sicherheitspolitik der Schweiz: Schweizerische Sicherheitspolitik im Wandel vom 1. Oktober 1990*, in BBl 1990 III 847.

31 For an analysis of the report, see Jon A. Fanzun, Andreas Wenger, 'Schweizer Sicherheitspolitik im Umbruch: Der Bericht 2000 vor dem Hintergrund des Kosovo-Konflikts', in *Bulletin 2000 zur schweizerischen Sicherheitspolitik* (Zürich: Forschungsstelle für Sicherheitspolitik und Konfliktanalyse der ETH Zürich, 2000), pp. 9–43.

32 On Switzerland's OSCE chairmanship, see Laurent Goetschel (ed.), *Vom Statisten zum Hauptdarsteller: Die Schweiz und ihre OSZE-Präsidentschaft* (Bern/Stuttgart/Vienna: Paul Haupt, 1997); Andreas Wenger, Christoph Breitenmoser, Heiko

Borchert, 'Das schweizerische OSZE-Präsidialjahr 1996', in *Bulletin 1996/97 zur schweizerischen Sicherheitspolitik* (Zürich: Forschungsstelle für Sicherheitspolitik und Konfliktanalyse der ETH Zürich, 1997), pp. 4–46.

33 For further reading, see Andreas Wenger, Christoph Breitenmoser, Patrick Lehmann, 'Die Partnerschaft für den Frieden – eine Chance für die Schweiz', in *Bulletin 1997/98 zur schweizerischen Sicherheitspolitik* (Zürich: Forschungsstelle für Sicherheitspolitik und Konfliktanalyse der ETH Zürich, 1998), pp. 45–102; Marcel Gerber, 'Schweizerische Rüstungskontrollpolitik in einem neuen internationalen Umfeld: das innovative Engagement für ein Personenminen-Verbot als Modell für die Zukunft?' in *Bulletin 1999 zur schweizerischen Sicherheitspolitik* (Zürich: Forschungsstelle für Sicherheitspolitik und Konfliktanalyse der ETH Zürich, 1999), pp. 77–98.

34 On the 1995 army reform, see *Bericht des Bundesrates an die Bundesversammlung über die Konzeption der Armee in den neunziger Jahren (Armeeleitbild 95) vom 27. Januar 1992*, in BBl 1992 I 850; *Armee 1995: Geschichte und Zukunft der Schweizer Armee* (ed.), Hansheiri Dahinden *et al.* (Geneva, 1998).

35 See *Bericht des Bundesrates an die Bundesversammlung über die Aussenpolitik der Schweiz: Präsenz und Kooperation – Interessenwahrung in einer zusammenwachsenden Welt (Aussenpolitischer Bericht 2000) vom 15. November 2000*, in BBl 2001 I 261; for further analysis, see Andreas Wenger, Jon A. Fanzun, 'Schweizer Sicherheitspolitik im Umbruch: Der Bericht 2000 vor dem Hintergrund des Kosovo-Konflikts', *Österreichische Militärische Zeitschrift*, Vol. 6 (2000), pp. 733–42.

36 See *Entwurf des Armeeleitbildes XXI: Konzeption der Schweizerischen Armee zu Beginn des 21. Jahrhunderts vom 2. Mai 2001* (Bern, 2001); for further analysis of the current army reform, see Markus Mäder, 'Euro-atlantischer Streitkräftewandel nach dem Kalten Krieg – wo steht die Schweizer Armee?' in *Bulletin 2001 zur schweizerischen Sicherheitspolitik* (Zürich: Forschungsstelle für Sicherheitspolitik und Konfliktanalyse der ETH Zürich, 2001), pp. 41–68; Andreas Wenger, Christoph Breitenmoser, Markus Mäder, 'Swisscoy-Einsatz im Kosovo: Erster Schritt der Schweizer Armee zur militärischen Normalität in der Sicherheitskooperation', in Jürg Martin Gabriel (ed.), *Schweizerische Aussenpolitik im Kosovo-Krieg* (Zürich Orell Füssli, 2000), pp. 119–40.

37 On the referendum on military law, see Andreas Wenger and Daniel Trachsler, 'Bewaffnete Teilnahme an Friedensoperationen – Schlüssel für die Umsetzung von "Sicherheit durch Kooperation" und Armee XXI', in *Bulletin 2001 zur schweizerischen Sicherheitspolitik* (Zürich Forschungsstelle für Sicherheitspolitik und Konfliktanalyse der ETH Zürich, 2001), pp. 11–39.

38 On the evolution of ESDP and its significance for Swiss security policy, see Andreas Wenger, 'Von Köln bis Nizza: Die Bedeutung der Gemeinsamen Europäischen Sicherheits- und Verteidigungspolitik für die Schweiz', in *Bulletin 2001 zur schweizerischen Sicherheitspolitik* (Zürich: Forschungsstelle für Sicherheitspolitik und Konfliktanalyse der ETH Zürich, 2001), pp. 99–124; Heiko Borchert and René Eggenberger, 'Selbstblockade oder Aufbruch? Die Gemeinsame Sicherheits- und Verteidigungspolitik der EU als Herausforderung für die Schweizer Armee', *Österreichische Militärische Zeitschrift*, Vol. 1 (2002), pp. 27–36.

3
The Long Road to Membership: Switzerland and the United Nations

Daniel Möckli

Introduction

Switzerland's policy towards the United Nations (UN) is paradoxical. On the one hand, the country has always been integrated in the UN system. It has joined all specialised agencies and has a long tradition of participating in various UN programmes and funds. It has also been one of the largest UN donors, contributing nearly half a billion Swiss francs in 1999. What is more, since the founding of the UN in 1945, Switzerland has been one of the organisation's most important conference sites. The city of Geneva hosts not only the European headquarters of the UN and eight UN-related international organisations but is also home for as many as 140 state missions and more than 120 non-governmental organisations (NGOs).[1]

On the other hand, Switzerland for a long time declined to join the United Nations. Non-membership was a defining feature of Swiss UN policy until March 2002, when a majority of the electorate and the cantons finally voted in favour of UN membership.[2] Before that Switzerland had been the only significant country to remain on the sidelines of the world organisation that since the 1970s had been quasi-universal in membership and at the time of Swiss entry (10 September 2002) counted 189 member states.

The conspicuous dichotomy between extensive Swiss engagement in the wider UN system and voluntary abstention from the political organisation for more than half a century raises important questions. Why did Switzerland opt against joining the United Nations for such a long time if the status of observer set obvious limits to its ability to pursue Swiss interests effectively? What caused the government to modify its UN policies in 1977 and aim for full membership? Why did the Swiss electorate reject accession in a first referendum held in 1986, but support it 16 years later? And how are we to interpret the positive outcome of the 2002 vote with respect to the future of Swiss foreign policy?

To account for the anomaly of non-membership and the recent change is to explain a number of peculiarities about Swiss foreign policy after 1945.

The UN and collective security were important factors affecting the Swiss position in international politics; in fact, they were perhaps as important as Cold War bipolarity and European integration. Therefore, the questions raised above have implications reaching beyond the UN and address the matter of Swiss foreign policy in general.

Recent research has rightly pointed out that Swiss foreign policy has always been conducted predominantly by the federal bureaucracy and transnational or transgovernmental networks rather than by the Federal Council itself.[3] With regard to the issue of UN membership, however, such a model of multiple sectoral foreign policies does not apply. Throughout the period in question here, it was the respective heads of the Federal Department of Foreign Affairs (until 1978 called the Department of Political Affairs) and the executive at large who were in charge of UN policies. Swiss relations with the world organisation were of strategic importance. They accordingly received attention at the highest levels.

I will argue that Swiss–UN relations are by and large a reflection of the country's changing interpretation of neutrality. During the immediate post-War period, both the government and the Swiss people identified so strongly with neutrality that there was little room for full membership. The Swiss government, or executive body called the Federal Council, was unwilling to redefine Swiss neutrality and subordinate it to the idea of collective security, preferring instead to pursue a distinctively autonomous course in matters of security. For the first three decades after 1945, it restricted Switzerland to participation in the 'technical' branches of the UN system not related to the sanctions regime. It was only in 1977 that the government decided to seek membership by arguing pragmatically – but implausibly – that UN collective security was so ineffective that it would not collide with Swiss neutrality.

Actually, non-membership developed into a characteristic feature of what became an isolationist mentality. It persisted among the voters even at a time when the Federal Council and Parliament had changed their minds and no longer viewed neutrality as an insurmountable obstacle. The 1986 vote was above all a popular manifestation in favour of preserving Switzerland's unique position in international affairs and of continuing a policy of non-interference in Cold War confrontations.

Only with the fall of the Berlin wall did the importance of neutrality begin to decline and UN membership become a possibility. On the conceptual level, the key turning point was the 1993 Foreign Policy Report in which the government at last qualified neutrality and declared that it did not clash with collective security. Of equal importance, however, was the intense public debate that set in on the future direction of Swiss foreign policy in an increasingly globalised and complex world. The 2002 vote to join the UN thus marked a second turning point. It ended Switzerland's status as observer and provided the country at long last with the possibility to influence decisions to an extent that corresponds with its broad engagement in the UN system.

Whether the recent vote stands for a change in Swiss identity, a move from a position of autonomy and neutrality to one of international co-operation and integration, remains uncertain, however. The Federal Council's one-sided campaign rhetoric, emphasising the compatibility of Swiss neutrality with UN membership, instead of showing the declining importance of neutrality, may well have cemented a popular belief that neutrality continues to serve as a cornerstone of foreign policy. If so, the barriers to true participation in international institutions will in the future be even more difficult to surmount.

3.1 The decision against UN membership

Many of the features that characterise Swiss policies towards the UN had their origins in the immediate post-War period. Swiss neutrality came under strong international pressure between 1943 and 1947, causing the Swiss government to review its foreign policy with the intention of adapting it to the newly emerging realities. In the process, the question of UN membership, one of the most pressing issues of the time, played an important role. Although after the Second World War neutrality was clearly in decline internationally, by the end of 1946 the Federal Council had decided to broaden rather than qualify the concept. At the same time, it developed a dualistic policy, manifesting a readiness to participate in those parts of the UN system considered to be compatible with neutrality but expressing reluctance in the security sphere.

At no time in its history was Switzerland under so much pressure and so isolated as during the final stages of the war and immediately thereafter. Its neutrality was challenged from two angles. First, there were Allied accusations that the Swiss were prolonging the war. The United States, in particular, no longer tolerated the right of neutrals to trade freely and demanded an end to all Swiss trade with Nazi Germany. The Soviets raised similar demands. This was all the more threatening, because Bern had no diplomatic relations with the Communist superpower.[4]

Second, the Allies pursued plans to institute a system of collective security that was bound to clash with Swiss foreign and security policy. The UN Charter outlawed war and replaced the traditional balance of power system with a commitment of each state to the security of every other state. This was a fundamental challenge to neutrality, which is a concept based on the legality of war. The Swiss dilemma was perfect: How could collective military (or economic) measures become compatible with a policy of abstention and non-interference?[5]

3.1.1 Neutrality versus collective security

In 1945/46, the Swiss managed to improve their relations with the Allies, but the UN question was more complex. The founding of the organisation did not take the Federal Council by surprise. As early as 1942, foreign minister Marcel Pilet-Golaz set up a unit to analyse Allied post-War plans. Most Swiss decision-makers were well informed about the new world organisation. But the government completely underestimated the speed and vigour with which the Allies would create the new body. In October 1944, Pilet-Golaz expected no organisation to emerge for three to five years. Yet when his successor, Max Petitpierre, took office in February 1945, he was confronted with the fact that the San Francisco Conference would begin within two months. Switzerland had defined no clear position at that time.[6]

The Federal Council was therefore not unhappy when the neutrals were not invited to San Francisco. It gave the government time to clarify its position. Not long thereafter, the neutrals were invited to join the 'peace loving countries' of the UN at the Potsdam Conference held in August of 1945, provided they agreed to adhere to the principles set forth in the UN Charter.[7] It was time for the Swiss government to take a public stand.

Petitpierre accelerated the foreign policy review process initiated by Pilet-Golaz. It soon became clear that under no circumstances would the Swiss be willing to renounce their neutrality entirely. Rather, in the summer of 1945, the key question was whether Switzerland would join the United Nations and subordinate its neutrality to the UN Charter, applying its traditional maxim only when collective security failed, or whether it would remain outside and pursue a purely unilateral security policy.[8]

Internal evaluations in the Department of Foreign Affairs showed a universal preference for maintaining traditional neutrality. Supporting UN sanctions would be contradictory to Swiss interests for a variety of reasons. First, the country had had a negative experience with qualified neutrality in the inter-War period. As a member of the League of Nations, Switzerland had adopted what it called 'differential' neutrality, participating in economic sanctions but preserving its military neutrality. The government and the electorate had been ready to join the organisation in 1920 in order to express Swiss solidarity with international efforts to promote a peaceful word order. However, during the Ethiopian crisis and in the wake of the League's failure, a disillusioned Switzerland returned to traditional or 'integral' neutrality in 1938.[9]

Second, in the immediate post-War era, Switzerland was surrounded by unstable neighbours, and with no peace treaties in sight, the future of Europe was uncertain. Germany, Italy and Austria were not eligible for UN membership, and it was conceivable that the UN might take action against any of them. This would put the Swiss once again in an awkward position.

Third, the hierarchical structure of the UN reinforced Switzerland's reluctance to join the UN sanctions regime. The power of the Security Council and the veto of the Permanent Five raised fears about being overruled in matters of national security. Such concerns were reinforced by the ongoing international condemnation of neutrality, both during the San Francisco Conference and after.[10]

It is important to note, however, that the decision against restricting the Swiss conception of neutrality was by no means influenced by such 'rational', interest-based reasons only. Two additional, if still insufficiently explored, factors had a large share in accounting for Swiss foreign policy preferences in the post-War period and for the strict course of neutrality vis-à-vis the UN in particular. One is the specific Swiss experience of war and the way it shaped post-War national identities. The fact that Switzerland in the Second World War was not attacked by Nazi Germany and managed to preserve its political and socio-economic stability forged a collective identity and role perception, very different from other continental states.

Comparing, for example, the Swiss case with the experience of another pre-War neutral such as Belgium may well help us to understand the different policies the two countries pursued towards both the UN and European integration. While Belgium, marked by the experience of military occupation, physical devastation and moral humiliation, did everything after 1945 to secure its independence and survival in collective arrangements, the Swiss had developed a deep emotional affinity to armed neutrality and more than ever trusted their traditional course of political and military autonomy.[11]

The other factor worth taking into account here is anti-Americanism. Considerable portions of the Swiss elite were not only ardent anti-Communists, but often also exceedingly ill-disposed towards US policies. Strong US pressure concerning Swiss trade relations with Nazi Germany (resulting in Swiss concessions in the economic negotiations of 1945 and the Washington Agreement in 1946) caused much bitterness in both the government and Parliament. Many politicians and diplomats accused the new superpower of hegemonic behaviour. They saw the United States as placing their power politics above law, which reinforced the government's inclination not to alter its neutrality.[12]

3.1.2 A special role for Switzerland?

Interestingly enough, the Federal Council in 1945/46 did not fully abandon the idea of UN membership. Foreign minister Petitpierre thought that membership combined with integral neutrality was worth striving for. As a result, the government decided that Switzerland would seek to accede to the United Nations as a 'special case'. Ideally the country would be recognised as a permanent neutral exempt from implementing UN sanctions. The Swiss government expected the United Nations to agree to a situation in which one member would have special rights and duties, offer its good offices in case of need or take charge of humanitarian services.

This formula of 'neutrality and UN membership' was also endorsed in November 1945 by a Consultative Commission that Petitpierre summoned to discuss government policy in a two-day seminar. After numerous presentations and intensive discussion, the nearly 50 participants, representing political, military, economic and academic circles, came to the conclusion that Switzerland should indeed join the UN. An overwhelming majority of the participants agreed with the Head of the Department of Foreign Affairs that official UN recognition of Swiss neutrality was a prerequisite to that step.[13]

It is not surprising that the many exploratory talks with foreign representatives that followed in subsequent months led to the realisation that not one country was prepared to support the idea of a special Swiss role within the United Nations. 'Neutrality is a word I cannot find in the Charter', was the laconic reply of UN General-Secretary Trygve Lie to the Swiss enquiry during his 1946 visit to Switzerland. His answer was typical of the international reaction.[14] Only Winston Churchill backed the Swiss position. However, in 1946 he was out of office. The Federal Council had grossly overestimated its position and the willingness of others to support the idea of Swiss uniqueness. The risk was too great that a Swiss precedent could lead to a wave of similar claims by other states in 'unique' positions.

When the UN went through its first enlargement round in August 1946, the Federal Council, faced with the choice of qualifying its neutrality or continuing on a course of abstention, decided unanimously for the latter. Petitpierre was still uneasy about the prospect of staying outside the UN. In a letter to the President of the UN General Assembly, Paul-Henri Spaak, he made a last effort to raise the idea of a special Swiss status in the UN. However, the very negative reaction of the Belgian foreign minister finally convinced Petitpierre, too, that the idea was hopeless.[15]

As a consequence, the Federal Council's 1946 annual report formulated three principles meant to serve as guidelines for Switzerland's UN policy. One, the government would continue to watch UN performance closely. Two, it would seek to participate in those UN organs compatible with neutrality. Three, the accommodation of UN agencies in Switzerland was to be encouraged and facilitated.[16]

Parallel to these decisions Petitpierre also terminated the general foreign policy review process. In a speech to Parliament in September 1947, he proclaimed the new formula of 'neutrality and solidarity'. The new Swiss doctrine was influenced by the decisions on neutrality and UN membership. It distinguished between 'political' and 'technical' international activities and outlined the Swiss intention to keep away from the former but strongly support the latter. This was a very pragmatic approach, of course, as it was left up to the Federal Council to decide what activities were 'political' and incompatible. Also, the doctrine was obviously a compensation strategy: abstention in important 'political' bodies would be compensated for by vigorous involvement in 'technical' co-operation, including humanitarian assistance, good offices and, above all, participation in 'non-political' international organisations.[17]

The analysis shows that it was not the Allies that blocked Swiss membership in 1945/46, as some traditionalist historians have argued.[18] The decisive factor was the position of the Federal Council; rather than qualify Swiss neutrality it even expanded its scope to embrace all 'political' international activity. Sweden, another neutral, took an alternative course. It joined the United Nations in 1946, supporting collective security when it was working well and practising neutrality whenever the Security Council was paralysed. The Swiss government was not prepared to accept any such restrictions to its neutrality. As the following section will show, Switzerland was satisfied with its position outside the UN.

3.2 Perceived benefits of absenteeism

The 1946 decision not to become a UN member was risky. At that time, it was uncertain whether collective security would work, and if it did, how the great powers would deal with Swiss neutrality. Yet, the advent of the Cold War and the ensuing polarisation meant that by the 1950s the Swiss found their autonomous course more practicable than they could have hoped for. More than ever, the Federal Council was convinced that non-participation was beneficial to both Switzerland and the UN, a role perception that was to mark Swiss foreign policy well into the 1960s. The Swiss government saw no reason to modify its UN stance. But it did make efforts to participate in those UN activities that accorded with integral neutrality.

The late 1940s was a time of great uncertainty, and the consequences of the government's decision were at first unclear. The Federal Council at that time took steps to legitimise neutrality internationally and domestically. In the public discourse the Swiss government, like numerous other representatives of the political and intellectual elites, ideologised Swiss neutrality and, by bestowing it with quasi-absolute character, raised it to the level of a myth. Neutrality became an end in itself – a determinant rather than an instrument of Swiss foreign policy. To foreign officials, the Federal Council explained the uniqueness of Switzerland and why it was compelled to pursue more rigid neutrality than others. At home, the incantation of neutrality concealed the imponderability that neutrality had entailed at the end of the Second World War and immediately thereafter.[19]

In actuality, the growing polarisation and ideologisation of world politics after 1947 raised doubts even among Swiss government officials about the usefulness of neutrality. Max Petitpierre, in particular, was well aware that any future foreign policy decisions of Switzerland would be perceived as favouring either East or West.[20] However, as the processes of militarisation and nuclearisation of the international system led to more stability in the 1950s, the Swiss realised that their freedom of action was expanding once more. An intermediate position between the two blocs again seemed possible. Furthermore, antagonism between the superpowers paralysed the UN and rendered collective security largely ineffective. The Korean War showed the limits of the idea of collective security and brought neutrality back into international politics. Balance of power politics celebrated a sort of revival, and traditional international law was now practised side by side with modern UN law.[21]

The Federal Council saw this as a confirmation of its UN policy. Switzerland's position outside the world organisation was not only seen as promoting national interests, but also as an instrument to support the world organisation and the general advancement of peace. The expectation was that by keeping out of world political struggles the country could offer its good offices and function as a model of peace and conflict resolution.[22] In the 1950s, non-membership became a defining feature of what gradually became a mentality of 'splendid isolation'.[23]

The Federal Council's 1954 guidelines on neutrality illustrate its new-found confidence. The policy paper became known as the 'Bindschedler Doctrine' after Rudolf Bindschedler, the influential legal advisor in the Department of Foreign Affairs who wrote it. The first version of the paper was formulated already in 1951. Against the background of the uncertainties and challenges brought about by the changing international environment (Korean War, the emerging transatlantic security alliance and the process of European integration), its original purpose was to provide basic internal guidance as to the Swiss course of neutrality.[24] When it was modified and published three years later, it contained four major additions, all of which confirmed and justified Swiss non-membership in the UN. First, the paper now explicitly held it that a neutral state like Switzerland must not sign any treaty on collective security; second, it argued that neutrality was incompatible with backing politically motivated economic sanctions of a group of states against other states; third, it ruled out participation in 'political' international organisations or conferences, at least as long as they were not universal in membership (a confirmation of Petitpierre's doctrine of 'neutrality and solidarity' of 1947); and fourth, the paper stressed the right of neutrals to offer their good services, which in Bindschedler's view no state involved could ever regard as an unfriendly act.[25]

What makes the 1954 version so interesting is that all these additions were characterised as 'neutral duties' (*Neutralitätspflichten*) rather than simple policy guidelines (in the sense of *Neutralitätspolitik*).[26] Bindschedler argued that in contrast to ordinary neutrals, a permanent neutral like Switzerland had to obey some neutral duties even in times of peace (so-called secondary neutral duties or *Vorwirkungen*). Rendering this contended legal interpretation of official policy and declaring Swiss accession to the UN as incompatible with international law contributed much to the ideological stance of the Swiss post-War conception of neutrality. It left no doubt that in the foreseeable future the government was determined to stay out of the world organisation.[27]

3.2.1 Participating in the wider UN system

The government's efforts to participate in 'technical' UN activities got an early start. In 1948, Switzerland set up an Observer Mission at UN headquarters in New York. Although it lacked a clear legal statute and was based only on an agreement with the UN General-Secretary, observer status allowed Switzerland to follow the activities of all principal UN organs, receive the necessary documentation, attend most meetings and at times even to participate in working out UN resolutions. But there were limits. Taking the floor in the General Assembly was an exceedingly complicated procedure. It was a sign of the difficulties Switzerland had in promoting its interests effectively.[28]

The sweep of Swiss participation in the general institutional framework of the UN system is remarkable. Table 3.1 lists the bodies in which Switzerland sat before accession to the main organisation in 2002. Already in 1948 it signed the statute of the International Court of Justice, the only principal UN organ admitting non-member states. Switzerland was also quick to join most specialised agencies, organisations that deal with specific social and economic issues in international relations. Already a member of several pre-War international organisations that became incorporated into the UN, the government between 1947 and 1949 also joined the newly established Food and Agriculture Organization, the World Health Organization, the International Civil Aviation Organization, the World Meteorological Organization and the United Nations Educational, Scientific and Cultural Organization. As other agencies were established later on, Switzerland was usually quick to accede to them, too.

The Federal Council also accepted an invitation to participate in various UN programmes and funds. For example, it decided to support the UN High Commissioner for Refugees, an office headed consecutively by two Swiss diplomats in the 1950s. The country also became active in entities such as the World Food Programme, the UN Conference on Trade and Development or the United Nations Children's Fund. In the latter it was to play a particularly prominent role.[29]

Although welcome to join, Switzerland at that time did not adhere to the Bretton Woods Institutions. Obviously, neutrality was not its only reason for abstaining from international organisations. The government did not conceal the fact that the primary motivation for non-membership was economic, for Swiss exporters expressed fears of discrimination in trade. This position was upheld throughout the Cold War. Switzerland joined the International Monetary Fund and the World Bank only in 1992.[30]

The Bretton Woods policy of the Federal Council, however, was an exceptional case that should not distort for us the general picture. More typical again were the government's efforts to establish Geneva as the UN's European headquarters. Even though Petitpierre failed in his effort to link UN recognition of Swiss neutrality with the idea of making Geneva the UN's

Table 3.1 Switzerland's integration into the wider UN system prior to its UN accession in September 2002

	UN entity	Founded	Swiss participation
Principal UN organs			
GA	General Assembly	1945	1948 observer
	Secretariat	1945	1948 contributions
ECOSOC	Economic and Social Council	1945	1948 observer
SC	Security Council	1945	
TC	Trusteeship Council	1945	
ICJ	International Court of Justice	1945	1948 membership
Specialised agencies			
ITU	International Telecommunication Union	1865/1947	1865 membership
UPU	Universal Postal Union	1874/1948	1875 membership
ILO	International Labour Organization	1919/1946	1920 membership
FAO	Food and Agriculture Organization of the United Nations	1945	1947 membership
ICAO	International Civil Aviation Organization	1944	1947 membership
WHO	World Health Organization	1946	1947 membership
UNESCO	United Nations Educational, Scientific and Cultural Organization	1945	1949 membership
WMO	World Meteorological Organization	1947	1949 membership
IMO	International Maritime Organization	1948	1955 membership
UNIDO	United Nations Industrial Development Organization	1966	1967 membership
WIPO	World Intellectual Property Organization	1967	1970 membership
IFAD	International Fund for Agricultural Development	1977	1977 membership
IBRD	Internat. Bank for Reconstruction and Development (World Bank)	1944	1992 membership
IDA	International Development Association (World Bank)	1959	1992 membership
IFC	International Finance Corporation (World Bank)	1956	1992 membership
MIGA	Multilateral Investment Guarantee Agency (World Bank)	1988	1992 membership
IMF	International Monetary Fund	1944	1992 membership

Table 3.1 *(Continued)*

	UN entity	Founded	Swiss participation
Programmes and funds (selective)			
UNICEF	United Nations Children's fund	1946	1947 membership
UNRWA	UN Relief/Works Agency for Palestine Refugees in the Near East	1949	1949 contributions
UNHCR	United Nations High Commissioner for Refugees	1950	1951 membership
WFP	World Food Programme	1961	1963 membership
UNCTAD	United Nations Conference on Trade and Development	1964	1964 membership
UNDP	United Nations Development Programme	1965	1965 membership
UNEP	United Nations Environment Programme	1972	1975 membership
UNDCP	United Nations Drug Control Programme	1990	1990 contributions
UNAIDS	Joint United Nations Programme on HIV/AIDS	1996	1996 membership
Others (selective)			
IAEA	International Atomic Energy Agency	1956	1957 membership
ECE	Economic Commission for Europe (ECOSOC)	1947	1972 membership
CD	Conference on Disarmament	1979	1997 membership

Source: Most of the data have been taken from François Nordmann und Dominique Petter, 'Die Rolle der UNO in der schweizerischen Aussenpolitik: Ausgezeichnete, aber unvollständige Beziehungen', *Volkswirtschaft*, No. 7 (1993), pp. 18–28; Jean-Pierre Keusch, 'Relations de la Suisse avec les organes subsidiaires et les institutions spécialisées du système des Nations Unies', in Alois Riklin *et al*. (eds), *Neues Handbuch der schweizerischen Aussenpolitik* (Bern/Stuttgart/Vienna: Paul Haupt, 1992), pp. 339–54; *UNO-Botschaft 2000*, Appendix 2. Some of the information is based on Internet research. The author would also like to thank Valentin Zellweger of the Swiss Mission to the United Nations for his help with collecting the data.

European headquarters, he realised how important it was for Switzerland to host the UN in what had previously been the League buildings. Geneva promised to bring those diplomatic networks to Switzerland that the country was bound to lose as a non-member of the UN. As early as the fall of 1946, Petitpierre persuaded his fellow members of the Federal Council to consent to all conditions put forward by the UN. As a result, many UN organisations found their way to the city of Calvin.[31]

In the early Cold War period, the government undertook two additional significant measures in order to emphasise its generally benevolent attitude towards the UN. First, in the wake of the first UN peacekeeping mission after the Suez crisis, it developed the practice of granting overfly rights to aircraft involved in UN missions, provided they did not carry troops or war equipment. This was a deviation from an otherwise very restrictive policy. Second, the government sought to assist peacekeeping missions by offering its good offices. In the Near East, in the Congo and in Cyprus Switzerland supplied the UN with transport capacities, medical staff and financial support. It even sent a large contingent of officers to Korea to monitor the armistice; this operation, however, confronted Switzerland with so many problems that after 1953 Swiss decision-makers usually took a more cautious stance towards such services.[32]

3.2.2 Shaping an isolationist swiss self-perception

In assessing Swiss–UN policy between 1947 and the late 1960s, two points stand out. First, the government was very successful in establishing Switzerland as a viable partner in the wider UN system, despite abstention from the central organisation. While Bern distrusted collective security and decided not to support the UN sanctions regime, it demonstrated from the beginning its solidarity with the general cause and actively supported many UN organs, especially in the socio-economic realm. In doing so, it managed to both win the appreciation of UN member states and to partly compensate for its lack of participation in the political organs. That the shortcomings of its abstention from the main organisation were not overly important was largely a consequence of the Cold War. That situation deadlocked the UN security system and, to the benefit of Switzerland, brought some international recognition for neutrality.

Second, in the early years of superpower confrontation, the Federal Council initiated or at least intensified developments that in the long run went counter to Swiss national interests. The process of giving neutrality a quasi-absolute quality and raising it to the central issue of any public foreign policy discourse turned out to be as counter-productive as the constant embracing of the notion of uniqueness and the related idea of a special Swiss role outside the UN. This rhetoric shaped an isolationist mentality that in later years proved hard to overcome. It was no surprise, therefore, that the Federal Council experienced negative repercussions when the question of

UN membership resurfaced and began to polarise the country. It is to that issue that we now turn.

3.3 Détente and fiasco at the polls

During the first two decades after the 1946 decision, the position of Switzerland outside the UN had found almost unanimous domestic approval. However, things began to change in the late 1960s. International developments caused the Federal Council to reassess its UN policies. By 1977 it declared UN membership a major goal of Swiss foreign policy. Faced with the familiar dilemma of reconciling neutrality with collective security, the government once again decided against subordinating neutrality to the obligations of the UN Charter. But it now argued that the Cold War had rendered the UN security system so ineffective that a collision between neutral law and collective security was unlikely. As could be expected, this argument – that Swiss neutrality and UN obligations were compatible at the practical level – triggered a great deal of controversy. As it turned out, in 1986 the electorate voted heavily against membership. This decision not only discredited the Federal Council's UN policy but also marked the beginning of a deep domestic polarisation regarding Switzerland's role in the international system.

Why did the question of UN membership gain new importance in the late 1960s? Two international developments are responsible. First, in the aftermath of the Berlin and Cuba crises, Cold War tensions subsided somewhat. Confronted with the threat of nuclear war and mutually assured destruction, the superpowers entered into a process of détente that resulted in arms limitation agreements as well as multilateral security talks in Europe. Together with Canada and the United States, 32 European states signed the 1975 Helsinki Final Act of the Conference on Security and Cooperation in Europe, recognising the Cold War status quo and expressing their willingness to improve inter-bloc relations.[33] Switzerland was a signatory, too.

Second, developments in the UN organisation itself were such that continued Swiss abstention led to growing marginalisation and increasing difficulties in safeguarding national interests. The UN was about to become universal in terms of membership. Whereas the organisation had originally been an alliance of the Second World War victors, by 1973 it included all former enemy states as well as all neutrals except Switzerland. Of particular importance to Bern was the accession of Austria in 1955 and the Federal Republic of Germany in 1973. Both neighbouring states were the object of great power confrontation and focal points of Swiss foreign policy. Also, the issues the UN dealt with began to proliferate. The growing interdependence and poly-centrism that marked world politics and the numerous new challenges ensuing from the process of decolonisation strengthened multilateralism and provided the world organisation with new responsibilities.

Non-member states found themselves increasingly excluded from vital debates and decisions, not least with regard to the further development of international law.[34]

Not surprisingly a number of Swiss – such as Karl Schmid, Max Imboden or Jean Rodolphe von Salis – began to express a sense of malaise and uneasiness about the isolationist Swiss mentality and the excessive self-restraint of Switzerland in international affairs.[35] It was mainly intellectuals who criticised the notion of Swiss uniqueness,[36] and it is telling that the government itself did not initiate the reassessment in the late 1960s. Pressure came from Parliament, which, having developed a growing interest in foreign policy, in 1967 demanded that the Federal Council prepare a report on Swiss–UN relations and on the possibility of joining while retaining neutrality.

The 1969 UN Report indicated that the disadvantages of non-membership now prevailed and that international appreciation for a state outside the UN had largely disappeared. However, at that time the Federal Council still did not officially embrace the membership option.[37] The executive body was divided about possible consequences. While foreign minister Willy Spühler made no secret of being in favour of UN membership, he failed to convince a majority of his colleagues.[38]

Yet the ice had been broken. Swiss membership in the UN was perceived by many to be a necessity, and the urgency was now such that the issue could no longer be shelved. It was characteristic of the Federal Council's reluctance, however, that it took eight more years and two additional reports before, backed by the report of yet another Consultative Commission, it declared in 1977, the UN adhesion as 'desirable'.[39]

3.3.1 How to reconcile the irreconcilable?

In public the Federal Council justified its reservations by emphasising primarily the insufficient familiarity of the Swiss electorate with the UN. The documents speak a different language, however. They leave no doubt that the real bone of contention was once more neutrality. As during the immediate post-War period, the review of Swiss UN policy revolved heavily around the 'problem', as it often used to be referred to, of how to reconcile UN membership with Switzerland's neutrality.[40] If Swiss decision-makers in the early 1970s became convinced that absenteeism was no longer justifiable, they were still at a loss as to just how membership could accord with traditional Swiss foreign policy principles.

It soon became apparent that the Federal Council was still not prepared to qualify Swiss neutrality in any meaningful way. While the period of détente was later referred to as a time when Switzerland developed 'multilateral enthusiasm',[41] the government's 1977 argumentation in favour of UN membership illustrates that the readiness to 'activate' Swiss foreign policy was limited to measures that did not diminish Swiss neutrality significantly.

It is true that some conceptual modifications were made at the time. The Federal Council finally gave up its distinction between 'political' and 'technical' activities, acknowledging that any issue in contemporary international relations naturally had a political dimension. Also, it modified its sanctions policy, arguing that it would support economic sanctions as long as they did not contradict neutral law. On the basic issue of acknowledging the primacy of modern UN law and of deactivating neutrality in the face of collective security, however, the government still took a negative stand.

Rather than switching to the Swedish position of 1946, the Swiss government in 1977 came up with the argument mentioned above that UN membership was now possible because the UN security system was ineffective. The Cold War realities would make a collision between neutrality and collective security unlikely. As a consequence, explicit UN acknowledgement of Swiss neutrality was no longer seen as prerequisite to accession.

The problem was not military, but rather economic sanctions. Military sanctions, so the Swiss government argued, could under no circumstances be imposed by the Security Council. Economic sanctions, however, posed a difficulty. Basically the Federal Council considered it improbable that the UN would ever agree on imposing economic sanctions inconsistent with neutral law. However, it reassured an evidently uneasy Parliament that should the improbable occur, it would retain neutrality rather than assume all obligations arising out of the Charter. As it elaborated in its 1981 Message on membership, Switzerland in such a case would ask the Security Council to be dispensed from the measure, and, if its demand were rejected, it still might deny the prerogative of the Charter and ignore the respective UN resolution.[42]

3.3.2 The 1986 vote

In retrospect that argument seems unnecessarily timid, yet it represented the spirit prevailing at the time. There was still boundless trust in neutrality as the foundation of Swiss security. It is hardly surprising that the government's flawed argumentation failed to persuade the people. Decades of isolationist rhetoric could not be undone by simply arguing that neutrality and collective security were compatible in the day-to-day practices of the Cold War. In March 1986, 75.7 per cent of the electorate and all 26 cantons rejected UN membership, leaving the government with an unprecedented foreign policy debacle.[43]

Of course, the flawed argumentation was not the only reason for the defeat of the referendum. There were three further contributing factors: the deteriorating international climate in the early 1980s, the lack of foreign policy awareness on the part of the public and insufficient leadership on the side of UN proponents.

The renewed tensions between the superpowers in the early 1980s undoubtedly had a negative effect on the vote. International events having a heavy impact on the Swiss,[44] the 'second Cold War', reinforced an inclination towards isolationism and a sceptical stance vis-à-vis the UN. The Soviet invasion of Afghanistan, the American Strategic Defence Initiative and the ongoing rivalries in the Third World convinced many Swiss of the undiminished validity of the country's unique role. If anything, this consolidated the Swiss self-image as an island of peace in an ocean of conflict.

The tensions did not help the image of the UN either. The failed mediation efforts of the UN General-Secretary in Central Asia, the Near East or in the war between Iraq and Iran received bad press. So did the serious financial crisis the UN ran into when the US Congress refused to pay its membership dues in 1985.[45] After its 1981 membership proposal, the Federal Council witnessed the faltering UN image and postponed the voting as long as possible. As it turned out, by 1986 things had not improved sufficiently to convince the Swiss that the UN was a useful forum for peace.

The international environment constituted a factor that was difficult to influence. That did not explain, however, why the government did so little to nurture foreign policy awareness and limited its language to repeated confirmations of neutrality's usefulness. Prior to the UN referendum, foreign policy had been the exclusive domain of a small circle of experts and politicians. As long as the Federal Council did not face a public vote, this did not hurt. However, this boomeranged once the poll became a necessity.[46] The UN vote constituted the first foreign policy referendum since 1920!

A lack of leadership also explains why UN proponents managed to mobilise so few votes. Neither the Federal Council nor Parliament succeeded in creating a positive UN image. In fact, many politicians were highly sceptical. All major parties were deeply divided, with few politicians willing to embark on a public campaign for UN membership. Long debates in Parliament demonstrated its conspicuous uneasiness with the bill; it demanded that the government issue four different declarations on neutrality instead of one, as planned. Initially the Department of Foreign Affairs developed a comprehensive information concept, but it was restrained by accusations that it was running a one-sided propaganda campaign. With the economic interest groups showing no interest in supporting the bill, there were insufficient means for a broad and sustainable campaign.[47]

Given the various obstacles the proponents encountered, it was quite easy for the opposing side to defend the status quo. It was chiefly the right-wing Swiss People's Party (SPP) that mobilised opposition to the bill. The SPP placed neutrality at the centre of its propaganda and turned the referendum into the emotional issue of preserving Swiss identity and securing national survival. The opponents denounced the UN as a useless and even Communist organisation that threatened Switzerland's uniqueness. They stirred up strong anti-government sentiments and accused the Federal Council of misrepresenting the interests of the country.[48]

There was no way the government could push its UN bill through. In 1986 the electorate opted for a policy of continuity rather than change, rejecting the government's reassurances that Swiss security would not be affected by membership in the world organisation. The voters overwhelmingly followed the SPP argument that neutrality and collective security were incompatible, thus embracing the position the Federal Council itself had maintained prior to its 1977 turnaround.

In 1986 the Federal Council stumbled over the very national self-image it had helped to shape in the early Cold War. Under the prevailing circumstances it had been impossible to alter the image within a few years time. The Swiss government had called upon ghosts that it now found very hard to dispel.[49] It was a far cry from the internationalist spirit prevailing in 1920 when a majority of the electorate had declared its solidarity with the League of Nations![50]

The negative outcome not only embarrassed the Federal Council but also the United Nations, since Switzerland was the first country ever to take a vote on membership. While the UN had more pressing business, the repercussions for the Federal Council were more far-reaching. It was clear for all to see that the incomplete U-turn of 1977 had been discredited and that the government was trapped. More fundamental even were the consequences that the UN vote had on Swiss foreign policy in general. Foreign policy had for the first time become a serious issue polarising the political elites and the public. As it turned out, the 1986 referendum was the beginning of a permanent debate about the international role of Switzerland. These discussions have severely limited the government's foreign policy options.

The SPP and an ad hoc committee against UN membership, naming itself 'Action for an Independent and Neutral Switzerland' in the wake of the referendum, were mainly responsible for mobilising the opposition against the UN bill. The same two organisations dominated the national foreign policy discourse from then on. Both groups did extremely well and managed to push the government into an overcautious and reactive stance. Gone were the days when foreign policy was a marginal public issue and when the government alone decided on important international issues. As for the issue of UN membership, it took 16 more years before the time was ripe to risk another vote.

3.4. The road to membership

After the fall of the Berlin Wall, the drawbacks of non-membership in the United Nations became ever more obvious. For domestic reasons, however, the Federal Council waited for more than a decade before reviving the issue. The period prior to the re-launch in 1997 was marked by a strategy of further consolidating co-operation with the UN and by preparing the ground for another vote. The new Foreign Policy Report of 1993 represented a milestone in these preparations, since the government finally acknowledged the primacy of the UN Charter and was now in the position to place its argumentation on a more solid base. For fear of controversial debates, however, the government refrained from making its qualified neutrality conception a campaign issue. It preferred to fall back on its old argument that Swiss neutrality would be compatible with UN membership. Once again, it was still the UN that had changed and not Switzerland! On the one hand the 2002 referendum was a major turning point in Swiss–UN relations, but on the other hand it may represent an expression of continuity, because the government's argumentation may reinforce the popular perception of neutrality as the corner stone of Swiss foreign policy.

Let us look more closely at the international and domestic changes that occurred between the embarrassing defeat of the first UN bill in 1986 and the successful vote of 2002. Undoubtedly, the key factor to explain the different outcome of the second referendum is the substantial shift that international relations have undergone since the end of the Cold War. The dissolution of bipolarity, coupled with the process of globalisation and the proliferation of transnational risks, has increased both the opportunity and the need for multilateral co-operation and global governance.[51] In the context of these developments, the usefulness of the United Nations, in spite of some setbacks, has risen considerably. Vetoes are far less common than they used to be. The UN, as the only organisation dealing globally with peace and security, finally received the significance and respect it had often lacked.[52]

3.4.1 The conceptual turning point of 1993

The changes at the international level had a profound effect on Swiss foreign policy. They influenced Swiss decision-makers and, to a somewhat lesser extent, the Swiss public as well. In 1993, the Federal Council responded to the new international situation with a radically modified foreign policy concept, which placed an emphasis on international co-operation and integration and significantly limited the scope of Swiss neutrality. The new concept meant a sharp break with tradition. Realising that the increased importance of UN sanctions would undermine a coherent and credible neutral policy and put Switzerland in opposition to the international community, the Federal Council finally came to acknowledge the primacy of the Charter obligations over the traditional law of neutrality.[53]

The Swiss government now regarded the world organisation as a legitimate global power and accepted the view that no neutrality could exist between the UN and an aggressor.[54] This narrowing of neutrality allowed the Federal Council to resolve the basic tension between neutrality and collective security. For Switzerland to take this step even as a non-member of the UN was a significant development. Between 1993 and 2002 the country participated in all economic sanctions of the UN, and even when it came to military measures, it was no longer neutral law but national interests that set the Swiss course.[55]

Although by 1993 the government had cleared away all conceptual hindrances to UN membership, it refrained from placing the membership issue before the public. The main reason for the postponement was that the domestic situation was less favourable than the international one. While most decision-makers now felt that observer status no longer constituted a viable alternative to membership, this view was obviously not yet held by significant parts of the electorate. In matters of international politics, domestic opinion was more polarised than ever. The Federal Council therefore decided to concentrate its efforts on one issue at the time and to place priority on European integration. As the electorate had rejected Swiss participation in the European Economic Area in 1992, the major challenge was to settle relations with the European Union.

Still, there was some movement on the UN front. After 1986 the Federal Council made great efforts to optimise its position as a benevolent bystander.[56] It now became more active in preventive action and peacebuilding, for instance. In fact, from 1989 onwards, the government made significant contributions in these fields. Medical units, military observers, civilian police, experts on democratisation, human rights and election monitoring were put at the UN's disposal. It also set up a pool of specialists for quick response to specific UN requests.[57] Taking up an idea that had been considered in the 1960s, the government even proposed a national blue helmet contingent for peacekeeping missions. However, in 1994 the bill was defeated at the polls.[58]

Other fields of increased engagement include arms control and disarmament and international criminal law. In the 1990s Switzerland was involved actively in the Ottawa process that led to the prohibition of anti-personnel mines, for example. It also played an important role in bringing about the Chemical Weapons Convention. Efforts at regulating trade in small arms and light weapons have also witnessed much backing by the Swiss government. With regard to the prosecution of war crimes, the country went to great lengths to ensure that the International Criminal Court agreed upon in Rome would not be toothless.[59]

These steps were mainly intended to demonstrate to the international community that Switzerland was ready to assume its share of international responsibility. At the same time, the Federal Council began to prepare the domestic ground for a second vote on accession. The conceptual modifications mentioned earlier were just one step to this end, albeit the most important. Other efforts included rather more symbolic events, such as Swiss President Adolf Ogi's joint alpine hike with UN General-Secretary Kofi Annan. The event was covered intensively by the national media and established a sense of familiarity with what is often perceived as an anonymous and faceless world organisation.

3.4.2 The second vote of 2002

In the late 1990s, the Federal government finally decided to embark on a second UN campaign. It had reason to believe that the international changes had worked to its advantage. Opinion polls revealed an increasingly favourable attitude towards the United Nations.[60] The UN's increased effectiveness and the fact that Switzerland, together with the Holy See, was the last state to sit on the observer bench in the General Assembly convinced many former sceptics that it no longer made sense to remain outside the UN. It was also encouraging that a vast majority of the political elite now strongly supported the idea of UN membership, the SPP being the only major party still opposed. Furthermore, this time the powerful economic interest groups stood behind the Federal Council and expressed their readiness to campaign actively for the UN cause.

The new campaign gained momentum in 1997 when Parliament asked the Federal Council to prepare a report showing how Swiss–UN relations had developed since 1986. The report was published on 1 July 1998, declaring the government's readiness to aim for 'the strategic objective of membership of the United Nations as soon as it is politically possible'.[61] The government also welcomed the launching of a public initiative in September 1998. Eighteen months later, more than 120 000 signatures were submitted. This accomplishment was very important to the Federal Council, since this meant that the second vote would be initiated by parts of the electorate rather than by the government. In the summer of the year 2000 a consultation process yielded broad support for the idea of accession. Finally, in the Message on UN Membership of 4 December 2000, the government recommended to Parliament that the electorate and the cantons be consulted.[62]

Despite the much-improved prospects for winning, the government unfortunately decided to argue largely along the lines of 1986 Report and to emphasise the compatibility of neutrality and UN membership. Rather than mentioning the conceptual changes of the 1993 Foreign Policy Report that allowed Switzerland to comply with all Charter obligations, the Federal Council time and again pointed out that Swiss neutrality would not be compromised by UN membership and that it would even gain increased international recognition. Although this position was legally tenable, it was highly simplistic.

Quite obviously Swiss decision-makers were still not prepared to make the declining relevance of neutrality an object of public debate. Fearing another defeat at the polls, the government was eager to prevent the UN vote from turning into a plebiscite on Swiss neutrality, even though it was neutrality that for more than half a century had kept the country out of the UN. Certainly, the Federal Council was right to refer to the changed international situation and the UN's improved performance. But it neglected to mention the domestic changes that were necessary to make UN membership feasible.

There are thus two sides to the positive verdict of March 2002. With regard to Swiss–UN relations, the referendum certainly marked an important turning point, similar to the conceptual changes of 1993.[63] The decision to join the United Nations had been long overdue, the Federal Council having pursued this goal for 25 years. With their positive vote, the electorate indicated that abstention from the world organisation was no longer perceived as a defining feature of Switzerland and that the idea of uniqueness had lost some of its value in recent years.[64]

However, taking into account the continuity of the government's message to the public, it may well be that the vote reinforced the popular belief in this maxim. From this perspective, it appears that far less changed in March 2002. The overwhelming majority of the population is still clinging to the idea of Swiss uniqueness in international affairs based on a particular concept of neutrality. The traditional Swiss self-perception is likely to persist, because many who voted for UN membership were also casting a positive vote for neutrality.

If that is the case, the chasm between the outward-oriented foreign policy of the government and the neutrality-focused perception of many Swiss people may even have widened. While the gap did not, finally, stand in the way of UN admission, it may prove to be a hindrance when such delicate issues as joining the European Union come before public vote. As far as EU supranationality is concerned, a domestic foreign policy discourse that focuses on the perseverance of neutrality will no longer do, of course. The vote of March 2002 may in the long run be remembered as a missed opportunity. It failed to provide a clear account of the parameters determining Swiss foreign policy in the post-Cold War era.

Conclusion

Although Swiss–UN relations have numerous dimensions, the issue that has dominated all others for much of the past six decades is neutrality. The question of joining or not joining preoccupied the country in the immediate post-War era and from the late 1960s onwards. The early Cold War period was the only time when Switzerland appeared to be united in rejecting UN accession.

Prior to 1977, it was the Federal Council that preferred to watch the UN as a bystander, unwilling to subordinate Swiss neutrality to the obligations of the UN Charter. After the Second World War, it had assessed the disadvantages of non-membership as tolerable. When the government finally changed its mind, it was up to the Swiss electorate to take a stand. The fact that for another quarter of a century a majority of the people hesitated to give an affirmative answer is an indication of the delicate and controversial nature of the issue. It also demonstrates how powerful the institution of direct democracy can be in shaping the course of Swiss foreign policy.

So is it expedient to regard the 2002 vote as a happy end to what proved a long and twisted story? Yes and no. On the positive side, by voting for UN membership, the electorate finally resolved the traditional foreign policy paradox. No longer is the country intimately integrated in the wider UN system while unable to adequately safeguard its interests on key UN issues. However, even after the success of the referendum, not yet all is well. With Swiss decision-makers over-emphasising the value of Swiss neutrality for short-term purposes, it may well be that in the long run they have curtailed their scope of action with regard to European integration. The dilemma between neutrality and full-scale multilateral participation may no longer apply to Swiss relations with the United Nations, but it will continue to haunt Swiss foreign policy in the years to come.

Acknowledgement

The author would like to thank Jürg Martin Gabriel and Thomas Fischer for their comments on an earlier draft.

Notes

1 For facts and figures on Swiss–UN relations, see *Botschaft über die Volksinitiative 'Für den Beitritt der Schweiz zur Organisation der Vereinten Nationen (UNO)' vom 4. Dezember 2000*, in BBl 2001 II 1183 (referred to in the following as 'UNO-Botschaft 2000'); *Bericht des Bundesrates über das Verhältnis zwischen der Schweiz und der Organisation der Vereinten Nationen (UNO) vom 1. Juli 1998*, in BBl 1998 V 5242 (referred to in the following as 'UNO-Bericht 1998').

2 Fifty-five per cent of the public voted in favour. However, since a cantonal majority was also required and only 12 of 23 cantons approved, that aspect of the vote was narrow.

3 See Thomas Gees, Andreas Kellerhans-Maeder and Daniela Meier, *Die Verwaltung der schweizerischen Aussenpolitik 1914–1978: Bundesrat und Bundesverwaltung: Entscheidungsprozesse und Netzwerke in der Landwirtschafts- und Umweltschutzaussenpolitik* (Zürich: Chronos, 2002); Peter Hug, Thomas Gees, and Katja Dannecker, *Die Aussenpolitik der Schweiz im kurzen 20. Jahrhundert. Antibolschewismus, Deutschlandpolitik und organisierte Weltmarktintegration – segmentierte Praxis und öffentliches Ritual*, NFP 42 Synthesis 49 (Bern: 2000).

4 On this issue, see Daniel Möckli, *Neutralität, Solidarität, Sonderfall: Die Konzeptionierung der schweizerischen Aussenpolitik der Nachkriegszeit, 1943–1947*, Zürcher Beiträge zur Sicherheitspolitik und Konfliktforschung 55 (Zürich: Forschungsstelle für Sicherheitspolitik und Konfliktanalyse der ETH Zürich, 2000).

5 Jürg Martin Gabriel, *Schweizer Neutralität im Wandel: Hin zur EG* (Frauenfeld: Huber, 1990); Stephen C. Neff, *The Rights and Duties of Neutrals: A General History* (Manchester: Juris Publishing, 2000); Adrian R. Schaub, *Neutralität und Kollektive Sicherheit: Gegenüberstellung zweier unvereinbarer Verhaltenskonzepte in bewaffneten Konflikten und These zu einem zeit- und völkerrechtsgemässen modus vivendi* (Basel: Helbing & Lichtenhahn, 1995).

6 Möckli, *Neutralität, Solidarität, Sonderfall*, pp. 35–92.
7 Gabriel, *Schweizer Neutralität im Wandel*, pp. 64–72.
8 Möckli, *Neutralität, Solidarität, Sonderfall*, pp. 92–111.
9 Gabriel, *Schweizer Neutralität im Wandel*, pp. 30–4; Carlo Moos, 'Ein Aufbruch von geringer Nachhaltigkeit: Zur Völkerbundsdebatte nach dem 1. Weltkrieg', in Sebastian Guex *et al.* (eds), *Krisen und Stabilisierung: Die Schweiz in der Zwischenkriegszeit*, Die Schweiz 1798–1998: Staat - Gesellschaft - Politik 2 (Zürich Chronos, 1998), pp. 47–60.
10 For example, US Secretary of State Stettinius in his opening address at San Francisco condemned neutrality explicitly, and the head of the French delegation during the conference even suggested a reference to the incompatibility of neutrality and collective security in the Charter. Jürg Martin Gabriel, *The American Conception of Neutrality After 1941*, updated and revised edition (Houndmills/Basingstoke: Palgrave, 2002), pp. 70–5.
11 Historical research on the nexus between Swiss collective identities and foreign policy has been neglected so far. Some ideas have been developed by Daniel Frei, *Neutralität – Ideal oder Kalkül? Zweihundert Jahre aussenpolitisches Denken in der Schweiz* (Frauenfeld/Stuttgart: Huber, 1967). For an interesting sociological-historical approach, see Kurt Imhof, Heinz Kleger and Gaetano Romano (eds), *Konkordanz und Kalter Krieg: Analyse von Medienereignissen in der Schweiz der Zwischen- und Nachkriegszeit*, Krise und sozialer Wandel 2 (Zürich: Seismo Verlag, 1996). An approach that could inspire further Swiss research has been developed by French historians. See Jean-Baptiste Duroselle, 'Opinion, attitude, mentalité, mythe, idéologie: Essai de clarification', *Relations internationales*, No. 2 (1974), pp. 3–23; Pierre Milza, 'Mentalités collectives et relations internationales', *Relations internationales*, No. 41 (1985), pp. 93–109; Etienne François, Hannes Siegrist and Jakob Vogel (eds), *Nation und Emotion: Deutschland und Frankreich im Vergleich, 19. und 20. Jahrhundert* (Göttingen: Vandenhoeck & Ruprecht, 1995). Also: Thomas Angerer, 'Für eine Geschichte der österreichischen Neutralität', in Michael Gehler and Rolf Steiniger (eds), *Die Neutralen und die europäische Integration 1945–1995* (Wien: Böhlau, 2000), pp. 702–8.
12 Möckli, *Neutralität, Solidarität, Sonderfall*, pp. 129–68. Signs of an elitist Swiss anti-Americanism can still be found in the 1950s, grounding on both strong US pressure on Switzerland to support Western economic warfare measures against the Eastern bloc and Swiss perceptions of ominous US Cold War policies. See, for instance, the diaries of Federal Councillor Markus Feldmann: Schweizerische Gesellschaft für Geschichte (ed.), *Markus Feldmann: Tagebuch 1923–1958, Bd. 5*, bearbeitet von Peter Moser, Krebs (Basel: 2002), pp. 149, 243, 265, 286 and 556.
13 Möckli, *Neutralität, Solidarität, Sonderfall*, pp. 120–28.
14 Möckli, *Neutralität, Solidarität, Sonderfall*, pp. 168–86, here p. 183.
15 Möckli, *Neutralität, Solidarität, Sonderfall*, pp. 186–205.
16 *UNO-Botschaft 2000*, here 1188. On the Swiss decision against UN membership in the immediate post-War period, see also Antoine Fleury, 'La Suisse et le défi du multilateralisme', in Georg Kreis (ed.), *Die Schweiz im internationalen System der Nachkriegszeit 1943–1950*, Itinera 18 (Basel: Schwabe, 1996), pp. 68–83; Peter Hug, 'Verhinderte oder verpasste Chancen? Die Schweiz und die Vereinten Nationen, 1943–1947', in Georg Kreis (ed.), *Die Schweiz im internationalen System der Nachkriegszeit 1943–1950*, Itinera 18 (Basel: Schwabe, 1996), pp. 84–97; Daniel Möckli, 'Vor einer neuen Uno-Abstimmung: Drei Erkenntnisse aus der Niederlage von 1986', in Kurt R. Spillmann and Andreas Wenger (eds), *Bulletin 2000 zur schweizerischen Sicherheitspolitik*, pp. 53–87, here pp. 56–9.

17 Möckli, *Neutralität, Solidarität, Sonderfall*, pp. 237–82.

18 See Reinhart Ehni, *Die Schweiz und die Vereinten Nationen von 1944–1947*, Tübinger Studien zur Geschichte und Politik 21 (Tübingen: Mohr, 1967); Reinhold Werner Hohengartner, *Schweizerische Neutralität und Vereinte Nationen 1945–1981: Die Problematik des schweizerischen UNO-Beitrittes im Spannungsfeld zwischen Bundesrat und Parlament*, Dissertationen der Universität Wien 236 (Wien: VWGÖ, 1993).

19 The process of ideologising Swiss neutrality after the Second World War was first described by Daniel Frei in 'Die Ära Petitpierre, 1945–1961 – Rückblick auf eine Epoche schweizerischer Aussenpolitik', in Louis-Edouard Roulet (ed.), *Max Petitpierre – Seize ans de neutralité active: Aspects de la politique étrangère de la Suisse (1945–1961)* (Neuchâtel: Baconnière, 1980), pp. 165–74. See also on this issue Matthias Kunz, *Aufbruchstimmung und Sonderfall-Rhetorik: Die Schweiz im Übergang von der Kriegs- zur Nachkriegszeit in der Wahrnehmung der Parteipresse, 1943–1950*, Bundesarchiv Dossier 8 (Bern: 1998); Sacha Zala, *Geschichte unter der Schere politischer Zensur: Amtliche Aktensammlungen im internationalen Vergleich* (München: Oldenbourg, 2001).

20 Daniel Trachsler, *Neutral zwischen Ost und West? Infragestellung und Konsolidierung der schweizerischen Neutralitätspolitik durch den Beginn des Kalten Krieges, 1947–1952*, Zürcher Beiträge zur Sicherheitspolitik und Konfliktforschung 63 (Zürich: Forschungsstelle für Sicherheitspolitik und Konfliktanalyse der ETH Zürich, 2002).

21 Gabriel, *American Conception of Neutrality After 1941*, pp. 123–45. On Swiss foreign policy in the early Cold War period, see Peter Hug, 'Vom Neutralismus zur Westintegration: Zur schweizerischen Aussenpolitik in der Nachkriegszeit', in Walter Leimgruber and Werner Fischer (eds), *'Goldene Jahre': Zur Geschichte der Schweiz seit 1945* (Zürich: Chronos, 1999), pp. 59–100. On Swiss good offices in particular, see the chapter by Thomas Fischer in the present volume. See also Andrew Williams, 'Finding a New Role in International Conflict Resolution: Switzerland after the End of the Cold War', in Michael Butler *et al.* (eds), *The Making of Modern Switzerland* (London: Macmillan, 2000), pp. 111–22.

22 In the Department of Political Affairs the idea of joining the UN was never entirely abandoned, however. Individual diplomats such as Alfred Zehnder (head of the Political Affairs Division) continued to strongly argue in favour of UN membership. In 1952 an exercise was even made in preparing drafts of both a formal Swiss application for membership and a UN resolution recognising Swiss neutrality (see Swiss Federal Archive, Nachlass Bindschedler, J.I.223/001 379, 25 September 1952). Petitpierre himself in 1959 raised the issue of UN membership and a generally more active Swiss foreign policy in the Federal Council. A majority of his fellow Councillors rejected any change of policy and characterised themselves as 'adherent to the old school'. See Roland Maurhofer, *Die schweizerische Europapolitik vom Marshallplan zur EFTA 1947 bis 1960: Zwischen Kooperation und Integration* (Bern: Paul Haupt, 2001), pp. 415–20. A comprehensive study in the Department of Political Affairs on the question of UN membership in 1960 equally concluded that the time was not yet ripe. See: Rudolf Bindschedler, 'Der Beitritt der Schweiz zu den Vereinigten Nationen', 11 July 1960, Swiss Federal Archive, Nachlass Bindschedler, J.I.223/001 381.

23 Jakob Tanner, 'Switzerland and the Cold War: A Neutral Country between the "American Way of Life" and "Geistige Landesverteidigung"', in Joy Charnley and Malcolm Pender (eds), *Switzerland and War* (Bern: Peter Lang, 1999), pp. 113–28, here p. 116.

24 See Swiss Federal Archive, 'Der Begriff der Neutralität', 28 December 1951, Nachlass Bindschedler, J.I.223/001 474. Petitpierre approved the document, with minor modifications, on 4 January 1952.

25 Both versions also contained a clause on Swiss neutrality being incompatible with joining a customs union, indicating that Switzerland would keep its distance from the process of European integration as well. The guidelines of 1954 are reproduced in Dietrich Schindler (ed.), *Dokumente zur schweizerischen Neutralität seit 1945: Berichte und Stellungnahmen der schweizerischen Bundesbehörden zu Fragen der Neutralität 1945–1983*, Schriftenreihe der Schweizerischen Gesellschaft für Aussenpolitik 9 (Bern/Stuttgart: Paul Haupt, 1984), pp. 15–9.

26 The existing literature so far has identified the four points in question simplistically as part of Swiss *Neutralitätspolitik*. The 'Bindschedler Doctrine' however adds them explicitly to the category of neutral law, emphasising that only those policies beyond the field of secondary neutral duties make up the realm of voluntary neutral measures.

27 It is indicative of the Swiss self-perception of the time that the Department of Political Affairs, despite Swiss non-membership in the UN, regarded it as a duty of the world organisation to support Switzerland in the event of a military attack. A draft appeal of 1952 for help held it that since the UN Charter did not restrict UN solidarity to member states only, Switzerland would be entitled to receive the benefits of collective security. See Swiss Federal Archives, Nachlass Bindschedler, J.I.223/001 381, 10 October 1952.

28 Paul Seger, 'Die Stellung der Schweiz als Beobachter bei den Vereinten Nationen in New York', *Schweizerische Zeitschrift für internationales und europäisches Recht*, No. 4 (1995), pp. 479–514.

29 For more information regarding Swiss integration into the UN system, see *Bericht des Bundesrates an die Bundesversammlung über das Verhältnis der Schweiz zu den Vereinten Nationen vom 16. Juni 1969*, in BBl 1969 I 1449 (referred to in the following as 'UNO-Bericht 1969'); Schweizerische Gesellschaft für die Vereinten Nationen (ed.), *Die Schweiz und die Vereinten Nationen* (Bern: Lang, 1970).

30 For an analysis of the Swiss decision against joining the Bretton Woods Institutions, see Stefan Rüesch, 'Neutralität oder Solidarität? Die Schweiz und die Bretton Woods-Institutionen 1944–1951', *Studien und Quellen*, No. 19 (1993), pp. 217–29.

31 Möckli, *Neutralität, Solidarität, Sonderfall*, pp. 218–25.

32 On these measures, see *UNO-Bericht 1969*, here 1509–20. See also the chapter by Thomas Fischer in this volume.

33 Christoph Breitenmoser, *Sicherheit für Europa: Die KSZE-Politik der Schweiz bis zur Unterzeichnung der Helsinki-Schlussakte zwischen Skepsis und aktivem Engagement*, Zürcher Beiträge zur Sicherheitspolitik und Konfliktforschung 40 (Zürich: Forschungsstelle für Sicherheitspolitik und Konfliktanalyse der ETH Zürich, 1996).

34 On the changes of the UN, see Evan Luard, *A History of the United Nations. Part II: The Age of Decolonization, 1955–1965* (London: Macmillan, 1989); Rolf Paul Haegler, *Schweizer Universalismus, UNO-Partikularismus: die Bedeutung des Universalitätsprinzips in der Frage des Beitritts der Schweiz zur Organisation der Vereinten Nationen, unter besonderer Berücksichtigung der Verhandlungen in der Bundesversammlung* (Bern/Frankfurt am Main/New York: Peter Lang, 1983), pp. 74–135.

35 On the writings of these authors, see Katharina Bretscher-Spindler, *Vom Heissen zum Kalten Krieg: Vorgeschichte und Geschichte der Schweiz im Kalten Krieg 1943–1968* (Zürich: Orell Füssli, 1997), pp. 404–54.

36 Ironically, some of these intellectuals (Swiss historian Edgar Bonjour would be an example) had had their share of responsibility in ideologising Swiss neutrality in the early post-War period.

37 *Bericht des Bundesrates an die Bundesversammlung über das Verhältnis der Schweiz zu den Vereinten Nationen vom 16. Juni 1969*, in BBl 1969 I 1449.

38 Elisabeth Glas, *Aufbruch der Schweiz in die multilaterale Welt: Die schweizerische Aussenpolitik 1965–1977* (Zürich: MA thesis, 1999).

39 The reports are: *Bericht des Bundesrates an die Bundesversammlung über das Verhältnis der Schweiz zu den Vereinten Nationen und ihren Spezialorganisationen für die Jahre 1969–1971 vom 17. November 1971*, in BBl 1972 I 1; *Bericht über das Verhältnis der Schweiz zu den Vereinten Nationen und ihren Spezialorganisationen für die Jahre 1972–1976 vom 29. Juni 1977*, in BBl 1977 II 813 (referred to in the following as 'UNO-Bericht 1977'). The Consultative Commission was set up in August 1973. Contrary to its predecessor of 1945, it had a broad mandate to evaluate the question of UN membership thoroughly and present its findings in a report. The report was completed by August 1975 but failed to find the approval of all members of the commission. For more information on the Commission, see the *UNO-Bericht 1977*. See also: Baslan Qurashi, *L'évolution de l'attitude officielle de la Suisse à l'égard d'une adhésion éventuelle à l'ONU de 1944 à 1978* (Wien: MA thesis, 1979).

40 Hans Haug, 'Das Problem der vollen Mitgliedschaft der Schweiz in den Vereinten Nationen', in Alois Riklin, Hans Haug and Hans Christoph Binswanger (eds), *Handbuch der schweizerischen Aussenpolitik*, Schriftenreihe der Schweizerischen Gesellschaft für Aussenpolitik 2 (Bern/Stuttgart: Paul Haupt, 1975), pp. 533–41; Rudolf Bindschedler, 'Das Problem der Beteiligung der Schweiz an Sanktionen der Vereinigten Nationen, besonders im Falle Rhodesiens', *Zeitschrift für ausländisches öffentliches Recht und Völkerrecht*, No. 28 (1968), pp. 1–15.

41 Carlo Jagmetti, 'Bilaterale und multilaterale Zusammenarbeit der Schweiz', in Alois Riklin *et al.* (eds), *Neues Handbuch der schweizerischen Aussenpolitik* (Bern/Stuttgart/Wien: Paul Haupt, 1992), pp. 211–20, here p. 217.

42 *Botschaft über den Beitritt der Schweiz zur Organisation der Vereinten Nationen (UNO) vom 21. Dezember 1981*, in BBl 1982 I 497, here 549–51.

43 Schweizerische Gesellschaft für praktische Sozialforschung (ed.), *Vox-Analyse der eidgenössischen Abstimmung vom 16. März 1986* (Bern: Forschungszentrum für schweizerische Politik, 1986).

44 See on this issue Daniel Frei, 'Die internationale Umwelt als Rahmenbedingung der schweizerischen Politik und die Gestaltung der schweizerischen Aussenbeziehungen', in Alois Riklin (ed.), *Handbuch Politisches System der Schweiz. Bd. 1: Grundlagen* (Bern: Paul Haupt, 1983), pp. 465–535; Daniel Frei, 'Die Schweiz im internationalen System', in Jürg Steiner *et al.* (ed.), *Das politische System der Schweiz* (München: Piper, 1971), pp. 63–233.

45 Philippe Grossen, *Das Bild der UNO in der Schweizer Tagespresse*, Zürcher Beiträge zur Politischen Wissenschaft 13 (Grüsch: Rüegger, 1986).

46 Möckli, *Neutralität, Solidarität, Sonderfall*, pp. 296f.

47 Stefan Glur, *'Rester à l'écart devient une démission': Bundesrat Pierre Aubert und die Uno* (Zürich: MA thesis, 1999); Laurent Goetschel, *Zwischen Effizienz und Akzeptanz: Die Information der Schweizer Behörden im Hinblick auf die Volksabstimmung über den EWR-Vertrag vom 6. Dezember 1992* (Bern/Stuttgart/Wien: Paul Haupt, 1994); Peter Ziegler, *Diplomatie, Diskretion und Information: Eine Studie zur Konzeption der Informationspolitik des Eidgenössischen Departements für auswärtige Angelegenheiten* (Aarau/Frankfurt am Main/Salzburg: Sauerländer, 1983); Möckli, *Vor einer neuen Uno-Abstimmung*, pp. 68–76.

48 Luzius Wildhaber, 'Das Schweizer Nein zu einer Vollmitgliedschaft in den Vereinten Nationen', *Europa-Archiv*, No. 15 (1986), pp. 461–8; Dieter Pfirter, 'Verhältnis Schweiz-UNO: Wie weiter nach dem 16. März 1986?' in Wolf Linder (ed.), *Aussenpolitik*, SVPW-Jahrbuch 28 (Bern: Paul Haupt, 1989), pp. 73–90;

Matthias Benz, 'Ja zur Schweiz – Nein zur Welt? Rückblick auf die Uno-Abstimmung 1986', *Neue Zürcher Zeitung*, 12 December 1995; Leonhard Neidhart, 'Hintergründe der Uno-Verwerfungslawine', *Neue Zürcher Zeitung*, 4 April 1986.

49 Frei, *Die Ära Petitpierre*, p. 168.

50 Carlo Moos, *Ja zum Völkerbund – Nein zur UNO: Die Volksabstimmungen von 1920 und 1986 in der Schweiz*, Schweizer Beiträge zur Internationalen Geschichte 4 (Zürich: Chronos, 2001).

51 Joseph S. Nye and John D. Donahue (eds), *Governance in a Globalizing World* (Washington, DC: Brookings Institution Press, 2000); Kurt R. Spillmann and Andreas Wenger, with the assistance of Daniel Möckli (eds), *Towards the 21st Century: Trends in Post-Cold War International Security Policy* (Bern *et al.*: Peter Lang, 1999).

52 *UNO-Botschaft 2000*, here 1190–6.

53 *Bericht über die Aussenpolitik der Schweiz in den 90er Jahren. Anhang: Bericht zur Neutralität vom 29. November 1993*, in BBl 1994 I 153 (referred to in the following as 'Bericht 93'). The findings regarding the Swiss UN policies were confirmed in the new foreign policy report of November 2000 that superseded the *Bericht 93*: *Aussenpolitischer Bericht 2000 – Präsenz und Kooperation: Interessenwahrung in einer zusammenwachsenden Welt vom 15. November 2000*, in BBl 2001 I 261. For a detailed analysis of the new UN policies, see Jürg Martin Gabriel, *Sackgasse Neutralität* (Zürich: vdf Hochschulverlag, 1997).

54 The need for a conceptual reorientation concerning neutrality and collective security became apparent during the Gulf War of 1990/91 when the Federal Council implemented the economic sanctions of the UN but applied neutrality towards UN-approved military measures. The Swiss government's revived position of differential neutrality not only amazed experts on neutrality law, but also hampered the military operations of the Allies, who were not granted overfly rights. See Dietrich Schindler, 'Kollektive Sicherheit der Vereinten Nationen und dauernde Neutralität der Schweiz', *Schweizerische Zeitschrift für internationales und europäisches Recht*, No. 4 (1992), pp. 435–79.

55 An overview of Swiss participation in individual UN sanctions is appended in the *UNO-Bericht 98*.

56 See here the excellent overview in the *UNO-Bericht 1998*. See also Thomas Bernauer and Sandra Lavenex, 'Abschied vom Sonderfall: Die 90-Prozent-Mitgliedschaft der Schweiz in den Vereinten Nationen', *Vereinte Nationen*, Issue 3 (2000), pp. 89–94; Hansrudolf Hoffmann, 'Die Schweiz und die UNO', in René Rhinow (ed.), *Die schweizerische Sicherheitspolitik im internationalen Umfeld* (Basel/Frankfurt am Main: Helbing & Lichtenhahn, 1995), pp. 57–72.

57 On the pool of experts, see the webpage of the Federal Department of Foreign Affairs, available at http://www.eda.admin.ch/sub_expool/g/home.html.

58 Robert Diethelm, *Die Schweiz und friedenserhaltende Operationen 1920–1995*, St. Galler Studien zur Politikwissenschaft 19 (Bern: Paul Haupt, 1997).

59 Jon A. Fanzun and Patrick Lehmann, *Die Schweiz und die Welt: Aussen- und sicherheitspolitische Beiträge der Schweiz zu Frieden, Sicherheit und Stabilität, 1945–2000*, Zürcher Beiträge zur Sicherheitspolitik und Konfliktforschung 57 (Zürich: Forschungsstelle für Sicherheitspolitik und Konfliktanalyse der ETH Zürich, 2000).

60 According to an annual survey, the ratio of respondents supporting UN accession rose from 30 per cent in 1990 to 60 per cent in 2001. Karl W. Haltiner *et al.*, *Sicherheit 2001: Aussen-, Sicherheits- und Verteidigungspolitische Meinungsbildung im Trend* (Zürich: Forschungsstelle für Sicherheitspolitik und Konfliktanalyse der ETH Zürich und Militärische Führungsschule an der ETHZ, 2001), p. 67.

61 *UNO-Bericht 1998*, here p. 5282.
62 For the development of the issue of UN membership in the Swiss political process, see *UNO-Botschaft 2000*, 1188–90.
63 Georg Kreis, 'Neue Verhältnisse – veränderte Haltungen: Die schweizerische Uno-Diskussion seit 1945', *Neue Zürcher Zeitung*, 4 January 2002.
64 Jean-Daniel Clavel and Alain M. Schoenenberger, *Sonderfall ade – die Schweiz auf neuen Wegen* (Zürich: vdf Hochschulverlag, 2000).

4

From Good Offices to an Active Policy of Peace: Switzerland's Contribution to International Conflict Resolution

Thomas Fischer

Introduction

The purpose of this contribution is to examine the practice of Swiss good offices since the Second World War and to analyse the impact of the end of the Cold War and the conceptual changes in Swiss foreign policy dating from 1993. This will reveal that the traditional categories of Swiss good offices – protecting power mandates, arbitration, good offices in a narrow sense and bilateral mediation – have decreased in number and importance since 1945, while at the same time international mandates and new approaches to international conflict management have become more relevant. In fact, Switzerland's role as an active contributor to multilateral missions and mediation only became possible when neutrality was reinterpreted to embrace active politics of peace.[1]

Since the end of the Cold War, civil conflicts having either a religious or ethnic background have begun to replace classical forms of war. It has therefore become necessary to modify established approaches to peaceful conflict settlement. Today, multilaterally co-ordinated third-party activities, mostly within the framework of the United Nations, play a much more important role than unilateral or bilateral measures initiated by single states. On the basis of its neutrality, Switzerland long considered itself predestined to act as an international go-between. In a recent example, however, the Swiss Federal Department of Foreign Affairs tried – in vain – to mediate in the Afghan civil war by applying traditional 'good offices' to a domestic conflict situation. That experience demonstrated clearly that bilateral activities conducted by a neutral state are by no means more successful than the activities of multilateral organisations.

From the time the Soviets withdrew in 1989, and especially after the Soviet-supported government lost power in 1992, Afghanistan experienced constant turmoil. In 1998, UN Secretary-General Kofi Annan set up a Special Mission to engage the authorities of neighbouring countries and the different Afghan factions in negotiations, but to no avail. After two rounds of intra-Afghan talks in early 1999, initiated by Kofi Annan's Special Envoy, Lakhdar Brahimi, the leaders of the unofficial Taliban government announced in the spring that they would not resume the negotiations under the auspices of the United Nations. In July 1999, the Taliban launched a military offensive against the northern United Front, which was under the leadership of Ahmed Shah Massoud, but they were unable to gain a decisive advantage.[2]

After Brahimi's failure, the Swiss initiated a bilateral mediation effort.[3] In the second half of 1999 and in early 2000, high-ranking Taliban representatives and delegates of the United Front met secretly in Switzerland. In order to establish contacts and to prepare the negotiations, each side was invited for separate talks with Swiss officials and representatives of the Swiss National Bank, the ICRC, and the State Secretariat for Economic Affairs. In the autumn of 1999, the talks were followed by a meeting of the conflicting parties in Switzerland, moderated by Andrej Motyl, a Swiss diplomat formerly stationed at the Swiss embassies in Teheran and Tashkent. However, when Motyl tried to resume the negotiations in Afghanistan, the atmosphere had cooled and the military conflict had resumed. The two parties met in Switzerland for the last time in March 2000, and when a new Taliban offensive was launched in August, the United Front refused to continue the talks. In the end, the Swiss initiative, just like the UN mediation effort, came to nothing.[4]

Today, good offices are part of a wide range of diplomatic and even military activities. As traditionally defined in international law, good offices constitute measures undertaken by a third party (a state, an international organisation, or a single citizen) to induce two conflicting countries to resume negotiations *without* the third party taking part in the actual negotiations.[5] The Swiss conception of good offices after the Second World War was broader, however. It included any initiative or measure taken by an international organisation, a state, its authorities or one of its citizens with the aim to contribute towards peaceful settlement of a conflict between other states.[6] This wider definition includes legal arbitration, good offices in a narrow (or technical) sense, mediation, conciliation, judicial settlement and the protecting power institution.[7]

Throughout the Cold War period, Switzerland tried to adhere to its policy of classical neutrality, which implies strict abstention from international conflict situations. However, this strict conception of neutrality came under much pressure towards the end of the Second World War and in the immediate post-War period. In order to avoid international isolation, a less traditional definition of neutrality was called for.[8] The provision of good offices became an important Swiss instrument to that effect. It was Max Petitpierre, head of the Department of Foreign Affairs from 1945 to 1961, who established a link between neutrality and solidarity, thereby emphasising that neutrality is more than a defensive concept based on abstention and passivity. For Petitpierre, neutrality implied the will and obligation to take on responsibilities abroad, particularly in the case of international conflicts. Together with an emphasis on humanitarian assistance, the Swiss government then promoted its availability for good offices, based on the formula of 'neutrality and solidarity'. At the time there was a strong conviction that a permanent neutral nation was in a privileged position to assist other nations in settling their conflicts.[9] However, the fear that neutrality would be damaged by political involvement, in fact, hindered the government from taking on assignments in a number of instances. This was particularly the case with mandates and mediation initiated under the auspices of the United Nations.

The establishment of the UN in 1945 created a new framework for the prevention and resolution of international conflicts, and the world organisation soon became the most important player in international conflict management.[10] Multilateral preventive diplomacy and peacekeeping replaced the traditional procedures of good offices and arbitration. Although not a member of the UN due to its neutrality, Switzerland retained its policy of good offices and tried to increase its influence by taking on international mandates, supervising armistices or internationally agreed plebiscites, offering hospitality to international organisations or conferences and providing various services to settle disputes and to soften the effects of war.[11]

However, since the Swiss concept was mainly meant to promote neutrality, it suffered from rhetorical overstretch. In fact, the country was most reluctant to participate in multilateral UN activities, and the significance of neutrality as a basis for good offices was highly overestimated. This only changed when the Cold War confrontation ended and the isolationist policy of neutrality lost its relevance. The conceptual changes affecting Swiss foreign policy since 1993 have emphasised a need for new instruments exercised in close international co-operation, including diplomatic, economic, humanitarian and even military measures.

In the following five sections, Switzerland's achievements in the field of good offices since 1945 will be discussed and evaluated. These include the country's activities as a protecting power, as a host for international organisations and conferences, as an arbitrator and mediator and also as an executor of international mandates. The concluding section will highlight recent changes in the Swiss concept of mediation and preventive diplomacy.

4.1 Serving as a protecting power

Much of Switzerland's reputation in the field of good offices is due to its experience as a protecting power. A state can become a protecting power by representing another state in a third state, in the absence of direct diplomatic relations between the latter two states. The protecting power task consists of maintaining an indispensable minimum of contact between belligerents, or between states that have broken off diplomatic relations for another reason, until hostilities cease and/or until both countries resume their ties.[12] Switzerland first acted as a protecting power in the Franco–German War of 1870/71, when it was entrusted with the interests of the Kingdom of Bavaria and the Grand Duchy of Baden in France. During the First World War, Switzerland had already assumed 36 such mandates before it reached the absolute peak of its activity in protecting foreign interests in the Second World War. By then, Switzerland was simultaneously representing the interests of 35 nations, with over 200 single mandates, including most of the belligerents and all of the big powers except for the Soviet Union.[13] At that time the Foreign Interests Section was by far the largest office of the Department of Foreign Affairs in Bern.

During the first period of the Cold War, from 1947 to 1963, Switzerland was – most likely due to its vast experience and availability – requested to act as a protecting power whenever international tensions rose. This was the case after the Suez Crisis of 1956, when several Western states turned to Switzerland to represent their interests in a number of Arab states – for example, Great Britain in Egypt and Syria; France in Egypt, Jordan, Iraq and Syria – raising the total number of Swiss mandates from 5 (in 1954) to 17 (in 1956). Most of these mandates were gradually rescinded in the course of events until the start of the 1960s, when the United States and several South American nations asked Switzerland to represent their interests in Cuba after the break of diplomatic relations between the United States and Cuba in 1961. This event raised again the number of Swiss mandates to 16 (in 1962). The mandate for the United States in Cuba became the most enduring one, and it included a spectacular airlift between Cuba and Florida instigated by the protecting power in 1965. The airlift enabled more than 260 000 Cubans who opposed the regime to emigrate to the United States over the next seven years.[14] Switzerland has also been representing Cuban interests in Washington since 1991, a mandate that was shifted by the Cuban government from Czechoslovakia to Switzerland after the dissolution of the Eastern bloc.

The Cold War crises of the 1950s and 1960s led to a clear increase in the number of Swiss mandates for protecting foreign interests, but the ongoing process of worldwide decolonialisation also had an impact on Switzerland's activities as a protecting power. From 1967 to 1973, for example, the Swiss represented American and British interests in Algeria.[15] When India and Pakistan severed relations in 1971, it was the first time that two developing countries asked Switzerland to represent their interests reciprocally.[16] Discussing the value of neutrality with Swiss members of Parliament, federal councillor and head of the Department of Foreign Affairs, Graber emphasised that this mandate confirmed the importance of neutral countries in world affairs, even as the focus was shifting from East–West to North–South conflicts in the 1970s.[17] In fact, following the outbreak of the Yom Kippur

War in the Middle East in 1973, the number of foreign interests represented by Switzerland reached its highest level since the Second World War with 25 assignments.

The rising Cold War tensions in the 1980s once more seemed to confirm the importance of Switzerland's role as a protecting power. This was particularly true for Switzerland's role in the Iran hostage crisis in 1979/80.[18] Nearly a year after the Islamic revolution led by Ayatollah Khomeini and the exile of Shah Reza Pahlevi to Egypt and Morocco, and finally to the United States for medical treatment, 52 US diplomatic staff members in Tehran were taken hostage. Islamic militants seized the embassy compound on 4 November 1979. Although formal diplomatic relations between the United States and Iran continued to exist, the American Embassy in Tehran could obviously no longer function under those circumstances. The American government therefore approached Raymond Probst, Swiss Ambassador in Washington, DC, and asked for Switzerland's informal support in Tehran. The fact that the Swiss had already represented US interests in Cuba, where they had proved their ability and usefulness to the United States in another difficult country, made Switzerland in the words of an American official the 'natural choice' for this task.

For five months Switzerland acted discreetly as a kind of de facto caretaker of US interests in Iran. The communication channel started with Ambassador Probst and his assistant, Franz Muheim, in Washington, DC, went through the Department of Foreign Affairs in Bern (Ambassador Edouard Brunner), and ended at the Swiss embassy in the Iranian capital (Ambassador Erik Lang). David D. Newsom, US Under Secretary for Political Affairs, called it the 'sensitive link'.[19] The Swiss government also offered to help by providing a Swiss civilian aircraft for transport when 13 hostages, women and African-Americans, were released early in the crisis. However, the Iranians disapproved of the special aircraft and chose another option.

The Swiss Channel subsequently served mainly to transmit urgent messages, and Ambassador Lang in Tehran became one of the prime sources of information on the spot. When diplomatic relations between the United States and Iran broke down on 7 April 1980, the Swiss link was already well established. It was only a matter of formality to assign to Switzerland the official mandate to represent US interests in Iran. In the course of events, the Swiss authorities were able to arrange for secret contacts through their embassies in both countries and even for top-secret meetings of emissaries from both sides on Swiss territory.[20] Yet the decisive breakthrough in the hostage crisis came only when, late in August 1980, the United States received word through Germany that the Ayatollah regime was ready to enter top-level negotiations. Finally, Algeria, which had previously been asked by Iran to represent its interests towards the United States, acted as an intermediary in protracted negotiations. This opened the way for decisive bargaining by US Deputy-Secretary of State Warren Christopher, which ultimately led to the release of all hostages in January 1981. The role of the Swiss in this final phase was limited to offering a reliable diplomatic back channel.[21]

Another important mandate was entrusted to Switzerland in the 1980s by Great Britain at the outbreak of the Falkland (Malvinas) Islands conflict.[22] The request to take care of British interests in Argentina reached Bern on 2 April 1982. The members of the Swiss embassy in Buenos Aires were informed accordingly, and after obtaining the consent of the Argentine government, they were able to fulfil the new task within hours. Apart from taking charge of the large British embassy and two consulates general, they also assumed the protection of 30 000 British subjects in the country. Since the Falkland Islands continued to be considered British territory by London, the interests of the British citizens on the Islands were excluded from the mandate.

The Swiss had to handle administrative matters, such as organising the repatriation of the British embassy staff as well as a number of journalists. Their task was facilitated by a mutual agreement that permitted four diplomatic and four consular officers of each of the conflicting parties to remain on the spot at the disposal of the protecting diplomatic mission. While Switzerland represented British interests in Buenos Aires, Argentina mandated Brazil with the role of its protecting power in London. After the hostilities on the Falkland Islands ended, it still took almost eight years until the two sides finally decided to resume diplomatic relations, and the Swiss and Brazil mandates ended in 1990. By then, Switzerland still held ten protecting power mandates, among others those for the United States in Cuba and Iran as well as one for Iran in Egypt.

During the two World Wars, neutrality and abstention from world politics definitely predestined Switzerland as a protecting power for nations at war. In the Cold War period, Switzerland's vast experience with such mandates, its lack of ambition in world politics, a wide-spread network of embassies and friendly relations with almost every nation seemed to be the key reasons that Switzerland was chosen as a protecting power. Last but not least, the Swiss were eager to prove the usefulness of their neutral position in times of troubled world affairs. In the meantime, however, the circumstances have changed. Despite a growing number of worldwide conflicts since the end of the Cold War, Swiss mandates for representing foreign interests have decreased continuously since the late 1980s. Three main reasons account for this development. First, several formerly hostile states resumed official ties after the end of the East–West confrontation. Second, the nature of worldwide conflicts in general changed from classic interstate disputes to intrastate conflicts and civil wars, in which classic diplomatic means and the protecting power institute in particular can no longer be applied. Third, the Swiss themselves became less keen to accept any possible mandate. This can best be illustrated by the events accompanying NATO's war in Kosovo in 1999.

As early as October 1998, when the likelihood of allied air attacks on Serbia could no longer be excluded, Great Britain and Germany sounded out the willingness of the Swiss Department of Foreign Affairs to represent their interests should diplomatic relations with Belgrade be severed. The Swiss authorities rejected this possibility at the time.[23] The official explanation, by Swiss foreign minister Flavio Cotti, that he could not guarantee that the embassy in Belgrade would stay open once allied air raids began, seems somewhat ephemeral. Following the new conceptual guidelines in the foreign policy of 1993 that departed from the strict neutrality policy during the Cold War years, it is more likely that the Swiss government, after vigorously condemning the Serbs for their expulsions in Kosovo, did not want any closer relationship with the misanthropist regime of Milosevic.[24] Nonetheless, the Swiss government changed its attitude in the course of the NATO operation against the Milosevic regime in the spring of 1999, by returning to its neutrality policy and offering its availability as a protecting power to other nations in Belgrade.[25] It took on the task of representing France in Belgrade and received an identical request from the United States.[26] While Switzerland, still with some reluctance, was now prepared to take on the US mandate, the assignment could not be effected in the end due to lack of Yugoslav consent.[27] After the end of the hostilities in former Yugoslavia, the mandate for France was handed back in November 2000, and by the end of the year 2001 Switzerland was only exercising five protecting power mandates; for the United States in Cuba and Iran, for Iran in Egypt, for Israel in Ghana and for Cuba in the United States.[28]

4.2 Hosting international organisations and conferences

Similar to its availability as a protecting power, Switzerland long regarded its readiness to host international organisations or conferences as an expression of international solidarity.[29] Switzerland's reputation as a host for international organisations originated with the establishment of the League of Nations in Geneva after the First World War. Switzerland also organised a number of important international conferences, among them are the peace conference between Turkey and the French–British Entente and Greece in Lausanne, which led to the conclusion of a peace treaty in 1923, and the conference between Germany and the Western powers in Locarno, which produced the so-called Locarno pact of 1925.

After the Second World War, the United Nations Organizations followed the former League of Nations to Geneva by making use of the Palais des Nations as its European headquarters. Although the main centre of the United Nations was established in New York, Geneva became the host of many special agencies and bodies of the United Nations System.[30] At present, more than 20 international intergovernmental organisations and more than 120 non-governmental organisations (NGOs) are located in

Geneva, and some 30 000 international officials and diplomats reside in the city. During the Cold War, Switzerland's political stability, its independent position between the blocs, its lack of a colonial past as well as its favourable geographical location, good communications and infrastructure were the main factors that enabled Geneva to become a centre of international relations. However, the times when Geneva seemed to be the 'logical' choice as a seat for an international organisation are gone. The end of the Cold War produced a wide range of potential residence cities for organisations and conferences: Geneva won the struggle for the seat of the World Trade Organization (WTO), but the Secretariat of the World Climate Convention was established in Bonn, the Secretariat for Biodiversity in Montreal and the Organization for the Prevention of Chemical Weapons in The Hague.[31]

Moreover, Switzerland's attitude towards hosting international conferences has changed considerably in the past few years. In the early Cold War years, the Swiss were proud to host a number of important conferences in Geneva, such as the Indo–China Conference of 1954 and the Laos Conference of 1961/62 on the neutralisation of the country, as well as the summit meeting of the 'Big Four' (USSR, USA, Great Britain and France) in 1955. The subsequent period of international détente in the late 1960s and early 1970s saw the Second Strategic Arms Limitation Talks (SALT II) between the United States and the Soviet Union from November 1972 on, the important second phase of the Conference on Security and Cooperation in Europe (CSCE) held in Geneva between 1973 and 1975, which lead to the Final Act of Helsinki,[32] as well as the Middle East Conference in 1973 following the Yom Kippur War.[33] At the height of the second Cold War in the early 1980s, Geneva hosted the initial Strategic Arms Reduction Talks (START), which led to the signing of the Soviet–American Agreement on the elimination of Intermediate-Range Nuclear Forces (INF) in 1987. In the same period the first superpower summit in over ten years took place in 1985: President Reagan and General-Secretary Gorbachev met between 19 and 21 November in Geneva, an event to which Switzerland has always referred with special emphasis.[34]

After the Cold War there was a general increase in the number of international conferences, most of them under the auspices of the United Nations or a group of states leading crisis management in a specific area of tension. Although Switzerland was the host of the International Conference on Former Yugoslavia in 1992, the decisive diplomatic talks to end the war in Bosnia were held elsewhere.[35] Today Switzerland no longer aims primarily at hosting international conferences but instead seeks to hold conferences at which it can contribute actively to international politics of peace. This was the case when the intergovernmental 'Human Security Network', consisting of 13 states working in close collaboration with NGOs, held its second meeting at ministerial level in Lucerne in 2000.[36] At this meeting the prevention of small arms and light weapons and the role of non-state actors in regions at risk were discussed, and Switzerland took a leading role not only as an organising state, but also as an active participant in the talks.[37]

4.3 Arbitration activities

Just like its role as a protecting power or as a host for international organisations and conferences, Switzerland's experience in international arbitration contributed considerably to its reputation regarding good offices. Yet, due to the fact that the instrument of arbitration is used less and less in international conflict management, Switzerland's role as an impartial arbitrator has lost much of its attraction.

As a small state that is best protected by the rule of law in international affairs, Switzerland has always been keen to promote dispute settlements through judicial means. In the late nineteenth century, Switzerland – and more often individual Swiss citizens appointed by the Federal Council – helped third states to settle their differences by taking on an arbitral role in over 20 cases. The Alabama case of 1872, between Great Britain and the United States during the American Civil War, was certainly the most prominent case. Yet, once the Permanent Court of Arbitration was established after the Second Hague Peace Conference of 1907 and the Permanent Court of International Justice was set up in The Hague by the League of Nations in 1922, it was no longer necessary to have a special court of arbitration for every conflict. Hence Switzerland's bilateral activity in this field lost much of its relevance. Thanks to Max Huber, who was elected to the Permanent Court of Justice and presided over it from 1925 to 1929, Switzerland – a full member of the League – was nevertheless instrumental in contributing to international jurisdiction.[38]

After the decline of the League of Nations, the International Court of Justice quickly replaced the Permanent Court of Justice as the principal judicial organ of the United Nations. Although Switzerland was the first non-member of the United Nations to adhere to the Court's Statute and to acknowledge the obligatory nature of its jurisdiction in 1948, it was no longer represented in the most important multilateral judicial organ by judges of Swiss nationality. Switzerland, therefore, tried to preserve its position by strengthening the notion of bilateral arbitration and by promoting multilateral arbitration procedures within the context of the Conference on Security and Cooperation in Europe (CSCE).[39] Yet, the Swiss project for the peaceful settlement of disputes between member states of the CSCE introduced as early as 1973 faced considerable resistance because of its obligatory character.[40] Only after the end of the Cold War did a meeting of CSCE experts in La Valetta produce a final draft for a European Court of Arbitration on CSCE (nowadays OSCE) matters, which was finally constituted in Geneva in 1995.

In recent decades, it seems that only disputes of secondary importance in interstate conflicts have been taken to the International Court of Justice, and international arbitration has only rarely been applied as an instrument of conflict management. Therefore, Switzerland has played a lesser role as a promoter and executor of international arbitration, both in quantity and relevance. As mentioned above, a substantial part of the efforts in peace politics has been transferred to the United Nations, and in post-Cold War conflicts political solutions are usually preferred to judicial ones.[41] Up to now the European Court for Arbitration on OSCE matters, which was initiated by the Swiss, has not been called upon a single time. In the field of peace politics, services such as participating actively in multilateral mediation efforts and taking over international mandates are much more prominent today. Consequently, arbitral activities are no longer mentioned as a primary goal in the official Swiss concept of preventive diplomacy and conflict management.[42]

4.4 Good offices and bilateral mediation

So far we have looked at traditional services provided by Switzerland, mostly *upon request* by a state or a group of states, to ease tension in international affairs. We now turn to the initiatives Switzerland promoted during the Cold War years as part of its 'active neutrality' politics: good offices (in their original sense) and bilateral mediation efforts that we would now call 'second track' third-party conflict resolution activities. These two terms differ in so far as good offices aimed originally at initiation or resumption of negotiations only, with no active participation of the third party; in a mediatory process, on the other hand, the third party tries to bring the conflicting parties to an agreement for peaceful settlement by actively participating in the process of negotiations. In practice the borderline between the two methods is often blurred.[43]

Before and after the First World War, Switzerland mainly promoted international jurisdiction and procedures of arbitration to settle international disputes. During the war, the Swiss government had made a few attempts to act as a mediator between the major powers, but most of them failed. In the Second World War, the absolute refusal of the Allies to even contemplate Hitler as a trustworthy negotiating partner and the demand for unconditional surrender made it difficult for Switzerland to initiate independent mediating efforts. The only successful initiatives were those undertaken by individual Swiss officials and representatives abroad to prevent needless sacrifice of lives and pointless destruction in the last stages of war in Western Europe.[44]

Invoking the concept of 'neutrality and solidarity' after the Second World War, Switzerland stressed its willingness to act as a facilitator and mediator in international conflicts, particularly in the emerging Cold War crises in which the United Nations was paralysed by the veto of the superpowers in the Security Council.[45] Yet, an examination of the early Cold War period shows that after the initiative in the Suez Crisis in 1956 failed, the Swiss government was extremely reluctant to offer its services as a mediator in the crises in Berlin and Cuba at the beginning of the 1960s.

After British troops left the Suez Canal region in the summer of 1956, Egypt's president, Gamal Abdel Nasser, immediately nationalised the company running the canal. Following these events, Israel, with the secret consent of Great Britain and France, invaded Egypt at the end of October 1956. As the Soviet Union was preoccupied with the rebellion in Hungary, the British and French seized the opportunity to support the Israeli intervention with air raids and landed their own airborne troops at Port Said. When, on 5 November, the Soviet Prime Minister, Nicolai Bulganin, demanded under threat of war that their troops be withdrawn from the canal region, there was a worldwide fear that the Hungary/Suez crises could lead to another world war.

On 6 November the Swiss government launched an urgent appeal to the president of the United States as well as to the governments of France, Britain, the Soviet Union and India (as the leading non-aligned power) to hold a summit meeting on the Suez question, which could be held in Switzerland.[46] Although the Swiss initiative was, according to the British Ambassador in Bern, 'a very interesting and significant departure from Switzerland's traditional aloofness, at the governmental level, from all those international political problems in which she is not directly concerned' and an 'unprecedented intervention of the Swiss Government into world politics',[47] Switzerland's offer soon turned out to be moot: by the time it reached Downing Street, the British cabinet was already about to take the decision to end the hostilities. The Swiss initiative therefore had no influence on the peaceful settlement of the crisis. By noon of 6 November, the British Prime Minister, Anthony Eden, had given in to American diplomatic pressure to hold the fire in the Middle East and to Soviet military threats and adopted a cease-fire resolution by the UN General Assembly of 2 November.[48]

The Suez Crisis illustrates clearly what a delicate matter it was for a small state to intervene in Cold War power politics. Not only had the Swiss authorities failed to contact in advance both the UN Secretary-General, who was already deeply involved in the crisis management, and the major powers, which irritated both the UN and the United States government, who supported the Secretary-General's efforts for peace. The Swiss were also criticised sharply by the French, who resented the comparison of British and French intervention in the Middle East with Soviet oppression in Hungary and disapproved of raising India to the level of a superpower. Only the Soviet Union and India reacted positively to the Swiss initiative. The public in Switzerland, on the other hand, reacted negatively to the issuing of an invitation to the Soviet Union, due to its intervention in Hungary, and the whole undertaking turned out to be more of an embarrassment for the Swiss government than anything else.[49]

Consequently, Switzerland declined to offer its good offices and to mediate actively between parties in conflict in the following years. When Cold War tensions reached their peak in 1961 (Berlin) and in 1962 (Cuban missile crisis), the Swiss Federal Department of Foreign Affairs adhered to a firm policy of abstention. During the Berlin crisis, the Swiss informed the US State Department that Switzerland would not make any approaches on either side because it considered this an abandonment of its policy of neutrality.[50] A year later, at the outbreak of the Cuban missile crisis, rumours in the national press had it that on 23 October 1962 the Swiss government had discussed the possibility of offering to mediate. Raymond Probst, assistant secretary in the political division of the Department of Foreign Affairs, denied these rumours instantly and categorically to the American Ambassador in Bern. In fact, the Swiss foreign minister, Friedrich Traugott Wahlen, had not even been present at the preceding session of the Federal Council due to an EFTA meeting of foreign ministers in Oslo.[51] By that time, Bern had definitely abandoned the idea that neutral Switzerland could actively mediate in Cold War crises involving the superpowers.

There is but one example in the Cold War years where Switzerland was called upon to offer its good offices and was able to play a decisive role in conflict settlement: the French–Algerian negotiations, which finally led to the independence of the Algerian Republic in 1962. When the resistance against the French domination at the beginning of the 1960s became increasingly violent, an exiled emissary of the Algerian government in Rome contacted Swiss Ambassador Olivier Long and asked him to establish contacts with French officials in order to find a possible peaceful solution of the conflict. Long, who had been a personal friend of the French minister for Algerian affairs, Louis Joxe, for over 25 years, first consulted the Swiss Department of Foreign Affairs. After obtaining an official mandate from foreign minister Max Petitpierre, he met with the French minister in January 1961. Joxe transmitted the contents of this peace initiative to General De Gaulle, who gave his consent to negotiations with the Algerians and thanked the Swiss for their help.

A French delegation headed by Georges Pompidou, later to become president, met with emissaries of the Algerian National Liberation Front (FLN) for the first time in February 1961 in Lucerne, Switzerland. Long and his team also organised the following round of secret talks between the two parties in May and July 1961. While the meetings themselves were held in Evian and Lugrin on the French side of Lake Geneva, the Algerian delegation was hosted in the villa of the Emir of Quatar in Bois d'Avault near Geneva. The Swiss played their role as facilitators by hosting the Algerians and assuring their security, by organising their transport (by helicopter or boat) to the meeting places on French territory and by providing the necessary means of communication and information. When the negotiation process was in danger of breaking down, Long acted as an intermediary by bringing the parties together again in February 1962 in Les Rousses near the French–Swiss border. This secret meeting paved the way for the final round of French–Algerian negotiations in Evian in March 1962, which led to the conclusion of a cease-fire agreement and ultimately to the independence of Algeria in July 1962. During the final phase of negotiations, the Algerian delegation was again hosted on the Swiss side of Lake Geneva, this time at the Hotel Signal de Bougy near Lausanne.[52]

Both Ambassador Long and Ambassador Probst, who was equally involved on the Swiss side in the final phase of the negotiations, later stated that in this case Switzerland had been able to demonstrate to other nations the usefulness of its neutral position in world politics. Yet, closer examination reveals that Switzerland was chosen as intermediary between the FLN and the French government primarily due to Long's personal relationship with French minister Joxe as well as Switzerland's lack of a colonial past, its geographical location and the availability and secrecy of Swiss facilities. Institutional neutrality was certainly not the main reason, except for the usual requirement of impartiality of a third-party mediator.

As far as we know, the Franco–Algerian negotiation process was the last occasion during the Cold War when Switzerland mediated successfully on its own.[53] Governmental statements to the contrary notwithstanding, there was no real need for neutral Switzerland's help in international crises beyond acting as a protecting power and providing humanitarian aid in the later Cold War years. The role of the main intermediary instead fell to the UN, a leading power, or to a state having closer relationships with the parties at dispute. The latter preference became obvious to Swiss diplomats during the Iran hostage crisis, where it was Algeria who played the mediator's part in the final phase of the crisis. As long as it was the primary goal of Swiss foreign policy to avoid any endangerment of its neutral status, the potential and possibilities to engage in mediation efforts were highly limited.

When the Swiss government tried to make use of its involvement as a protecting power in the Falkland conflict by arranging informal conversations between the British and the Argentineans in Bern on 18 July 1984, the problem of initiating talks without setting an agenda became obvious. Following an approach by British Ambassador Powell-Jones, the Swiss Department of Foreign Affairs organised an informal meeting between high-ranking diplomats from both countries. However, the talks broke down on the first day, as the two delegations held fundamentally opposing views as to whether the major point of controversy, sovereignty over the Falkland Islands, should form part of the conversations. Had the British known in advance that the Argentineans would insist on the inclusion of the sovereignty issue, they would have rejected the meeting in advance.[54] Consequently, the British foreign minister declared the talks a disappointing and frustrating experience and stated that he did not see any prospects for continuing the dialogue in the near future.[55] In this case, the specific arrangement of the talks served to poison the atmosphere even more and produced new tensions between the parties.

A similar development could be observed in 1988, when the Swiss Federal Department of Foreign Affairs was asked by South African lawyer Richard Rosenthal to sound out the possibilities of talks between the Government of P.W. Botha and the African National Congress (ANC) to put an end to the apartheid system. The first steps undertaken by Swiss Ambassador Quinche in Pretoria and Secretary of State Brunner were promising. Yet the initiative broke down in summer 1988 when the newly elected Swiss foreign minister René Felber urged P.W. Botha in a private meeting in Bern to proceed with the talks. This failure was most likely due to the fact that the South African foreign minister Pik Botha, who also took part in the conversation, was obviously unaware of the initiative. Therefore P.W. Botha rebuffed Felbers approach and denied all knowledge of the Rosenthal channel, because he did not want to admit secret contacts with the ANC.[56]

The possibilities for Switzerland to act successfully as a go-between remained limited after the end of the Cold War. When, in 1990, Switzerland was asked by the president of Afghanistan, Muhammed Nadjibullah, and by different Afghan factions to mediate in the emerging intra-Afghan conflict, Swiss diplomats engaged in various activities: several meetings of representatives of the Afghan opposition were held in Switzerland in 1991, and former Secretary of State Klaus Jacobi embarked on various missions to Kabul to prepare the handing-over of power and the establishment of a widely accepted government, but to no avail.[57]

Although the transition from the communist regime to the opposition in the following year was relatively well regulated, the different Afghan factions soon engaged in a civil war over power in Kabul. In 1995, the new Afghan president, Burhanuddin Rabbani, asked Switzerland again for its help in mediating the conflict, yet this renewed request was declined. Although it was reported that there were voices opting for an active engagement of Switzerland in the Afghan case in the Department of Foreign Affairs, the answer from the Swiss foreign minister, Flavio Cotti, remained negative. As long as the UN special mission led by Mahmoud Mestiri and the Office of the UN Secretary-General in Afghanistan (OSGA) – established in Jalalabad in January 1995 – were present in the country, Switzerland did not want to interfere.[58]

Chances to mediate successfully in this conflict without the assistance of a leading world power, an international organisation, or a group of like-minded states were small. This fact is illustrated by the most recent failed attempt of Swiss diplomacy at active intervention in 1999/2000.[59] In the course of the United States' military action against the Taliban regime following the terrorist attacks on New York City on 11 September 2001

Switzerland once more offered its territory to the United Nations as the site for a conference on possible future government structure of Afghanistan. Yet while Vienna and Berlin were also mentioned as possible hosts, the United Nations finally chose Bonn as the conference site.[60]

While the Swiss government's Foreign Policy Report of 1993 introduced important *conceptual* changes in promoting peace and security as a primary goal of foreign policy, it took several years for a shift in Swiss *politics* in the field of bilateral initiatives – from the rather passive offering of traditional good offices to a more active strategy of contributing to the peaceful settlement of international conflicts. Today, about one third of the means of the Department of Foreign Affairs for civil activities in peace promotion is spent on bilateral activities in preventive diplomacy, confidence building measures and mediating efforts, including projects for democratisation, human security and for the establishment of further capacities in peace promotion.

The following two projects illustrate the Swiss government's new approach to preventive diplomacy and conflict management without the involvement of an international organisation. Since 1998 Switzerland has been – together with other third parties, state and non-state actors – engaged in the 'Arusha peace process' for Burundi by actively supporting international efforts for peace in the Great Lake region in central Africa. While the role of facilitator and mediator in the Burundi conflict was assigned first to Julius Nyerere, former president of Tanzania, and in autumn 1999 to Nelson Mandela, former president of South Africa, Switzerland's main contribution consisted in delegating an expert on federalism to the 'international commission on democracy and good governance', over which it presided together with South Africa. In the course of its work, the commission won the confidence of all rebelling factions and was able to negotiate the basic constitutional framework that should be guaranteed in a democratic, pluralistic and multicultural Burundi once the actual conflict was resolved.

The mandate of the international commission officially ended when the warring factions signed a peace agreement in neighbouring Tanzania in 1999. Yet the war in Burundi continues, and Switzerland is on stand-by to continue negotiations.[61] What is new in the Burundi case, as compared to earlier attempts at mediation, is that Switzerland worked in close co-operation with other states, such as South Africa and Tanzania, from the very beginning. It also restricted itself to a specific domain in which it has particular knowledge and competence: constitution building and democracy.

In another long-standing intrastate conflict, in Colombia, Switzerland was asked by the government and one of the rebellion movements, the Ejército de Liberación Nacional (ELN), to supervise the peace talks they had recently begun. Together with France, Spain, Norway and Cuba, a group of states called Países amigos (friends of the peace process), Switzerland has been moderating and facilitating the meetings of the two parties since early 2000 in order to build an atmosphere of confidence and to keep the peace talks going. In February 2000, a government delegation and representatives of the Fuerzas Armadas Revolucionarias de Colombia (FARC), the largest rebellion movement in the country, were invited to Switzerland to establish contacts and prepare negotiations.

Switzerland was present when FARC and the government held peace talks in June 2000 in Colombia, and from March 2001 onwards an international commission of ten states, including Switzerland, was formally engaged in organising the negotiation process between the two parties.[62] However, despite all third-party efforts, the process broke down again after another rebellion offensive caused more than a hundred deaths and casualties at the beginning of 2002. It has not been resumed since.[63]

In Colombia as in Burundi, the Swiss initiative sought to combine traditional good offices with more active involvement by fostering alliances and establishing a network of like-minded states and other actors motivated and qualified to contribute to the systematic search for peaceful conflict resolution. In an active approach, the third party not only provides neutral ground or personnel for negotiations in case of immediate crisis, but also acts as a 'friendly state' towards the parties in dispute, remaining engaged on a long-term basis.

The most recent example of this approach to conflict settlement is Switzerland's engagement in the Sudan conflict. Josef Bucher, former ambassador to various Northern African and Sub-Saharan states and today Switzerland's official 'ambassador for conflict resolution', had held longstanding relations with the Sudanese government in Karthoum. This is why both the Sudanese government and the Sudan People's Liberation Army (SPLA), who engaged in a blood shedding civil war in central Sudan, turned to Switzerland when they were looking for neutral ground for ceasefire negotiations for the Nuba mountain region in response to an American initiative. In the talks, which were held under Swiss–American patronage on the mountaintop of the Bürgenstock in central Switzerland in January 2002, Josef Bucher again played a decisive role.[64]

4.5 International mandates

While bilateral activities in conflict mediation generally declined, international mandates became more and more important with the establishment of the United Nations system. Switzerland had already had some experience with this type of mandate from the period before 1945. As a full member of the League of Nations, it had contributed on a number of occasions to the resolution of conflicts arising in the border regions of the German Reich in the aftermath of the First World War. Former Federal Councillor Felix Calonder was thus appointed mediator for Upper Silesia and Prof. Carl Jacob Burckhardt, the High Commissioner of the League of Nations in Danzig. Switzerland also prepared and observed the execution of the Saar Plebiscite in 1935.[65]

After the Second World War, a new opportunity to contribute to international efforts for peace arose in connection with the Korean War. Since Switzerland had not joined the newly founded United Nations in 1946, it was eager to show that neutrality was more than abstentionism. Therefore, Switzerland reacted positively when sounded out by the US State Department in 1951 on whether it would co-operate in a neutral commission to supervise an eventual armistice agreement between United Nations' forces in the south and the North Korean People's Army.[66] When the armistice was finally concluded on 23 July 1953, two commissions with Swiss participation were installed, the Neutral Nations Supervisory Commission (NNSC) to observe the peace agreement and the Neutral Nations Repatriation Commission (NNRC), whose task was to implement the regulations concerning prisoners of war unwilling to return to their homeland.

The main difficulty with these two commissions was their composition, which besides Switzerland included Sweden, Poland and Czechoslovakia in the NNSC plus India in the NNRC. While the latter completed its task of discharging the prisoners of war by the end of February 1954, Switzerland and Sweden, the two permanently neutral nations in the NNSC nominated by the Commander in Chief of the UN forces, were in constant disagreement with the two other member states of the commission, Poland and Czechoslovakia. The latter two states were neutral only in so far as they had not participated in the hostilities in Korea, but they clearly supported the point of view of the Korean People's Army and the Voluntary Forces of the Chinese people, who had designated them as 'their' members in the commission.

In the summer of 1956, after less than three years, the commission was forced to withdraw its inspection teams in the north and in the south. The Swiss had originally shown great interest in participating in the commission to demonstrate the usefulness of their permanent neutrality in Cold War conflicts, yet the NNSC turned out to be practically ineffective. Its mandate was soon reduced to preventing renewed escalation and military incidents between north and south on the borderline at the 38th parallel. Despite these problems, the Swiss government decided to remain in the NNSC (and is to this day), although it cut the size of its delegation from 140 persons in the initial phase to a minimum of five military officers.[67] Yet, in response to the negative experiences with the mandate in Korea, which had in fact damaged the image of Swiss neutrality, the Federal Department of Foreign Affairs elaborated a catalogue of conditions to be fulfilled for future mandates.[68]

When the first official peacekeeping mission in the history of the United Nations, the United Nations Emergency Force (UNEF) for the Middle East, was established in 1956 in the aftermath of the Suez Crisis, it was clear that the neutral non-member Switzerland would not contribute any troops.[69] However, UN Secretary-General Dag Hammarskjöld turned to Switzerland with a request for Swiss national airline (Swissair) airplanes for the transport of troops under UN command from Naples to the area of operations in Egypt.[70] The Swiss government agreed upon the condition of Egypt's consent.

A similar request was sent to Switzerland again in 1960, when the United Nations embarked on a large operation (ONUC) to prevent the newly independent Congo, formerly a Belgian colony, from falling apart. Again Swissair provided means for the transport of troops, and the Swiss government participated in the supply of foodstuffs to the Congo. Besides the UN civil mission to build up and strengthen the social and political structures, the Congo was in need of French-speaking personnel from countries other than Belgium or France. Switzerland agreed to participate with a larger number of civil experts in finance, business, employment and judicature, as well as with a medical team of 25 persons, provided that the Swiss personnel were recruited and financed directly by the UN and that no Swiss citizens were employed for military or police action.[71]

Switzerland did not always react positively to such requests during the first phase of the Cold War, however. When the superpowers and the UN were seeking inspection personnel for an international verification mission in the settlement of the Cuban missile crisis in 1962, the Swiss government declined to offer its services. As foreign minister Wahlen explained to the American Ambassador in Bern: 'Normally [we] would say yes to such [a] request, but our representation of other nations in Cuba – particularly [the] United States – raises [the] question [of] dual interests. We would therefore expect to decline.'[72] The execution of a protecting power mandate (for the United States in Cuba) obviously hindered the provision of assistance due to the Swiss fear of losing its absolute neutrality, which was considered a prerequisite for a protecting power. In general, the Swiss government was less reluctant to assume mandates during the Cold War as long as they were of a 'technical' nature and had few political implications.[73] Furthermore, in all its activities the Department of Foreign Affairs adhered to the conditions established after the failure of the Korean mission to safeguard its neutrality in the execution of such mandates.

Nevertheless, on various occasions throughout the Cold War, a few Swiss individuals served the UN Secretary-General as special envoys in regions at risk. Among the first to fulfil this type of task were diplomats Victor Umbricht, as Senior Financial Adviser and President of the Monetary Council of the United Nations Mission in Congo (1960), and Edouard Zellweger, as special representative of the Secretary-General in Laos (1960/61). In order to trace the reasons why Swiss officials were chosen as personal representatives of the UN Secretary-General, the case of Ambassador Ernesto Thalmann's observation mission to Jerusalem in 1967 in the aftermath of the Six-Day War is particularly enlightening: when the UN General Assembly requested a detailed report on the situation in East

Jerusalem, which was de facto annexed by Israel, Burmese UN Secretary-General U Thant first intended to entrust a Swede with the fact-finding mission. When Israel rejected this proposition, he turned to the Swiss government. Out of two possible Swiss candidates indicated by the Secretariat General, U Thant chose Ambassador Thalmann, a former Swiss observer at the United Nations in New York, whom he knew personally.[74] As the Swiss mission in New York explained in the message transmitting the Secretary-General's request to foreign minister Willy Spühler, 'it was not because Switzerland was not a member of the United Nations that U Thant finally decided to ask for a Swiss representative for this mission (...) but due to the quality and competence of the two Swiss diplomats in question.'[75]

Thalmann's two-week mission to Jerusalem to gather information on the assumption of control by Israel's authorities produced a lengthy report that was considered well balanced by both sides and by the Secretary-General. Consequently, it was submitted to the UN General Assembly. U Thant himself later wrote that he had chosen Thalmann because he was 'highly respected for his political acumen and impartiality'[76] throughout the UN. If Thalmann had not been known personally to the Secretary-General and the parties involved, Switzerland – irrespective of its neutral status – would most likely have been ignored in this search for a special envoy to the Middle East.

Some years before, in the conflict of the divided island of Cyprus, it had become evident that the Swiss were not always welcome as the UN Secretary-General's personal representatives in crisis regions. In March 1964 the US State Department and the British urged U Thant to nominate a Swiss personality as UN mediator in the crisis, proposing the names of Ambassador August Lindt, former High Commissioner for Refugees of the United Nations, Paul Rüegger, a long-standing diplomat and former president of the International Committee of the Red Cross and former foreign minister Max Petitpierre. Although the Turkish and Greek governments were supposedly in favour of this proposition, the leadership in Nicosia would not give its consent to a Swiss mediator. The Archbishop and President of the Cypriotic Republic, Makarios III, rejected Petitpierre or any Swiss citizen on the grounds that a Swiss mediator, coming from a neutral, multicultural and federal country, would most likely prefer a 'cantonal solution' to the conflict.[77]

The choice of a Swiss representative proved to be luckier when the East African Community (EAC) and the World Bank were looking for a mediator in the late 1970s. After the Community of Kenya, Tanzania and Uganda had collapsed in 1977 due to increasing political and financial difficulties, Ambassador Victor Umbricht, given the rank of a United Nations Under Secretary-General, acted as mediator. He recommended proposals for the permanent and equitable division of the assets and liabilities of the former EAC and assisted the states in reaching a definitive settlement.[78] After seven years, a mediation agreement could be signed by all parties involved, and

Umbricht continued to act as a co-ordinator of future regional co-operation in East Africa for some time.[79] The fact that Umbricht had acted as a UN special representative on various previous occasions (Congo, Bangladesh), as well as his knowledge of financial and monetary administration, certainly contributed to his choice as mediator for the dissolution process of the EAC.

The examples mentioned show that during the Cold War, the Swiss contribution to international, and especially United Nations, peace missions consisted mainly of individual missions and was limited strictly to civil action or financial support.[80] This was about to change in 1986, when Switzerland prepared a request to become part of the United Nations. Although the government's plan to become a full member was clearly rejected by Swiss voters in a national referendum, an internal inquiry of the Department of Foreign Affairs showed that Switzerland could contribute most effectively to international crisis management by participating in multilateral efforts for peace. For this reason, and despite the negative vote on UN membership, the Swiss government decided in 1988 to substantially increase its financial and logistic efforts for peace operations.[81]

In 1988, Switzerland for the first time dispatched a complete medical unit for the care of the United Nations Transition Assistance Group (UNTAG) to Namibia. It consisted of 150 persons, mainly doctors and nurses, and ground transportation and two airplanes.[82] Two years later, when free elections for a constitutional assembly were organised as a final step to Namibian independence, Switzerland contributed more than 30 observers to the international supervision of the election process.[83] The UNTAG experience became a precedent for the support of similar UN missions in the early 1990s, such as the Mission des Nations Unies pour le référendum au Sahara occidental (MINURSO), where Switzerland again participated with a medical unit. This was also the first time that a Swiss became the head of a UN mission. Between 1990 and 1992 Ambassador Johannes Manz, given the rank of a special representative of the United Nations Secretary-General, was in charge of the mission.[84]

In the same period, Ambassador Edouard Brunner, former secretary of state, was called upon by the United Nations Secretary-General to act as his special representative in the Middle East to promote understanding and peace between the Arabs and Israel. In 1993 Brunner was entrusted with the task of finding a resolution to the conflict between Georgia and the Abkhazian region within the framework of the United Nations Observer Mission in Georgia (UNIMOG). While in the Middle East process the credit for the signing of the Oslo Peace agreement in 1994 clearly went to Norway and the United States,[85] Brunner was more successful in mediating a ceasefire agreement in 1993/94 in the Abkhaz conflict.

However, political progress in the negotiations on the status of autonomy of Abkhazia remained slow. Although a further round of talks between the Georgian and the Abkhaz parties was held in Geneva in November 1994, no agreement could be reached, and a few days later the Abkhaz parliament adopted a new constitution declaring the region a sovereign republic. Apart from the difficulties in the Abkhaz region, the fact that Brunner was at the same time head of the Swiss embassy in France complicated his task. His double mandate was criticised publicly by one of Brunner's former colleagues, Ambassador Paul Stauffer.[86] When the assignment in Georgia became more demanding and the new UN Secretary-General, Kofi Annan, was looking for a special representative to reside permanently in the country, the choice fell to Brunner's former assistant, Liviu Bota of Rumania. Ambassador Brunner could not have accepted this new assignment due to his accreditation at the Swiss embassy in Paris.[87]

On the whole, Swiss activities within the framework of UN diplomacy remained limited due to non-membership and because the government's plan to recruit its own blue helmets for UN peacekeeping missions was foiled by a negative referendum vote in 1994. At the same time, the Swiss contribution to international peace support operations of the Organisation for Security and Cooperation in Europe (OSCE) increased constantly after the end of the Cold War. Switzerland had already played a vital role within the group of the neutral and non-aligned member states of the Conference for Security and Cooperation in Europe (CSCE), when newly arising Cold War tensions in the 1980s nearly led to the breakdown of the Conference in 1984.[88]

Yet with the shifting of the balance of power after 1989, Switzerland lost its role as a power broker in the revitalised CSCE (since 1994 OSCE). It subsequently concentrated on the newly established capacity of the organisation to secure peace and democracy, particularly in the context of the violent process of dissolution of former Yugoslavia. Since 1991, Switzerland has taken part in various OSCE missions to the Balkans by recruiting and assigning experts in human rights, democracy, constitution building and forensic medicine, as well as civil observers, policemen, custom officers and coroners.[89] When Switzerland held the chair of the OSCE in 1996, free elections were organised in Bosnia, and more than 100 Swiss observers were additionally placed at the disposal of the organisation to supervise this process.[90]

Apart from Switzerland's contributions of personnel to UN and OSCE missions in the Balkans, where Switzerland was present with hundreds of civil experts, one Swiss representative in particular deserves to be mentioned for his mediating efforts within the framework of the OSCE in the Caucasus region: In 1995 and 1996, Swiss diplomat Tim Guldimann was head of an OSCE support group in Chechnya with the mission to initiate and facilitate negotiations between the pro-Russian local government in Grozny and the Chechens fighting for independence. At first, the Chechens were resolutely opposed to any OSCE activity, but after their leader Dschohar Dudaev died in a missile attack in April 1996, his successor Selimkhan Jandarbiev was more amenable to negotiations and agreed to meet the Russian President Boris Yeltsin.

The ceasefire agreed upon on 27 May 1996 in Moscow in the presence of Tim Guldimann did not persist, however, and Grozny was taken by the Chechens in early August 1996. This time it was Yeltsin's newly nominated security adviser, General Alexander Lebed, who brokered another ceasefire in Chechnya together with the military commander of the Chechens, Aslan Maskhadov. Subsequent endeavours by Guldimann finally led to the signing of an agreement between Jandarbiev and Russian Prime Minister Victor Tschernomyrdin in October 1996 in Moscow. They confirmed the ceasefire negotiated by Lebed and Maskhadov and called upon the OSCE support group to supervise the return of the prisoners of war and to organise presidential and parliamentary elections in Chechnya – a task that placed high demands on Guldimann's small group.

A few months later, the first round of elections were held as provided, and after the second round Maskhadov was inaugurated as the new president in March 1997.[91] Guldimann and his group had thus been successful in facilitating talks in the initial phase, in spring 1996, between Moscow and the Chechens and in organising free elections after General Lebed had re-established the ceasefire in August 1996. Unfortunately, the work and the presence of the OSCE could not prevent a second outbreak of the war in the long run. In 1999 the relaunch of Russian military operations in the southern border region vitiated the political progress achieved in the preceding years within just months.[92]

Today, more than two thirds of the money spent for Swiss peace support represents contributions to multilateral operations and missions of international organisations, namely the UN and the OSCE.[93] In 1991, 98 per cent of the Swiss support consisted of strictly financial contributions to international peace missions and only 2 per cent of the means were spent on Swiss personnel or projects. By 1999, the numbers had changed remarkably: 85 per cent of the budget for peace activities was now spent on personnel missions and contributions to projects with Swiss participation, whereas only 15 per cent made up direct financial contributions. On the whole, 235 Swiss civil experts were on peace missions abroad in 1999.[94] While Swiss personnel, during the Cold War were deployed only on very rare occasions and personal contributions to international peace missions remained mostly individual, the need for experts in preventive diplomacy, forensic medicine, justice, democracy and human rights had become particularly evident in the aftermath of the Balkan wars in the 1990s. The response of the Federal Department of Foreign Affairs to this development was the creation of a corps of civil experts that could be placed flexibly and rapidly at the disposal of UN or OSCE peace support missions.[95] The systematic registration of Swiss civil experts from previous international missions as well as recruitment and instruction of new personnel began in January 2001 with the aim to build up a capacity to deploy 100 persons at a time on long-term missions.[96]

Conclusions

Since the end of the Cold War it has become evident that the classical concepts of international law for the peaceful settlement of *inter*-state disputes, such as protecting power mandates, arbitration, good offices (in a narrow sense) and hosting international conferences, have been replaced and amended. New forms and instruments of international conflict prevention and management have been established that are more appropriate to the requirements of third-party intervention in *intra*-state conflicts having either religious or ethnic backgrounds. International civil missions in the field of human security, constitution building, civil administration and economic development led by the UN and the OSCE are sent into crisis regions together with military deployments in order to co-ordinate the stabilising and mediating efforts multilaterally. The tendency towards multilateral activities in conflict management is, however, not a recent development; it has only become more articulated with the enhanced possibilities for action within the framework of the United Nations and the OSCE since the end of the Cold War.

Compared to the World War years, Swiss good offices (in a broader political sense) have declined since the foundation of the United Nations in 1945. Switzerland at first tried to promote itself as a go-between in international conflicts by invoking the notion of 'neutrality and solidarity'. Yet examination of specific cases of Cold War crises reveals that after the unsatisfactory Korea mission and a failed attempt to initiate an international peace conference in the Suez Crisis, the Department of Foreign Affairs was prepared to act only when there was absolutely no risk of endangering neutrality. In practice, Switzerland restricted itself to offering logistic support and services, and hardly ever took the initiative in political questions. Under these circumstances, 'active neutrality' was obviously not much more than a flowery phrase, and the concept of good offices suffered from rhetorical overstretch.

In fact, there were only four occasions during the Cold War period on which Switzerland actually engaged in political mediation efforts on its own, and only one of them – the French–Algerian negotiations – was a success. The argument that permanent neutrality predestined Switzerland to act successfully as an intermediary in conflicts where the UN would be paralysed and great power interests would be at stake proves undeniably to be unfounded when we analyse the past fifty years more closely. Certainly, Switzerland played a fairly important role as a protecting power and as a host for international organisations and conferences throughout the Cold War. Still, the concept of good offices as the basis of an active politics of peace seems to have been no more than a slogan to gloss over the negative aspects of neutrality and abstention from UN membership.

An active contribution to international conflict prevention and management became possible only with the conceptual changes in Swiss foreign policy of 1993, when efforts to promote peace were no longer linked with neutrality. Neutrality was no longer the sole corner stone of Swiss foreign policy; the goals of Swiss foreign policy now outlined included the safeguarding of ecological balance and Swiss economic interests abroad, the relief of worldwide poverty, the attainment of peaceful understanding among peoples, the observance of human rights and the promotion of democracy.

While this further enhanced the scope of Swiss activities in the field of multilateral preventive diplomacy and conflict management, especially with Swiss participation in UN and OSCE peace support missions in the Balkans, it reduced the notion of good offices to its traditional meaning. In the latest report on Foreign Policy, issued in 2000, the Swiss government explained the shift in its approach to conflict prevention and management by emphasising the importance of broad and active support of international peace missions, including diplomatic, economic and humanitarian aid.[97] The traditional good offices provided by a single state were incorporated into a concept of conflict management that relies strongly on international co-operation, with state and non-state actors alike. The end of the Cold War had a decisive influence on this shift in policy, since it paved the way for a redefinition of Swiss activities to promote peaceful solutions to international crises according to the needs of the parties involved and not primarily according to the requirement of the strict safeguarding of neutrality.

Acknowledgement

The Author would like to thank Jürg Martin Gabriel and Daniel Möckli for their comments on an earlier draft and Barbara Schedler for her help with the English.

Notes

1 Swiss military activities in the field of international peacekeeping and its efforts in arms control and reduction are discussed in separate publications and are therefore not taken into consideration here. Also excluded from this chapter is the subject of humanitarian aid, which deals with the consequences of conflicts and not with their prevention or peaceful resolution.

2 UN General Assembly, Official Records, *Report of the Secretary-General on the work of the Organization*, Fifty-fourth Session, Supplement No. 1 (A/54/1), 31 August 1999, para. 83.

3 Since 1990, Swiss diplomacy had been involved in the Afghan civil war. See more in the following section on good offices and bilateral mediation.

4 Artur K. Vogel, 'Bin Laden diskret loswerden: In Afghanistan hätte die Schweiz beinahe Weltpolitik gemacht', *Weltwoche*, 20 September 2001, p. 9; 'Schweiz organisierte Afghanistan-Gespräche: Abbruch wegen Offensive', *Neue Zürcher Zeitung*, 2 November 2000, p. 14.

5 The Hague Convention for the Pacific Settlement of International Disputes (1907) states explicitly that 'Powers strangers to the dispute have the right to offer good offices or mediation even during the course of hostilities' (Art. 3, para. 2), and that 'the exercise of this right can never be regarded by either of the parties in dispute as an unfriendly act' (Art. 3, para. 3).

6 This widely accepted definition is taken from: Konrad Stamm, *Die Guten Dienste der Schweiz: Aktive Neutralitätspolitik zwischen Tradition, Diskussion und Integration* (Bern: Herbert Lang, 1974), p. 5.

7 Michael E. Dreher, *Die Institution der Guten Dienste im Völkerrecht* (Zürich: Dissertation, 1980), p. 103f. Mediation and conciliation go beyond good offices in the sense that the third party takes active part in the negotiations and submits its own proposals for settlement of the dispute.

8 Edgar Bonjour, *Geschichte der schweizerischen Neutralität: Kurzfassung* (Basel/Stuttgart: Helbing und Lichtenhahn, 1978), p. 106.

9 This argument was repeatedly brought forward by Raymond Probst, former Secretary of State in the Swiss Department for Foreign Affairs. Raymond R. Probst, 'Die "Guten Dienste" der Schweiz', in *Annuaire de l'Association suisse de science politique* (Lausanne: 1963), pp. 21–5; Raymond R. Probst, *'Good Offices' in the Light of Swiss International Practice and Experience* (Dordrecht/Boston/London: Martinus Nijhoff Publishers, 1989), pp. 13–5; Raymond R. Probst, 'Die Schweiz und die "Guten Dienste"', in Alois Riklin, Hans Haug and Raymond Probst (eds), *Neues Handbuch der schweizerischen Aussenpolitik*, Schriftenreihe der Schweizerischen Gesellschaft für Aussenpolitik 11 (Bern/Stuttgart/Wien: Paul Haupt, 1992), p. 660f.

10 More than a quarter of all international mediation efforts since 1945 has fallen under the responsibility of the UN. Marquis, Lionel und Gerald Schneider, 'Wer kommt als Vermittler zum Zuge? Überschätzte und unterschätzte Anforderungsfaktoren für Mediationstätigkeiten', *Schweizerische Zeitschrift für Politische Wissenschaft*, Vol. 2, Issue 3 (1996), p. 72f.

11 Raymond Probst, *'Good Offices' in the Light of Swiss International Practice and Experience*, p. 11; Pierre Du Bois, 'Neutrality and Political Good Offices: The Case of Switzerland', in Hanspeter Neuhold and Hans Thalberg (eds), *The European Neutrals in International Affairs* (Vienna: Wilhelm Braumüller, 1984), p. 7f.

12 The protecting power mandate is founded in Art. 45 and 46 of the 1961 Vienna Convention on Diplomatic Relations, and Art. 8 of the 1963 Vienna Convention on Consular Relations.

13 Reto Borsani, *La Suisse et les bons offices* (Geneva: IUHEI, 1994), p. 16.

14 See Wayne S. Smith, 'The Protecting Power and the US Interests Section in Cuba', in David D. Newsom (ed.), *Diplomacy under a Foreign Flag: When Nations Break Relations* (London: Hurst, 1990), pp. 99–112; Raymond Probst, *'Good Offices' in the Light of Swiss International Practice and Experience*, p. 114f.

15 Cf. William Eagleton, 'Evolution of the US Interests Sections in Algiers and Baghdad', in David D. Newsom (ed.), *Diplomacy under a Foreign Flag: When Nations Break Relations*, pp. 90–8.

16 According to Probst, the Swiss, at the request of both parties, also embarked on some mediating efforts, which helped to pave the way for an agreement on the

repatriation of prisoners of war and civilians – an agreement that finally led to the restoration of diplomatic relations between New Delhi and Islamabad in 1976. Raymond Probst, *'Good Offices' in the Light of Swiss International Practice and Experience*, p. 114.

17 Foreign minister Graber in a speech to the Parliamentary Committee on Foreign Affairs of the Council of States. Swiss Federal Archives, Bern, E 1050.12 1995/512, 3, Kommission für auswärtige Angelegenheit des Ständerates, 10 January 1972.

18 For the Swiss role in the US–Iran hostage crisis, see the following first hand accounts: Raymond R. Probst, 'The "Good Offices" of Switzerland and Her Role as Protecting Power', in David D. Newsom (ed.), *Diplomacy under a Foreign Flag: When Nations Break Relations*, pp. 18–31; David D. Newsom, 'The Sensitive Link: The Swiss Role in the US–Iran Hostage Crisis', in David D. Newsom (ed.), *Diplomacy under a Foreign Flag: When Nations Break Relations*, pp. 32–43. For the context of the Swiss activities in the larger context of American diplomatic efforts, see: Harold H. Saunders, 'Diplomacy and Pressure: November 1979–May 1980', in Warren Christopher, Harold H. Saunders *et al.* (eds), *American Hostages in Iran: The Conduct of a Crisis* (New Haven: Yale University Press, 1985), pp. 72–143, especially p. 88f.; and Harold H. Saunders, 'Beginning of the End', in Warren Christopher, Harold H. Saunders *et al.* (eds), *American Hostages in Iran: The Conduct of a Crisis*, pp. 281–96.

19 Based on the title of David D. Newsom's article on the Swiss role in the hostage crisis, which was first published in a commemorative publication for Ambassador Probst: David D. Newsom, 'The Sensitive Link: The Swiss role in the US–Iran Hostage Crisis', in Edouard Brunner *et al.* (eds), *Einblick in die schweizerische Aussenpolitik: zum 65. Geburtstag von Staatssekretär Raymond Probst* (Zürich: Verlag Neue Zürcher Zeitung, 1984), pp. 291–303.

20 Harold H. Saunders, 'Beginning of the End', in Warren Christopher, Harold H. Saunders, *et al.* (eds), *American Hostages in Iran: The Conduct of a Crisis*, pp. 285–87.

21 Ibid., pp. 289–96; Cf. Raymond Probst, *'Good Offices' in the Light of Swiss International Practice and Experience*, p. 116f.

22 Ibid., p. 117f.; Raymond R. Probst, 'The "Good Offices" of Switzerland and Her Role as Protecting Power', in David D. Newsom (ed.), *Diplomacy under a Foreign Flag: When Nations Break Relations*, p. 29f.

23 After the opening of the NATO air campaign, the British interests in the Serb Republic were officially represented by Brazil and German interests by Japan.

24 'Schlechter Start für Gute Dienste', *Neue Zürcher Zeitung*, 16 April 1999, p. 13; 'Cotti a refusé de protéger les intérêts allemands et anglais à Belgrade', *La Liberté*, 10 June 1999, p. 35.

25 This attitude is best represented by the official explanation of the Federal Council of 21 April 1999 on the war in Kosovo: 'The Federal council first of all confirms its readiness to take on any assignment that is likely to contribute to a political solution of the conflict – be it by lending its good offices, representing the diplomatic interests of other nations or by offering its territory to negotiators of the parties to the conflict' (Translation by the author).

26 Switzerland was only the second choice after Sweden, which had previously been rejected by Milosevic as a US protecting power because Washington had objected to Yugoslav interests being represented by China in the United States.

27 'Gute Dienste nach wie vor gefragt', *Neue Zürcher Zeitung*, 21 April 1999, p. 15.

28 Information from the Foreign Interests Section of the Swiss Foreign Department, dated 10 October 2001.

29 Jon A. Fanzun and Patrick Lehmann, *Die Schweiz und die Welt: Aussen- und sicherheitspolitische Beiträge der Schweiz zu Frieden, Sicherheit und Stabilität, 1945–2000*, Zürcher Beiträge zur Sicherheitspolitik und Konfliktforschung 57 (Zürich: Forschungsstelle für Sicherheitspolitik und Konfliktanalyse der ETH Zürich, 2000), p. 101.

30 The special agencies in Geneva include the World Health Organization (WHO), the World Intellectual Property Organization (WIPO), the World Meteorologic Organization (WMO), the General Agreement on Tariffs and Trade (GATT), and most recently the World Trade Organization (WTO), the International Bureau of Education (IBE), as well as the International Telecommunications Union (ITU) and the International Labour Organization (ILO), which were established previously to the founding of the UN. Further United Nations bodies located at Geneva are the Economic Commission for Europe (ECE), the Conference on Disarmament, the United Nations Conference on Trade and Development (UNCTAD), the Office of the United Nations High Commissioner for Refugees (UNHCR) and the Commission on Human Rights, whereas the Economic and Social Council (ECOSOC) alternates its regular sessions between New York and Geneva. Other important independent international organisations located in Geneva are the European Free Trade Organization (EFTA), the European Organization for Nuclear Research (CERN), the International Committee of the Red Cross (ICRC) and the Interparliamentary Union (IPU).

31 *Bericht des Bundesrates über das Verhältnis zwischen der Schweiz und der Organisation der Vereinten Nationen (UNO) vom 1. Juli 1998*, p. 26.

32 Subsequent CSCE expert meetings took place in Montreux 1978 (peaceful settlement of disputes), in Bern 1986 (human contacts) and in Geneva 1991 (national minorities).

33 The tensions in the Middle East would again be the subject of discussions in Geneva at the 1983 United Nations Conference on Palestine and once more when the special sessions of the UN General Assembly in 1988 and the Security Council in 1990 on the Palestine question were transferred from New York to the European headquarters of the UN.

34 For an overview of selected conferences organised in Geneva between 1945 and 1991, see the table in: Jean-Pierre Vettovaglia, 'La Suisse en tant que pays d'accueil d'organisations et de conférences internationales', in Alois Riklin, Hans Haug and Raymond Probst (eds), *Neues Handbuch der schweizerischen Aussenpolitik*, p. 784.

35 The talks to end the war in Bosnia were organised and headed by American Ambassador Richard Holbrooke in Dayton, Ohio, in the United States. Richard Holbrooke, *To End a War* (New York: Random House, 1998).

36 The first such meeting took place in 1999 in Lysoen, Norway.

37 Eidgenössisches Departement für auswärtige Angelegenheiten, *Gewalt vorbeugen, Frieden mitgestalten, Demokratie stärken: Die Friedenspolitik der Politischen Direktion des EDA* (Bern: Juli 2001), p. 4.

38 Raymond Probst, *'Good Offices' in the Light of Swiss International Practice and Experience*, p. 49f.

39 Rudolf L. Bindschedler, 'Verfahren zur friedlichen Streiterledigung', in Alois Riklin, Hans Haug and Hans Christoph Binswanger (eds), *Handbuch der schweizerischen Aussenpolitik*, Schriftenreihe der Schweizerischen Gesellschaft für Aussenpolitik 2 (Bern/Stuttgart: Paul Haupt, 1975), pp. 875–89.

40 Christoph Breitenmoser, *Sicherheit für Europa: Die KSZE-Politik der Schweiz bis zur Unterzeichnung der Helsinki-Schlussakte zwischen Skepsis und aktivem Engagement*,

Zürcher Beiträge zur Sicherheitspolitik und Konfliktforschung 40 (Zürich: Forschungsstelle für Sicherheitspolitik und Konfliktanalyse der ETH Zürich, 1996).

41 Jon A. Fanzun and Patrick Lehmann, *Die Schweiz und die Welt: Aussen- und sicherheitspolitische Beiträge der Schweiz zu Frieden, Sicherheit und Stabilität, 1945–2000*, p. 109.

42 Eidgenössisches Departement für auswärtige Angelegenheiten (EDA), Politische Abteilung III/B, *Konzept friedensfördernde Massnahmen (Legislaturperiode 2000–2003)*, December 1999, p. 5.

43 The Hague Convention for the Pacific Settlement of International Disputes (1907) set up the same rules for offering and handling good offices and mediation (Art. 2–8).

44 Raymond Probst, *'Good Offices' in the Light of Swiss International Practice and Experience*, pp. 38–40.

45 Raymond R. Probst, 'Die "Guten Dienste" der Schweiz', p. 22f.

46 The Swiss at the same time notified the UN Secretary-General of their initiative. Raymond R. Probst, 'Die "Guten Dienste" der Schweiz', p. 28.

47 Ambassador Lionel Lamb, cited in: Mauro Mantovani, *Schweizerische Sicherheitspolitik im Kalten Krieg (1947–1963): Zwischen angelsächsischem Containment und Neutralitäts-Doktrin* (Zürich: Orell Füssli Verlag, 1999), p. 209, fn. 4.

48 Ibid., p. 210f.

49 Ibid., p. 212f.

50 Ibid., p. 215.

51 Thomas Fischer, *Die guten Dienste des IKRK und der Schweiz in der Kuba-Krise 1962*, Beiträge der Forschungsstelle für Internationale Beziehungen 30 (Zürich: Zentrum für Internationale Studien der ETH Zürich, October 2000), p. 12f.

52 Marc Perrenoud, 'La Suisse et les accords d'Evian', *Politorbis*, Vierteljährliche Zeitschrift zur Aussenpolitik (ed.) Zentrum für Analyse und prospektive Studien, EDA, No. 31 (2/2002), pp. 8–37; Olivier Long, *Le dossier secret des Accords d'Evian: Une mission suisse pour la paix en Algérie* (Lausanne: 24 heures, 1988).

53 A later attempt in the 1960s by Ernesto Franzoni, a Swiss member of parliament, to initiate talks for a peaceful solution in the Biafran Civil War failed, since Swiss intermediaryship did not meet the requirements of all parties. Pierre Du Bois, 'Neutrality and Political Good Offices: The Case of Switzerland', p. 14.

54 Edouard Brunner, *Lambris dorés et coulisses: Souvenirs d'un diplomate* (Geneva/Paris: Georg, 2001), pp. 61–6.

55 Victor H. Umbricht, *Multilateral Mediation: Practical Experiences and Lessons – Mediation Cases: The East African Community and Short Comments on Mediation Efforts between Bangladesh–Pakistan–India and Vietnam–USA* (Dordrecht: Martinus Nijhoff Publishers, 1989), p. 227f.

56 Richard Rosenthal, *Mission Improbable: A Piece of the South African Story* (Cape Town/Johannesburg: David Philip Publishers, 1998); Edouard Brunner, *Lambris dorés et coulisses: Souvenirs d'un diplomate*, pp. 77–9.

57 Reto Borsani, *La Suisse et les bons offices*, p. 27.

58 Philipp Dreyer, 'Kabul bittet Bern vergebens um Vermittlung', *Tages Anzeiger*, 15 June 1996, p. 3.

59 See the introduction to this chapter.

60 'Schweiz will Afghanistan-Konferenz durchführen', *Neue Zürcher Zeitung*, 19 November 2001, p. 10; 'Keine Nationaltrauer um entgangene Konferenz', *Neue Zürcher Zeitung*, 22 November 2001, p. 15.

61 Eidgenössisches Departement für auswärtige Angelegenheiten, *Gewalt vorbeugen, Frieden mitgestalten, Demokratie stärken: Die Friedenspolitik der Politischen Direktion des EDA* (Bern: Juli 2001), p. 10.
62 Ibid., p. 8f.
63 'Kolumbiens Friedensprozess gescheitert', *Neue Zürcher Zeitung*, 22 February 2002, p. 1.
64 'Suche nach Teilfrieden im Sudan', *Neue Zürcher Zeitung*, 15 January 2002, p. 2; 'Einigung zwischen Khartum und den Rebellen', *Neue Zürcher Zeitung*, 21 January 2002, p. 5; 'Josef Bucher – Schlichter zwischen Streithähnen', *Neue Zürcher Zeitung*, 18 February 2002, p. 9.
65 For these cases, see Raymond Probst, *'Good Offices' in the Light of Swiss International Practice and Experience*, pp. 81–6, 88–94.
66 Sources: Denise Bindschedler-Robert, 'Les commissions neutres instituées par l'Armistice en Corée', *Annuaire suisse de droit international* (Lausanne: 1953), pp. 89–130; Raymond R. Probst, 'Die "Guten Dienste" der Schweiz', p. 29f.; Peter Duft, *Das Mandat der Neutralen Überwachungskommission in Korea* (Zürich: 1969); Institut für Geschichte ETHZ (ed.), *Dreissig Jahre Schweizerische Korea-Mission 1953–1983* (Zürich: Archiv für Zeitgeschichte, 1983); Marius Schwarb, *Die Mission der Schweiz in Korea* (Bern/Frankfurt a. M./New York: Peter Lang, 1986); Raymond Probst, *'Good Offices' in the Light of Swiss International Practice and Experience*, pp. 94–8; Jürg Martin Gabriel, *The American Conception of Neutrality After 1941*, updated and revised edition (Houndmills/Basingstoke: Palgrave, 2002), pp. 132–7.
67 After the end of the Cold War, Poland and Czechoslovakia were expelled from the commission. The commission was no longer welcome in North Korea as such, but Sweden and Switzerland, together with Poland – although no longer present on the spot – continued their work.
68 The conditions were formulated by the later Secretary of State Raymond Probst and included: requests by all parties to the conflict, a common and clearly defined mandate by the parties, the innocuousness of the mandate for the status of permanent neutrality, a concrete chance of success, the guarantee of freedom of action for the Swiss government, as well as a limitation to the duration of the mandate. Robert Diethelm, *Die Schweiz und friedenserhaltende Operationen 1920–1995* (Bern/Stuttgart/Wien: Paul Haupt, 1997), p. 157.
69 Troops were sent by Brazil, Denmark, Finland, India, Indonesia, Yugoslavia, Canada, Colombia, Norway and Sweden.
70 Planes were equally made available by the United States and Canada.
71 Raymond Probst, *'Good Offices' in the Light of Swiss International Practice and Experience*, p. 154f.; for more detail, see Robert Diethelm, *Die Schweiz und friedenserhaltende Operationen 1920–1995*, pp. 158–75.
72 Telegram from the American Embassy in Bern to the Secretary of State, 1 November 1962. Cited in Thomas Fischer, *Die guten Dienste des IKRK und der Schweiz in der Kuba-Krise 1962*, p. 22.
73 In 1963, for example, the Swiss consulate-general in Saigon took over the safekeeping of sensitive documents and the transmission of coded messages and material for the United Nations Fact Finding Mission on the violation of human rights in South Vietnam to the General Secretariat of the United Nations. 'Schweiz und UN: Gute Dienste der Schweiz für die UN-Untersuchungskommission in Südvietnam', Swiss Federal Archives, Bern, E 2003 (A) 1984/84, 699, Direktion für Internationale Organisationen, 23 June 1964.

74 The other potential candidate was Ambassador Paul Jolles, another leading figure of Swiss diplomacy at the time.

75 Telegram Swiss Observer Mission NY to foreign minister Spühler, 27 September 1967. Cited in Robert Diethelm, *Die Schweiz und friedenserhaltende Operationen 1920–1995*, p. 187, fn. 92 (Original in French, translation by the author).

76 U Thant, *View from the UN* (Newton Abbot/London: David & Charles, 1978), p. 282.

77 I owe these details to one of my colleagues in Zurich, Claude Nicolet, who recently published his dissertation on American foreign policy in Cyprus. Claude Nicolet, *United States Policy towards Cyprus, 1954–1974: Removing the Greek–Turkish Bone of Contention* (Mannheim: Bibliopolis, 2001). Cf. Robert Diethelm, *Die Schweiz und friedenserhaltende Operationen 1920–1995*, p. 186, fn. 87.

78 In the early 1970s, Victor Umbricht had already acted as Chief of the United Nations Relief Organization for Rehabilitation and Reconstruction of Bangladesh (1972–3).

79 Victor H. Umbricht, *Multilateral Mediation: Practical Experiences and Lessons – Mediation Cases: The East African Community and Short Comments on Mediation Efforts between Bangladesh–Pakistan–India and Vietnam–USA* (Dordrecht: Martinus Nijhoff Publishers, 1989).

80 Except for the Korean mission, the Swiss military department only once placed one of their officers at the disposal of a mission abroad in the Cold War period. When chemical weapons were used during the first Gulf War between Iran and Iraq, Colonel Ulrich Imobersteg, Chief of Chemical Weapons Defence of the Swiss Army, was sent on three missions (in 1984, 1986 and 1987) to investigate the situation at the front together with a Swedish, a Spanish and an Australian expert.

81 *Bericht des Bundesrates über die Friedens- und Sicherheitspolitik der Schweiz vom 29. Juni 1988.*

82 Swiss diplomacy had been involved before in UN action in Namibia, when Swiss diplomat Alfred Escher was sent on a mission as the UN Secretary-General's personal representative in 1972.

83 Numerous similar mandates for Swiss personnel to participate in international supervision of elections followed in Eastern Europe, Africa, Asia and Latin America.

84 At the same time, Swiss professor Walter Kälin, a human rights specialist, was entrusted with a UN fact-finding mission to Kuwait in 1991 to inquire about the violation of human rights during the Iraqi occupation in the previous year.

85 Jane Corbin, *The Norway Channel: The Secret Talks that Led to the Middle East Peace Accord* (New York: Atlantic Monthly Press, 1994).

86 Paul Stauffer, 'Über Gute und nicht ganz so gute Dienste: Eine Zuschrift', *Neue Zürcher Zeitung*, 3 August 1994, p. 12.

87 Another reason for terminating Brunner's mandate might have been the fact that he had made some public statements in Georgia strongly supporting Russian and Abkhaz positions.

88 Andrew Williams, 'Finding a New Role in International Conflict Resolution: Switzerland after the End of the Cold War', in Michael Butler, Malcolm Pender and Joy Charnley (eds), *The Making of Modern Switzerland, 1848–1998* (Houndmills, Basingstoke/London: Macmillan, 2000), p. 119.

89 See Andreas Wenger und Jeronim Perovic, *Das schweizerische Engagement im ehemaligen Jugoslawien: Über Grenzen und Möglichkeiten der Aussenpolitik eines neutralen*

Kleinstaates, Zürcher Beiträge zur Sicherheitspolitk und Konfliktforschung 36 (Zürich: Forschungsstelle für Sicherheitspolitik und Konfliktanalyse der ETH Zürich, 1995), pp. 23–5.

90 Armin Ritz, 'Friedenspolitik vor neuen Herausforderungen', *Neue Zürcher Zeitung*, 11 April 1997, p. 13.

91 See Tim Guldimann, 'Die OSZE-Unterstützungsgruppe in Tschetschenien – Ein Erfahrungsbericht', in Laurent Goetschel (ed.), *Vom Statisten zum Hauptdarsteller: Die Schweiz und ihre OSZE-Präsidentschaft* (Bern/Stuttgart/Wien: Paul Haupt, 1997), pp. 109–25.

92 By that time, Tim Guldimann was already in charge of a new OSCE mission in Croatia to supervise the observance of human rights and the return of the refugees in the demilitarised border region of Eastern Slavonia.

93 In 2001 Switzerland spent approximately 40 Mio. Swiss francs on bilateral and multilateral peace support activities. Norway, in comparison, spends five times more on similar undertakings.

94 Eidgenössisches Departement für auswärtige Angelegenheiten (EDA), Politische Abteilung III, *Jahresbericht der Sektion Friedensfragen* (Bern: 1999), p. 8.

95 Eidgenössisches Departement für auswärtige Angelegenheiten (EDA), Politische Abteilung III/B, *Konzept friedensfördernde Massnahmen (Legislaturperiode 2000–2003)*, December 1999.

96 *Neue Zürcher Zeitung*, 5 December 2000, p. 13. So far, 600 to 700 names have been registered in a database; in addition to the corps of civil experts a diplomat in the Foreign Department, Josef Bucher, was nominated ambassador for conflict mediation.

97 *Aussenpolitischer Bericht 2000 – Präsenz und Kooperation: Interessenwahrung in einer zusammenwachsenden Welt vom 15. November 2000*, pp. 29–34. The annex to the report states clearly that Switzerland's status of neutrality since the end of the Cold War has lost its meaning as a prerequisite for the offering of good offices, Annex p. 7f.; Permanent neutrality is not even mentioned in the study by the Federal Department of Foreign Affairs on the comparative advantages of Switzerland in international conflict prevention. See Eidgenössisches Departement für auswärtige Angelegenheiten (EDA), Politische Abteilung III/B, *Konzept friedensfördernde Massnahmen (Legislaturperiode 2000–2003)*, December 1999, p. 4.

5

The International Committee of the Red Cross and its Development Since 1945

Hans-Peter Gasser

Introduction

The history of the International Committee of the Red Cross (ICRC) is closely tied to that of Switzerland, and as a consequence of two world wars the relation became especially intimate. To this day the ICRC president is generally a former Swiss diplomat, and the 20 individuals constituting the actual Committee are still exclusively Swiss. Times are changing, however. During the Cold War, and particularly since the fall of the Berlin Wall, the world outside and inside the ICRC has evolved. The ICRC was created to function in classical wars among state actors. Today, such wars are rare and the ICRC is experiencing the difficulties encountered by all agencies engaged in international conflict management. The internal ICRC dynamics are also changing and, most particularly, the ICRC is increasingly becoming an actor in its own right. The purpose of this article is to look more closely at the evolution of the ICRC's mission and, most particulary, to trace the changing nature of its relation to Swiss foreign policy.

The chapter has four parts. It begins with a look at international humanitarian law. Without this legal foundation the ICRC would lack its *raison d'être* and its international legitimacy. The second part examines the ICRC as a player *sui generis* on the international scene (private roots but international tasks) and gives a general overview on its activities as humanitarian actor in armed conflict situations. Part three follows the development of the ICRC since the end of the Second World War, and part four examines the relationship between the ICRC and Switzerland. The conclusion of the article contains a list of questions which the ICRC may well have to answer in the near future.

5.1 International humanitarian law and the ICRC

Inter arma silent leges: There is no law in times of war. This blunt and (at first sight) sadly realistic statement is attributed to Cicero, the great Roman philosopher and statesman. It could also originate from a neutral observer of twenty-first century warfare – or from political leaders or their advisors, who claim that their country's (alleged) national interest is the sole norm to be respected when using force in international relations.

Political and military history has shown that the reality is much more complex, and this for three reasons. First, no state denies that there are normative constraints to limit the use of force, be it at the international level or within a State's own jurisdiction. They are rules derived from generally accepted custom, from international treaties and from other statements considered to be binding (for example, resolutions of the United Nations Security Council). That body of rules is called international humanitarian law (or international law of armed conflict or law(s) of war).

Second, these constraints are heeded by the armed forces of states and by other entities in the conduct of armed conflict. This does not mean, of course, that all constraints are respected at all times, but failure to respect them is considered to be a breach of international law. Third, institutions have been set up at the international level to promote compliance with the rules governing armed conflict and to act if serious violations occur.

The behaviour of states is a clear evidence that international humanitarian law as a set of constraints which limit the right to use force in an armed conflict is a compelling reality. But let us begin with a short look at history.

The modern period of organised humanitarian action in aid of war victims started with Henry Dunant's outcry after witnessing the useless suffering and anguish of wounded soldiers who died without care or moral support after the Battle of Solferino (northern Italy) in 1859.[1] Their neglect was not due to deliberate cruelty on the part of any military authority, but to the absence of any structure to assist victims of warfare. In his bestselling book *A Memory of Solferino*, Dunant called for two steps to be taken simultaneously, both of them very practical indeed: (1) to establish a private organisation in each country with the task of caring for the wounded in wartime, as a subsidiary to the (then non-existent) medical services of the armed forces, and (2) to conclude an international agreement declaring medical personnel neutral on the battlefield and thus creating the necessary conditions for assistance to wounded soldiers. The first proposal led to the formation of National Red Cross Societies, at first in all European countries and later all over the world. The second proposal resulted in the adoption in 1864 of the (original) Geneva Convention for the protection of war victims, the nucleus of modern international humanitarian law. That treaty was, by the way, the first multilateral treaty that codified norms governing a specific aspect of international concern.

Nowadays the treaty of 1864 is more of historical interest. The law has been further developed through many stages and codification procedures, in particular in 1929, 1949 and 1977. After the addition in 1929 of a convention on the protection of prisoners of war, based on the experience of the First World War, international humanitarian law was rewritten in 1949, taking into account the lessons learned from the Second World War. The four 1949 Geneva Conventions for the protection of war victims are today the basic documents codifying humanitarian rules to be respected in armed conflict.[2] Adopted in 1977 after lengthy and arduous negotiations, the two Additional Protocols adapt the law to modern conditions of military conflicts, not only for traditional forms of warfare but also for asymmetric conflicts or for civil wars and other forms of armed violence.[3]

Henry Dunant was an excellent communicator. He conducted a thoroughly modern though very personal campaign to spread his ideas and pave the way for action by the international community of his time. A group of Geneva citizens joined him and brought Dunant's two proposals closer to realisation: together they initiated the creation of Red Cross Societies at the national level and convinced the Swiss government to convene a Diplomatic Conference to elaborate and finally to adopt the 1864 Convention. This informal group later became the International Committee of the Red Cross, with its headquarters in Geneva. Since 1863 the ICRC has always been at the heart of what is now the International Red Cross and Red Crescent Movement. It has also always been closely involved in the development of international humanitarian law.

This chapter intends to examine the development of the ICRC since the Second World War and tries to understand how it has adapted to the various changes in the environment, in particular, since the end of the Cold War. This analysis should ultimately give a clear impression of the ICRC as it responds to humanitarian concerns at the beginning of the twenty-first century. There can be done no more than recall some basic facts which characterise a complex institution with a particularly difficult scope of action. By attempting to ask the right questions the author hopes to arouse the reader's interest in a unique international organisation and to give pause for thought on the response to be given to humanitarian disasters caused by war.

5.2 The ICRC as a non-state actor

The Statutes of the International Red Cross and Red Crescent Movement define the ICRC as follows:[4]

> The International Committee, founded in Geneva in 1863 and formally recognized in the Geneva Conventions and by International Conferences of the Red Cross, is an independent humanitarian organisation having a status of its own. It co-opts its members from among Swiss citizens.

Without being an international treaty, these Statutes have nonetheless been adopted by the International Conference of the Red Cross and Red Crescent, at which states are represented at the same level as the Red Cross and Red Crescent Movement itself. However, the Statutes, though government-approved, are not the ICRC's legal basis. They merely acknowledge its existence. Their basic message is of a political character: states have undertaken to guarantee that the ICRC can perform its activities as 'an independent humanitarian organisation having a status of its own'. In legal terms, the ICRC is at first sight a private institution incorporated under Swiss law, just like any other association such as a football club or church choir. Its membership is made up of individual persons and not of states, as is the case in fully fledged international governmental organisations. Its employees are not international civil servants; their terms of employment are governed by Swiss law. Moreover, neither the members of the governing board (the 'Committee') nor *the* personnel of the ICRC enjoy full immunity from prosecution in the event of an alleged violation of domestic law, as do members of the diplomatic corps or international civil servants. In short, the ICRC does not have the status of an international organisation with its specific rights, privileges and immunities. It is striking to see such an institution in a place like Geneva with its numerous international organisations.

However, the activities performed and the mandates accomplished make it clear that the ICRC is a player on the international scene which deals, directly and in its own right, with governments of all states party to the Geneva Conventions (that is all states) and with international organisations such as the United Nations or regional governmental organisations. For example, the ICRC is a party to agreements with states and international governmental organisations. It has concluded a number of agreements on the status of its delegations in countries where its delegates are called upon to carry out their humanitarian tasks. It seems that the doctrinal question of whether the ICRC is a subject of international law is of little concern to states which expect it to take action. As a result of international practice the ICRC today undoubtedly has the legal capacity to conclude agreements within its area of jurisdiction. In other words, the ICRC is recognised *de facto* as an international organisation by the international community.

This quasi-international status is alluded to in the four 1949 Geneva Conventions on the protection of war victims and their 1977 Additional Protocols. Through these treaties, states parties assign specific tasks to the ICRC to be performed during armed conflict, such as visiting prisoners-of-war or monitoring compliance with the Geneva Conventions in an occupied territory. The Conventions also recognise the ICRC's self-chosen role of taking initiatives to resolve problems of a humanitarian nature caused by armed conflict. That 'right of initiative' is particularly important in the context of non-international armed conflict, that is in a conflict between government forces and one or more non-State entities. Whereas any contact by a third State with a rebel group fighting against the government of another State would be considered an unjustified political interference in the latter's internal affairs, the ICRC has the explicit right, and even the mandate, to make that move – for humanitarian matters only, of course.

It is not the ICRC's legal basis and structure that determine its status on the international scene, but the tasks actually performed. This unique mixed status seems to be an appropriate solution enabling a humanitarian organisation to act in the midst of war.

As governments are apparently satisfied with the way the ICRC performs its tasks, or they see no alternative solution, no requests are being made today for changes to the organisational structure. This has not always been so. At the end of the Second World War, when the post-war legal order was formulated and the United Nations system established, ideas were voiced, but not actually pursued, to incorporate the ICRC into the United Nations system. Others would have preferred to transform the ICRC into a separate international organisation. During the decolonisation period and the advent of new states on the international scene in the 1960s, the question whether the ICRC should be placed under the umbrella of the UN and thus under the control of its member states, was again raised. Again, no action was taken and the ICRC, with its unique set-up, continues to perform its mandate as before.

Is the ICRC a non-governmental organisation (NGO)? Yes, because it is not a governmental organisation: it is composed of private individuals and not of states/governments. No, because the ICRC carries out tasks assigned to it by states through international treaties, and deals with governments on the same footing as any international governmental organisation. The following examples will serve to corroborate the ICRC's ad hoc and role-adapted status on the international scene:

- The General Assembly of the United Nations has granted observer status to the ICRC. The ICRC's position is distinguished from that of other non-governmental organisations by the fact that the UN General Assembly extended its invitation to the ICRC by a special resolution entitled 'Observer status for the International Committee of the Red Cross, in consideration of the special role and mandates conferred upon it by the Geneva Conventions of 12 August 1949'.[5] That title clearly expresses the intention of the member states. The ICRC also has observer status with the African Union, the Organisation of American States, the Council of Europe and others.
- On 19 March 1993 the Swiss government concluded a Status Agreement with the ICRC.[6] In it, the Swiss Confederation guarantees the ICRC 'independence and freedom of action', assures the inviolability of its premises and grants immunity from legal process and execution for ICRC authorities and staff for the conduct of their official activities.
- States engaged in conflict have repeatedly requested the ICRC to carry out specific tasks of a humanitarian nature, such as setting up the (governmental) Tripartite Commission to settle humanitarian issues left unresolved after the 1990/91 Gulf War and in particular to ascertain the fate of missing persons.[7]

These examples show that governments do not hesitate to think laterally and seek solutions beyond the confines of existing categories, or 'boxes' – if to do so is in their well-informed interest. And last but not the least, the ICRC has been on the scene for almost 140 years, and states have never regarded its unique and (in legal terms) hybrid set-up as an obstacle. Even though governments have no direct, institutional influence on decisions taken by the ICRC, it has acquired an exceptional degree of legitimacy.

5.2.1 The ICRC's main tasks

The main task of the ICRC is to work for due respect for any individual human being's right to receive humane treatment and survive in dignity, even in times of war or other situations of widespread violence. These 'humanitarian minima' are part of the heritage of mankind. They have been codified for situations of armed conflict by international humanitarian law, in particular the 1949 Geneva Conventions and their 1977 Additional Protocols, which all parties to an armed conflict – including non-State groups engaged in hostilities against their government – are bound to respect. At the same time, states party to the Geneva Conventions have entrusted the ICRC with a large number of activities to be carried out in the context of armed conflict. Governments and rebel groups are thus bound to respect and promote the ICRC's activities on behalf of persons affected by war. It may be safely said that the ICRC's role in conflict is today generally accepted, and is unquestioned either by states or the United Nations or by rebel groups of any kind.

The humanitarian action of the ICRC is not limited to situations covered by the Geneva Conventions, that is international and non-international armed conflict. It has always claimed to have a right of initiative in humanitarian matters in situations other than war, especially in circumstances such as internal tensions and disturbances which may be akin to civil war. In such circumstances the ICRC concentrates on places of detention and the treatment of people held there for political reasons. Though an individual State may not accept the ICRC's offer to visit its prisons, states as a whole have not objected to the existence of such a 'right of initiative' – which implies, at least, the obligation of governments to consider the ICRC's proposal and not to deem it an unacceptable interference in their internal affairs.

The ICRC likes to explain its activities in terms of two key notions: *protection* and *assistance*.

Protection – Parties to an armed conflict have to respect the rights and interests of persons who belong to the adverse party but are under their direct control or otherwise affected by their military operations. The main categories of 'protected persons' are prisoners-of-war, civilians in detention, inhabitants of occupied territory, displaced persons and the civilian population at large insofar as it is exposed to hostilities. ICRC delegates work to ensure that these particularly vulnerable groups receive maximum protection. They rely on several techniques to influence the authorities or persons in charge, ranging from on-the-spot attempts to bring about changes to formal diplomatic approaches at the highest political level of the state or rebel group concerned. ICRC practice has shown that meaningful 'protection' is possible only if its delegates have direct access to persons and premises. The ICRC is particularly highly qualified for its own specialised protection work, in which it has accumulated a great deal of experience and whose relevance is now generally recognised. That experience is, however, focused mainly on working to obtain better conditions for those who are actually under enemy control (detention, occupied territory). Persuading parties to an armed conflict to spare the civilian population during their military operations is a different matter. Effective ways of exerting pressure on governments and military commanders and convincing them to respect the basic obligation of distinguishing between military targets and civilian persons and objects are still to be found.

Assistance – Populations affected by armed conflict should be allowed to live as normal a life as possible under those circumstances. Parties to an armed conflict are under an obligation to provide assistance such as water, food, medical care and so on to people in need, be they detained or living in occupied territory. If the authorities who are responsible fail or are unable to meet that obligation, ICRC delegates must be authorised to step in, distribute relief and organise medical care. In providing assistance to war victims the ICRC does not stand alone. A large number of international organisations and non-governmental organisations are also active in that field.

Intermediary in humanitarian matters – In the words of the Statutes, the ICRC 'may take any humanitarian initiative which comes within its role as a specifically neutral and independent institution and intermediary'.[8] It can take initiatives and act as a facilitator for the conclusion of agreements between parties to an armed conflict, for instance for the repatriation of prisoners or to set up procedures to search for missing persons.

Specific tasks relating to international humanitarian law – The text of the original Geneva Convention of 1864 was drafted by the ICRC, which also played a decisive role in the preparation and convening of the Diplomatic Conference by the Swiss government. The same applies to the subsequent revision procedures. Thus the preparation of new international humanitarian law has always been firmly in the hands of the ICRC, which has the necessary expertise to make meaningful proposals. Governments also rely on the ICRC's expertise for explaining and spreading knowledge of the Geneva Conventions and other humanitarian treaties, in particular to members of their armed forces. Finally, the ICRC has a general obligation to work for the faithful application of the Geneva Conventions and to defend them against politically motivated attempts to weaken their effectiveness in protecting victims of armed conflict.

The ICRC's determination to be as close to the victims as circumstances (including security considerations) allow is the undoubtedly justified hallmark of the Geneva-based institution.

5.2.2 The ICRC's internal structure

The International Committee of the Red Cross is governed by a board which numbers between 20 and 25 members, all of them Swiss citizens: the 'Committee'. The President and one of the two Vice-Presidents are in the full-time service of the institution, while the others are part-time. The Committee, meeting *in plenum* (the 'Assembly'), formulates policy, defines general objectives and institutional strategy, and approves the budget and accounts. Chaired by the ICRC President, the Assembly tends to take its decisions on a collegial basis. A number of the Assembly's responsibilities are delegated to the Assembly Council. Composed of five members, including the President and the two Vice-Presidents, the Assembly Council oversees the administration's activities. The Directorate is the executive body in charge of running the ICRC's affairs. It is headed by a Director-General and comprises the Director of Operations, the Director for International Law and Cooperation with the (Red Cross and Red Crescent) Movement, and the directors in charge of human resources, financial affairs and communication respectively.

The ICRC acts through what it calls its delegates. They have the authority to represent the institution and to speak on its behalf in their contacts with parties to an armed conflict or during negotiations with governments, international organisations or insurgent groups. While almost exclusively Swiss in the past, the delegates are today of increasingly international origin. They are either general field delegates or have specific skills. Among the latter there are medical doctors, water and sanitation engineers, legal advisors, relief specialists, communication experts, administrators and many other professionals.

In 2002, the ICRC had a total of 63 delegations in all five continents, staffed by approximately 1200 delegates and 8500 local personnel. About 800 people were employed at its headquarters in Geneva. Most delegations are based in conflict areas. Today, all ongoing armed conflicts are covered by ICRC delegations, working on both sides. Several are regional delegations, such as those in Nairobi, Buenos Aires or Washington, or liaison offices, such as the bureaux in New York (United Nations) or Brussels (European Union, NATO). In 2001 the ICRC spent a total of 830 million Swiss francs. It is financed by voluntary contributions from governments (85 per cent of the total amount), by contributions from National Societies and by private donations. As it is not an international governmental organisation for which states parties automatically have to provide the necessary funding through regular contributions, the ICRC has to convince governments of their moral obligation to enable it to carry out its humanitarian work. In particular, it has to show that the money is well spent in its relief operations. The system works, as the ICRC has never had to forego a relief operation for lack of funding, and at the end of the year income and expenditure are usually balanced. A remarkable number of 82 governments made a contribution to the 2001 budget. The United States is the largest donor, followed by the United Kingdom and Switzerland. The European Union is also a major contributor. The ICRC works to ensure a broad financial basis for its humanitarian operations. Each contribution, however modest, is seen by the ICRC as an expression of support for its activities.

5.3 The ICRC since 1945

At the close of the Second World War – beyond all doubt the most horrific event in the history of mankind – the ICRC could look back with some satisfaction on the work accomplished to assist war victims, often under the most difficult circumstances. Its delegates made 11 200 visits to prisoner-of-war and internment camps, distributed 470 000 tons of relief supplies to POWs and civilian internees, and delivered around 120 million personal messages across the lines. At the end of the war its Central Tracing Agency had compiled a total of 36 million files.[9] On the other hand the plight of the civilian population, and especially the appalling conditions in concentration camps which remained beyond the reach of ICRC delegates, made it abundantly clear that the Geneva Conventions had to be revised. In particular, international law had to protect the civilian population in occupied territory from the horrors of war. Moreover, the Spanish Civil War (1936–9) clearly showed that people in the throes of a civil war also urgently needed protection by an international treaty. Following up an initiative taken by the ICRC, Switzerland convened a Diplomatic Conference which, on the basis of drafts prepared by the ICRC, adopted the four Geneva Conventions for the protection of victims of war on 12 August 1949.[10] The new Convention on the protection of civilians (the Fourth Geneva Convention) and Article 3 common to the four Conventions, with its essential minimum guarantees for victims of internal warfare, were designed to respond to those challenges, and in particular to the tragedies of the Nazi death camps. Furthermore, the new law gave the ICRC a better basis for its work in aid of persons affected by warfare.

With hindsight, the process of drawing the necessary conclusions from the experience of the Second World War seems to have gone quite smoothly and without major problems, at least where humanitarian policy was concerned. It took the Diplomatic Conference less than four months to draft and adopt four comprehensive international treaties on this complex subject. The ICRC itself faced tougher times and had to overcome difficult obstacles in endeavouring to adapt its own role to the new post-war conditions. It was not always easy to realise that the world was not the same as before the war. In particular, the adoption of the Charter of the United Nations and the creation of the UN Secretariat as an international body, along with several organisations with specific tasks, meant that the ICRC was no longer alone on the international scene. Moreover, at the end of the war and particularly after the events of 1948 in Eastern Europe, the world split into two camps separated by a rigid boundary, the Iron Curtain. In the eyes of the communist world, the ICRC was not surprisingly considered to be part of the Western bloc, and the Soviet Union backed the fight to revise the institution's political and legal status. Yet, the first and most vigorous proposal to internationalise the ICRC came from within the Red Cross Movement, from the Chairman of the Swedish Red Cross, Count Bernadotte.[11] The proposal was discussed at the Red Cross Conference held in Stockholm in 1948...and withdrawn by the author himself. He realised that to internationalise the ICRC might well paralyse its ability to take decisions on controversial issues, as had happened in so many international governmental organisations.

Although the Soviet Union and its allies, as well as China, continued to co-operate with the Red Cross Movement, the ICRC had no access to conflict areas under their control. Thus in the Korean and Vietnam Wars, ICRC delegates were only allowed access to prison camps in South Korea and in South Vietnam. Nor were the ICRC's offers of service accepted by Eastern Germany in 1953, by Hungary in 1956 (except during the short period when Imre Nagy was in power) or by Prague in 1968. (In those circumstances governments were not, however, under an obligation to grant the ICRC access to their territory.) The civil war in Kampuchea, after the ouster of Pol Pot in 1979, was the first conflict in Communist-controlled territory where the ICRC could organise a huge relief operation in favour of displaced persons. In the same year the ICRC was authorised to assist China and Vietnam in the repatriation of prisoners-of-war captured during the short border war of 1979.

In the period between 1945 and 1989, the ICRC was called upon to exercise its mandate in a number of wars which had the rather 'classic' objective of controlling people, territory or resources: the Suez conflict in 1956, the succession of wars in the Middle East, starting in 1967 (the ICRC was present in Palestine as early as 1947/48) and still with no end in sight; the various clashes between India and Pakistan over Kashmir; and the war between Iran and Iraq. Decolonisation and wars waged for the independence of former colonial territories brought a new dimension to the ICRC's activities.[12] The civil war in Nigeria during 1967–70 was the first major conflict to take place within a former colonial country. The ICRC was ill-prepared for coping with the sheer magnitude of a relief operation in unfamiliar political and geographical terrain.[13] Its experiences during the Biafra war convinced the Committee to substantially strengthen its organisational capacity to mount large-scale relief operations in aid of civilian victims of armed conflict.

Brief mention should be made of two rather extraordinary issues, both of which doubtless influenced the ICRC in its search for the right policy to be pursued during the Cold War. During the Cuban missile crisis in October 1962 the ICRC offered its services to the UN Secretary-General to perform any task which might defuse the impending confrontation between the two nuclear superpowers.[14] U Thant thereupon proposed to the United States and the Soviet Union that ICRC personnel act as observers to ascertain that no further missiles were being shipped to Cuba. The Soviet Union ordered its vessels to turn around and return to their bases, and no action by ICRC personnel was needed. Nevertheless, the ICRC's decision was a remarkable expression of its willingness to take on a task in a situation where no other international institution was able to act.

On more than one occasion the ICRC has had to get to grips with the question whether nuclear weapons were illegal and as such prohibited by international law, or at least whether their use in an armed conflict was incompatible with international humanitarian law. Less than a month after Hiroshima and Nagasaki the ICRC, in a circular letter to the National Societies, voiced its opinion for the first time on this new and terrible weapon. While not broaching the question of the legality of nuclear weapons as such, President Max Huber's analysis leaves no doubt of his views on this weapon of mass destruction.[15] Several years later, at the International Conference of the Red Cross in 1957, the ICRC submitted a set of draft rules intended to serve as the basis for a revision of the international rules on the conduct of hostilities and the protection of the civilian population. The exercise failed miserably, for the sole reason that the ICRC had included a provision declaring the use of nuclear weapons to be incompatible with international humanitarian law.[16] Discussions in the 1960s and 1970s on the development of international humanitarian law – which resulted in the adoption of the two 1977 Additional Protocols – were possible only on the understanding that the legal status of nuclear weapons would not be discussed and that the new law would not be applicable to the use of nuclear weapons. These two examples show that during the Cold War, the ICRC's work was influenced by the policy of mutual exclusion pursued by the superpowers.

The period following the end of the Second World War is also characterised by the emergence of a multitude of non-governmental organisations. Ever since the Nigerian/Biafran war, organisations like Oxfam, Doctors without Borders or church-related organisations have been providing assistance of all kinds to civilian populations affected by armed conflict. Suddenly, the ICRC and the Red Cross or Red Crescent Societies were no longer alone on the scene. In addition, UN bodies such as the UN refugee organisation UNHCR, the

World Food Programme and the WHO undertook to take a much greater share in wartime humanitarian action. Coordination of the various organisations' relief operations thus became indispensable, and was also requested by the donors. Exchange of views to that effect and practical co-ordination occur at different levels and in different places, both between the respective headquarters and in actual conflict areas. The ICRC has a permanent invitation to the meetings of the Inter-Agency Standing Committee, which brings together the various UN bodies concerned with international relief operations. Closer links with the United Nations have not only been established at the level of technical co-operation. Since 1990 the ICRC has been following UN affairs as an observer at the General Assembly. Contacts with the Secretary-General's office are also frequent. Of late the ICRC President has been invited on several occasions to address the Security Council on topics of concern to the ICRC, such as the protection of the civilian population in armed conflict.

In other domains it was somewhat more difficult for the ICRC to accept 'competitors'. While the success of relief operations did not necessarily depend on the special position of the ICRC, it responded more critically to moves by other bodies to address protection issues. It had, for instance, great difficulty in accepting the initiative by the Council of Europe to create a mechanism to combat torture,[17] an initiative subsequently emulated by the UN.[18] The ICRC regarded visits to places of detention as its own prerogative, at least in situations of internal strife and armed conflict, and was convinced that attempts by 'political' bodies to do the same could only be detrimental to the detainees' interests. The quality of the work done by these new bodies gradually dispelled initial scepticism about such an intrusion into what was considered to be ICRC terrain.

5.3.1 The end of the Cold War

The fall of the Berlin Wall in 1989 heralded the end of the Cold War and opened up a new area which was no longer held in thrall by the competition between the superpowers. While this historic event fundamentally changed the framework for international relations, it did not do away with the use of military force to settle conflicts. On the contrary, new wars broke out in the Balkans, the Caucasus and Central Asia (Afghanistan), and none of the 'old' conflict areas came to rest, either in the Middle East or on the Indian subcontinent, in Latin America or in Africa with its numerous local wars. And the ICRC had to continue and sometimes step up its activities to help the victims of all these armed conflicts.[19] In the humanitarian sector not much has changed – protection and assistance for war victims remained and still remains as necessary as ever. True, more and more conflicts are of a non-international character, with government forces fighting against sometimes rather amorphous groups, while in other situations, in the absence of any state authority, various groups fight against each other. Such hostilities are sometimes closer to organised criminality than to armed conflict. Despite the frequent references to so-called asymmetric conflicts, in which usually government forces are ranged against much weaker rebel fighters, these conflicts are in fact not new. Colonial wars and wars of national liberation had the same characteristics. The waning of the superpowers' interest in those areas makes the seemingly unending conflicts there even harder to resolve. For the ICRC, they mean a greater investment in terms of personnel and relief supplies and a worsening of security conditions for its delegates.

The end of the Cold War restored vitality to the United Nations. The UN Charter's mechanisms to settle disputes between member states (Chapters VI and VII) were able to function for the first time since 1945. Secretary-General Boutros Ghali launched an ambitious 'Agenda for Peace'. In the event of a threat to international peace, armed intervention under the authority of the UN Security Council became possible (Balkans, Rwanda). And the idea of a general 'right of intervention' in the internal affairs of a State which violated fundamental human rights was also put forward. For the ICRC, with its mandate to defend humanitarian concerns in an existing armed conflict, these developments did not change the parameters for action very much. However, ICRC delegates found new players on the operational scene who also claimed the right to perform tasks of a humanitarian nature: members of peacekeeping forces, or Blue Helmets. The ICRC had to make considerable efforts to convince all concerned that humanitarian activities should remain in the hands of humanitarian organisations, whereas the task of military forces was to ensure the security of humanitarian personnel and the victims alike.

An important and positive development was achieved in the field of criminal justice: the creation of an International Criminal Court (ICC) with jurisdiction over war crimes, that is a grave breache of the Geneva Conventions and their Additional Protocols.[20] The ICC in no way supplants domestic criminal jurisdictions, which are under an international obligation to bring war criminals to justice. In accordance with the Rome Statute the ICC can institute proceedings only when domestic courts fail to act or if there is a serious miscarriage of justice. Although the Court itself will hardly have many cases to try in the near future, the mere existence of an international jurisdiction should be a strong signal to the community of states that impunity for war crimes will no longer be tolerated. The fact that the United States does not share this view gives cause for concern. The existence of a new permanent international criminal jurisdiction does not, however, affect the activities of the ICRC. At its request the ICC's Rules of Procedure specify that ICRC delegates do not have to testify in criminal proceedings.[21] The ICRC considers this measure necessary to safeguard the confidential character of its dealings with parties to an armed conflict.

After the events of 11 September 2001 in New York and Washington, the ICRC published the following declaration:[22]

> Since the attacks of 11 September 2001 in the United States which negated the most basic principles of humanity, people all around the world share a sense of uncertainty, a feeling that what is most precious to us all – life and dignity – is under threat. Thousands of Afghan men, women and children have once again abandoned their homes over the past few days in an elusive search for safety, and in dozens of countries in Africa, the Americas, Asia, the Middle East and Europe, the number of people for whom armed violence is an inescapable reality runs into the hundreds of thousands.
>
> The International Committee of the Red Cross (ICRC) strives to protect and assist all people affected by armed conflict wherever they are, without any distinction based on religion, race or nationality. It does this whatever the reasons for armed violence, its only criteria being humanitarian: what people need to preserve life and a measure of dignity.
>
> To remain at the victims' side is the aim of the ICRC and its partners in the International Red Cross and Red Crescent Movement. Working out of more than two hundred offices worldwide, the ICRC steadfastly pursues this goal. Despite the temporary withdrawal of the organisation's expatriate staff from Afghanistan, one thousand local Afghan employees and their colleagues from the Afghan Red Crescent Society are continuing to carry out humanitarian work in the country, particularly in the medical field.
>
> The purpose and the essence of international humanitarian law are to minimize the effects of war on people not taking part in the hostilities, and to protect their lives and physical integrity. Those engaged in armed hostilities must maintain a firm stance against acts that indiscriminately inflict physical and mental suffering. These fundamental principles are the common heritage of all nations and all civilizations.
>
> Humanity is the founding principle of the International Red Cross and Red Crescent Movement. At a time when the fabric of human society risks being torn asunder by outrageous acts of violence, the ICRC and the entire Red Cross and Red Crescent Movement stand ready to do their utmost to ensure that humanity prevails.

This text is the opposite of many nationalistic and at the same time apocalyptic statements made by some governments. While clearly condemning the crimes committed by the hijackers ('which negated the most basic principles of humanity') the ICRC recalls three basic facts:

- There are victims of violence all over the world, in particular also in Afghanistan.
- The ICRC is prepared to bring humanitarian assistance and protection to *all* persons affected by warfare, without any discrimination.

- International humanitarian law is part of the common heritage of all nations and all civilisations. It has to be respected under all circumstances. Its provisions prohibit any killing of civilians and seek to reduce suffering and destruction to a minimum.

These are a basic and, many would have thought before the debates following 11 September 2001, an uncontroversial expression of what humanity requires of all those who engage in armed hostilities. The statement, however, that the Geneva Conventions must be respected under all circumstances, irrespective of the motivation or cause for recourse to war or the presumed guilt of the detained enemy fighter, no longer seems generally acceptable as a matter of course.

The US-led armed attack on Afghanistan in October 2001 and the establishment of new authorities in Kabul had only one, but a decisive, immediate effect on the ICRC's operations: it enabled ICRC delegates to return to the country which they had had to leave in September, shortly before the downfall of the Taliban regime. They are now running a vast programme to bring humanitarian relief to all people whose living conditions have drastically deteriorated as a result of the long war against the Soviet Union, of the Taliban regime and of the US-led military operations. Delegates also visit detainees in Afghanistan and those held by the United States in Guantanamo.

The aftermath of 11 September 2001 raises *inter alia* the following questions, which are of interest in reflecting on the future of international humanitarian law:

- Will it be possible to preserve the essence of the Geneva Conventions in a period which tends to adopt a black and white approach even in the domain of international humanitarian law, an approach which is incompatible with the results of a long historical development dedicated to promoting the concept of equal justice for all, even in war?[23] Certain conclusions drawn from the events in New York and Washington and based on 'just war' considerations are but one example of a threatened decline of international humanitarian law. The events in the Middle East, where since 1967 the occupying power (with US connivance) has not recognised the (evident) applicability of the Fourth Geneva Convention – which protects the basic rights of inhabitants in occupied territories – to the territory conquered in the Six-Day War, bode ill for future respect for international humanitarian law.
- Will states and the international community stand up and take the defence of international humanitarian law, even against those who refute its *raison d'être*?
- Will it be possible for the ICRC not only to preserve but also to strengthen its own independence in a bipolarised – or, even more likely, in a multipolarised – world? Will it remain possible, even under changed

circumstances, to get the message across that its independence is not only a condition for humanitarian action but also an element of international security?

Despite 11 September and its aftermath, life went on for the ICRC. Its delegates were and still are deployed throughout four continents, visiting detainees of all categories, caring for the wounded, repairing drinking water installations in conflict areas, distributing relief, restoring contact between family members separated by hostilities, searching for missing persons, and so on. They experience on a daily basis the much discussed concepts of internal armed conflict with outside intervention, asymmetric conflict, transnational conflicts and other forms of non-classic warfare. In terms of their humanitarian implications these so-called 'new forms of conflict' are known as conflicts which never end.

5.4 The ICRC and Switzerland

The ICRC is an international institution incorporated under Swiss law, with its headquarters in Geneva, Switzerland. Members of its governing Committee must be of Swiss nationality. For a long time staff members were recruited almost exclusively from among Swiss citizens, the exceptions being staff drawn from neighbouring European countries. While the employment policy of the ICRC has radically changed in recent years and more and more posts are now held by non-Swiss, it is still perceived as a Swiss institution firmly rooted in (international) Geneva. The Swiss government and most of the Swiss media never conceal their satisfaction at having a humanitarian institution in the country, whose worldwide activities broaden the rather narrow scope of Switzerland's own foreign policy.

But Switzerland is not only the seat of the ICRC and one of its main financial contributors, it is also a party to the Geneva Conventions and their Additional Protocols. What happens if the Swiss government, in its capacity as a party to the Conventions, puts forward ideas or proposals which the ICRC considers to be unhelpful to the humanitarian cause?

And, finally, the Swiss government is the depository of the Geneva Conventions, a mandate which includes various tasks of a more or less administrative nature. The depository may, however, have to take politically sensitive decisions on controversial issues such as the admission or not, as party to the Conventions, of an entity which does not possess all the attributes of a sovereign State, for example the request of the Algerian Provisional Government to become party to the 1949 Geneva Conventions prior to the country's independence in 1962. The ICRC may have a divergent opinion as to whether such a decision is politically opportune or not.

To sum up, what are the relations between the ICRC and the Swiss government today? Is there complete independence or full control by Bern over Geneva, or vice versa, in humanitarian policy issues? Has Switzerland any obligations towards the humanitarian organisation? Let me characterise the situation by mentioning three points.

(1) There are quite obviously neither personal nor institutional links between the Swiss government and the ICRC. Although presidents and other members of the Committee have been former high government officials, they have all been chosen and co-opted by the Committee. They have not been seconded to Geneva by Bern, and all have given up their position in the Swiss administration. In 1917 the then President of the ICRC, Gustave Ador, was elected a member of the Swiss Federal Council and Head of the Department of Foreign Affairs. During his tenure in Bern he remained a member of the Committee, but did not exercise his function as president. Despite the dual role of one of its most distinguished members, the Committee managed to keep its distance from Bern in the final months of the First World War.

The situation was somewhat different in the Second World War. One member of the Committee, Philipp Etter, was simultaneously in charge of the Swiss government's assistance operations, and was also a member of the government. Although such close links between Bern and Geneva doubtless also had positive effects, especially for the organisation of relief operations, Etter had a crucial influence on an important decision taken by the Committee on 14 October 1942: the refusal to issue a public statement on the situation of the civilian population under the control of the Axis powers, although the first bits of information about German concentration camps were at that time filtering through to neutral Switzerland, the main Western allies and the ICRC.[24] The Committee itself was afraid that by taking a public stance on the situation of civilians, it might annoy the German authorities to such an extent that they would close the doors to POW camps which ICRC delegates were visiting on a regular basis (POWs of the Allies). Etter's reasoning was different. He cited two basic arguments for neutral Switzerland's interest in not interfering in the internal affairs of neighbouring Germany: first, Swiss territory was encircled by German troops (except for the border with fascist Italy), and second, Switzerland's economic survival depended on German goodwill. This is not the place to examine all the aspects of the Committee's controversial decision (which, incidentally, was contested by some of its members). There is no doubt that on that occasion the Swiss government did exert pressure on the Committee to steer a course which would not collide with Swiss national interests as perceived by the Swiss Federal Council. But there is insufficient evidence for the claim that dependence on Bern was a general pattern during the Second World War and could have impaired the ICRC's standing as a neutral and impartial humanitarian player. Moreover, close co-operation with the Swiss government and its diplomatic outposts was at times essential for the ICRC, especially for relief operations.

Since 1945, no active member of the Swiss government has ever been elected to membership of the Committee. But former federal counsellors have joined the Committee after their departure from active political life and have made outstanding contributions to the work of the ICRC. The same holds true for members of Parliament or high-level officials from federal and cantonal administrations. Several former Swiss ambassadors have also been co-opted by the Committee. In particular, the present President and his two predecessors were high-level Swiss officials before they were elected to the ICRC presidency.[25] Is this evidence of undue interference by Bern in the ICRC's personnel policy? – Switzerland is a small country, and potential candidates with extensive experience, on the international scene and a proven record for successfully managing what is (not only by Swiss standards) quite a large organisation, are rare. They might be found in government or academic circles, but since Switzerland was not a member of the United Nations until late 2002[26] and is still not part of the European Union, the possibility of recruiting members of the Committee among senior international officials (diplomats or civil servants) of Swiss nationality is rather limited. As long as there is no broader source of experienced international personnel with Swiss nationality, suitable candidates will have to be found in Bern rather than elsewhere.

Certain questions remain. Does the Swiss government unduly influence the selection of ICRC presidents? And does Switzerland use the ICRC as an instrument of Swiss foreign policy? There are undoubtedly frequent contacts between Bern and Geneva, especially at the working level, on questions such as the implementation and development of international humanitarian law. But informal contacts are certainly no less frequent between the ICRC and legal or relief experts of other governments or international organisations. To the author's knowledge, no government or international organisation has ever complained about too close links between Bern and Geneva. The rest is conjecture. In conclusion, there is no clear evidence of the existence of undue influence, at least since the end of the Second World War. However, the ICRC's present governing elite are of Swiss nationality, have received their education in Swiss schools and universities and live in a Swiss environment. Is there any reason to believe that the Swiss perception of international problems and Swiss approaches to solving them should be absent in Geneva? That Swiss affinity probably creates links that are much stronger than any outside attempt to influence individual decisions.

(2) After the end of the Second World War and during the Cold War, Swiss foreign policy maintained its neutrality while at the same time remaining firmly anchored in the West, a somewhat contradictory undertaking which, however, had the full support of the Swiss population. This policy did not clash with the ICRC's determination to develop or strengthen its ties with all states and all political forces in the world, the only approach which can create the

necessary conditions for it to deploy its humanitarian activities on all sides of a possible conflict. Similarly, the ICRC has always been in contact with third-party governments if such contacts were useful to gain access to victims of armed conflict. In that regard, Swiss diplomacy has also helped the ICRC in its endeavour to establish communication with parties to an armed conflict. Yet Switzerland's policy maxim of absolute neutrality has always restricted Swiss initiatives. Nonetheless, it has reacted by every available means when ICRC delegates have been taken hostage. In such cases Switzerland has not only given the ICRC diplomatic support, but has also taken action in its capacity as the state of origin of kidnapped Swiss nationals.

(3) The fall of the Iron Curtain changed the political parameters, but less so the Swiss attitude towards the ICRC. There is no reason to expect interest in its activities to decline. On the contrary, conservative movements continue to stress Switzerland's unconditional obligation to support the ICRC – and thus to abstain from pursuing a more proactive foreign policy which, in their view, would detract from Switzerland's 'absolute' neutrality. The Swiss government has, however, given added priority to an active policy of promoting human rights. It is not impossible that under this general heading Swiss policy will also strengthen its commitment to foster the development of international humanitarian law. A recent poorly conceived initiative to 'develop' international humanitarian law on the basis of the events of 11 September 2001, launched by a private group and supported by the Swiss authorities, does not augur well for future processes to strengthen the law of Geneva.

Concluding remarks

In the period since 1945, with its watershed events of 1989/91, the ICRC has pursued a remarkably stable course guided by fundamental principles which are intrinsic to the Red Cross, in particular the principles of humanity, independence and impartiality (or non-discrimination), while simultaneously showing astonishing flexibility in addressing actual conflict situations. Governments seem to appreciate this policy. Today, the ICRC's approach to new problems of humanitarian action seems to be in the interest of states and also, surprisingly enough though not in all circumstances, of insurgent movements. This relative satisfaction with the institution probably also stems from rather cynical considerations, such as promoting humanitarian action as a substitute for tough political decisions or supporting Red Cross activities as a moral act to quieten a bad conscience.

One difficult issue seems to have been laid to rest once and for all: the status of the ICRC as a private institution with public mandates is no longer cast in doubt. There are probably two reasons for this. First, it has been generally understood that an independent ICRC is in the interest of everyone. Second, the ICRC has proved in recent years that it is capable of acting on the international scene as if it were part of the international system. While its roots remain in Switzerland, an international environment in and around it has been created by its permanent contact with international players – states and international organisations, in particular the United Nations – coupled with the progressive internationalisation of its staff. At the same time, the ICRC is now actively opening up to other cultures and civilisations, not least by hiring staff members from other continents. Lastly, the ICRC has increasingly accepted that international humanitarian law is but one chapter of international law as a whole, and that bridges have to be built to human rights law, refugee law and international criminal law.

The ICRC may in future be confronted more and more with the limits of humanitarian action. Is it possible to 'protect' persons affected by armed conflict without publicly denouncing the illegal and possibly criminal behaviour of those responsible for the harm done to the victims? In other words, can the ICRC continue to assume its (self imposed) role of 'guardian' of international humanitarian law without taking a stand on horrendous war crimes and their perpetrators? If long-term humanitarian action over several decades is likely to prolong a war (for example in the Middle East), what should be the response of a humanitarian agency?

At the end of this chapter one point should never be forgotten: in war, humanitarian policy can only bring relief (in its broad sense) to those who suffer. War is always the result of failure of governments to settle a conflict with peaceful means. Neither international humanitarian law nor humanitarian organisations such as the ICRC may do that and thus bring peace. The responsibility is with the governments.

Notes

1 On the history of the ICRC see in particular François Bugnion, *Le Comité international de la Croix-Rouge et la protection des victimes de la guerre* (Genève: CICR, 1994). An English version of this book will be published in 2003: *The International Committee of the Red Cross and the Protection of War Victims* (Houndmills, Basingstoke: ICRC and Macmillan, forthcoming). See also Caroline Moorehead, *Dunant's Dream: War, Switzerland and the History of the Red Cross* (London: HarperCollins, 1998); John F. Hutchinson, *Champions of Charity: War and the Rise of the Red Cross* (Boulder: Westview Press, 1996); David P. Forsythe, 'The International Committee of the Red Cross and humanitarian assistance: A policy analysis', *International Review of the Red Cross*, No. 314 (1996), pp. 512–31; David P. Forsythe, *Humanitarian Politics: The International Committee of the Red Cross* (Baltimore and London: The Johns Hopkins University Press, 1977).

2 Convention (I) for the Amelioration of the Condition of the Wounded and Sick in Armed Forces in the Field, Convention (II) for the Amelioration of the Condition of Wounded, Sick and Shipwrecked Members of Armed Forces at Sea, Convention (III) relative to the Treatment of Prisoners of War, Convention (IV) relative to the Protection of Civilian Persons in Time of War, all four adopted on 12 August 1949 – 190 states parties.

3 Protocol Additional to the Geneva Conventions of 12 August 1949, and relating to the Protection of Victims of International Armed Conflicts (Protocol I) and Protocol Additional to the Geneva Conventions of 12 August 1949, and relating to the Protection of Victims of Non-International Armed Conflicts (Protocol II), both adopted on 8 June 1977 – 160 and 155 states parties, respectively.
4 *Statutes of the International Red Cross and Red Crescent Movement* (1986), Article 5. The Statutes are the basic law of the International Red Cross and Red Crescent Movement. They assign the various tasks to the components of the Movement: the National Red Cross and Red Crescent Societies, their International Federation and the ICRC. They have been adopted by the International Conference of the Red Cross and Red Crescent, at which delegates of the various Red Cross and Red Crescent bodies assemble with delegates of the states party to the Geneva Conventions. In accordance with the Geneva Conventions states may use the red crescent on a white ground to indicate the medical services of their armed forces, in lieu of the original emblem: the red cross on a white ground. National Societies may likewise opt for the red crescent as an emblem. Several Muslim countries and National Societies have done so. There is no difference in status and both names and emblems have the same legal connotation. Israel does not accept either of these two emblems and names. This has no effect on the status of Israel as party to the Geneva Conventions (which it has ratified), but its National Society cannot be formally recognised unless and until the First Convention is amended to allow the use of a third emblem.
5 General Assembly Resolution 45/6, 16 October 1990.
6 Text published in *International Review of the Red Cross (IRRC)*, No. 293 (April 1993), pp. 152–60.
7 See Christophe Girod, *Tempête sur le désert: le Comité international de la Croix-Rouge et la guerre du Golfe 1990–1991* (Bruxelles: Emile Bruylant, 1995).
8 *Statutes of the International Red Cross and Red Crescent Movement*, Article 5, para. 3.
9 Bugnion, *Le Comité international de la Croix-Rouge et la protection des victimes de la guerre*, p. 272f.
10 See note 2.
11 Bugnion, *Le Comité international de la Croix-Rouge et la protection des victimes de la guerre*, p. 1147.
12 See Jacques Freymond, *Guerres, révolutions, Croix-Rouge* (Geneva: Graduate Institute of International Studies, 1976).
13 See Thierry Hentsch, *Face au blocus: La Croix-Rouge internationale dans le Nigéria en guerre (1967–1970)* (Geneva: Graduate Institute of International Studies, 1973).
14 Thomas Fischer, 'The ICRC and the Cuban missile crisis', *IRRC*, No. 842 (June 2001), pp. 287–309. Opinions differ as to whether U Thant was the first to ask the ICRC to accept such a task or whether the ICRC spontaneously offered its services to the Secretary-General.
15 370th Circular letter of the ICRC, 5 September 1945.
16 Draft Rules for the Limitation of the Dangers incurred by the Civilian Population in Time of War, submitted to the XIXth International Conference of the Red Cross (1957).
17 European Convention for the Prevention of Torture and Inhuman or Degrading Treatment or Punishment, 26 November 1987.
18 Optional Protocol of 18 December 2002 to the (United Nations) Convention against Torture and Other Cruel and Inhuman or Degrading Treatment or Punishment, 10 December 1984.

19 See Simone Delorenzi, *Contending with the Impasse in International Humanitarian Action: ICRC Policy since the End of the Cold War* (Geneva: ICRC, 1999); Michèle Mercier, *Crimes without Punishment: Humanitarian Action in former Yugoslavia* (London: Pluto Press, 1995).

20 Rome Statute of the International Criminal Court, 17 July 1998. While 139 states had signed the Rome Statute, 87 were formally bound by the treaty at 31 December 2002. The United States actively opposes the ICC. The drafters of the Rome Statute had the benefit of the experience acquired by the International Criminal Tribunal for the former Yugoslavia and the International Criminal Tribunal for Rwanda.

21 ICC Rules of Procedure and Evidence. On the ICRC's position, see in general: Gabor Rona, 'The ICRC's privilege not to testify: Confidentiality in action', *IRRC*, No. 854 (March 2002), pp. 207–19.

22 ICRC, Communication to the press 01/33, 21 September 2001.

23 Proposals have been made in the US to amend the Geneva Conventions in a way which would clearly exclude those persons from international protection whom the government declares to be 'illegal fighters'.

24 Jean-Claude Favez, *The Red Cross and the Holocaust* (Cambridge: Cambridge University Press, 1999); and Bugnion, *Le Comité international de la Croix-Rouge et la protection des victimes de la guerre*, p. 1172.

25 Alexandre Hay (1976–87) was Director-General of the Swiss National Bank, Cornelio Sommaruga (1987–99) was Secretary of State in charge of international economic affairs, and Jakob Kellenberger, the present ICRC President, was Secretary of State in the Swiss Federal Department of Foreign Affairs.

26 Switzerland has, however, been an active member of all subsidiary institutions of the UN system.

6

Swiss Human Rights Policy: From Reluctance to Normalcy

Jon A. Fanzun

Introduction

Switzerland – like all countries – cultivates a positive self-image containing the domestic core elements of a republican system of government, direct democracy, federalism and the rule of law. Neutrality and humanitarianism complement the picture in foreign policy. While neutrality has lost some of its aura in recent years, the positive image of Switzerland's humanitarian tradition remains uncontested. The International Committee of the Red Cross (ICRC) and Switzerland's active promotion of international humanitarian law are cited as evidence of the country's humanitarian tradition.

The Federal Council has at times declared that promoting human rights is a constant and integral part of Swiss foreign policy. However, such constancy cannot be found in the period following the Second World War, because for decades, human rights played no role in Swiss foreign policy. Human rights have become more important only in recent years. It was not until 1993 that the Federal Council explicitly defined the promotion of human rights as one of its foreign policy objectives. Rather than constancy then, there has been an uneven process in the course of which human rights have gained increasing importance.

In the early years after the Second World War, Switzerland – in contrast to comparable European countries – was sceptical of the internationalisation of human rights. This reticence was closely intertwined with the country's foreign policy isolation and its rigid understanding of sovereignty. In the 1970s, Switzerland developed a more co-operative foreign policy. It signed the European Convention on Human Rights (ECHR) and began to participate in international efforts to protect human rights. An important opportunity was the Conference on Security and Cooperation in Europe (CSCE, since 1994 Organization for Security and Cooperation in Europe, OSCE).

Foreign minister Pierre Aubert initiated a new phase of Swiss human rights policy in the late 1970s. In view of the increased international focus on human rights, he made the issue one of his foreign policy priorities. In the

1980s, and as part of the discussion on UN membership, human rights became a regular topic on the Swiss political agenda. However, given the continued isolationism prevailing in parliament and in the public at large, the new departure remained within narrow confines. The step towards a comprehensive human rights policy was taken only after the end of the Cold War, in the context of a general foreign policy change. In the 1990s, Switzerland took actions to catch up in the area of human rights. It ratified numerous human rights conventions and, for the most part, cast off its previous reservations.

This chapter will examine the development of Swiss human rights policy since the end of the Second World War. I will argue that with respect to human rights policy, Switzerland moved from its exceptional, unique position among nations to a normal position and ultimately developed a policy comparable to that of other western countries. In tracing the process I will sketch out the essential features of Swiss human rights policy.

The essay has four parts. Part one begins with some remarks on the general relation between foreign policy and human rights. It then turns to Swiss human rights policy and presents the position held in the early post-War years. Part two discusses Switzerland's first experiences with international human rights protection in connection with the Council of Europe (CoE) and the CSCE. Part three deals with the activation of human rights policy in the 1980s. The fourth and concluding part analyses the development of Swiss human rights policy since the end of the Cold War.

6.1 Between humanitarianism and reluctance

Human rights were traditionally a matter of domestic but not of international politics. Foreign policy and international law dealt with the issues of war and peace; in these questions the rights of individuals had no place. This changed after the Second World War. In the treaty establishing the United Nations, member states pledged themselves to take action towards the achievement of universal respect for and observance of human rights. As a consequence, they were compelled to devote more attention to human rights in foreign policy. However, it soon became apparent that the relation between human rights and foreign policy was fraught with tensions. The concept of universal human rights gives a central place to the individual, strives to overcome national borders and emphasises what all people share in the sense of a global civil society. The world of classical foreign policy, in contrast, is a world of states in which foreign policy is meant to assure national sovereignty. It is within this controversial context that the promotion of human rights must operate.[1]

The dividing line between advocates and critics of human rights policy corresponds rather precisely to the distinction between idealists and realists. The realist worldview has no room for norms like human rights, for international politics is characterised as an unbridled struggle for power in an anarchic environment dominated by sovereign states. The goal of foreign policy is to assure the existence of the state and to maximise its interests. To follow a set of individualistic ethics, according to this view, would endanger the material and security interests of the state.[2] In contrast, the idealist view stresses the importance of rules and norms in international relations. From this perspective international law is an authority standing above power. Idealism eliminates the realist dichotomy between domestic and foreign policy. The norms that prevail at home should also be valid in international politics. In this sense, the promotion of international human rights is a legitimate foreign policy concern serving state and citizens alike.[3]

Whether or not a state follows an active human rights policy depends upon its foreign policy conception. As a rule, a realist foreign policy will be sceptical of human rights. In contrast, an active human rights policy is usually the expression of an idealist orientation. The actual foreign policy practised by most states is a mixture of realist and idealist elements.

6.1.1 Humanitarian tradition

Swiss foreign policy, too, is marked by the tension between realism and idealism. Since the founding of the Confederation in 1848 there has been a realist and an idealist tradition. In the Swiss context, realism is a combination of 'raison d'état' and perpetual neutrality. Idealism, on the other hand, is expressed in an open, co-operative foreign policy emphasising solidarity.[4] As elsewhere, Swiss foreign policy never knew the absolute contrast between foreign abstinence and openness. Switzerland was always both open and closed. This is not to say that the weighting of realist and idealist components did not change over time, and shifts usually had a direct effect on Switzerland's humanitarian and human rights engagement. But it is important to know that Swiss political identity, and thus its foreign policy, developed in a direction opposite to the general trend in Europe.[5]

Switzerland practised a relatively idealist and outward-looking foreign policy in the second half of the nineteenth century and the first decades of the twentieth. It was a period when the rest of Europe was nationalistic and involved in wars. At that time Switzerland felt that it had a mission to fulfil for the promotion of peace, justice and democracy. The country believed that it served as a moral and political model for other countries, and it tried to be useful internationally. The government organised numerous conferences, created a number of international agreements and organisations and engaged actively in codification and development of international law. Switzerland was very active at this time and pursued a relatively modern and co-operative foreign policy.[6]

During this period the Confederation assumed a pioneering role in supporting the concept of humanitarianism in international politics, as shown by its efforts in international law and the ICRC. Humanitarian engagement was viewed as a natural complement to and as a legitimisation of neutrality.[7] Neutrality as practised at the time did not hinder the country from launching international initiatives or from joining the new League of Nations in 1920. However, League membership turned out to be both the high and final point of Switzerland's idealist foreign policy.[8]

6.1.2 Neutrality and solidarity

The end of the Second World War marked a break in international politics and sounded the bell for the decline of classical international law and its notion of state sovereignty. Collective security, as propagated by the United Nations, was incompatible with a state's right to wage war. Furthermore, the promotion and protection of human rights was declared to be an international concern and a main objective of the new organisation.[9] As early as 10 December 1948, the UN General Assembly adopted and proclaimed the Universal Declaration of Human Rights. When the Council of Europe was set up a parallel effort was undertaken ending in what by its full name is called the Convention for the Protection of Human Rights and Fundamental Freedoms (European Convention on Human Rights, ECHR, for short). It was signed in November 1949 in Rome and put into force in September 1953. Just a few years after the end of the Second World War, the cornerstones for universal and European human rights protection had been laid. The new emphasis on human rights, a movement that had begun during the Second World War, represented a moral, legal and political break with the international order that had ruled prior to 1945. Unfortunately, the two proclamations were soon to be overshadowed by the outbreak of the Cold War.

In contrast to most other countries, the end of the Second World War was not a historical turning point for Switzerland. The country had survived the war unharmed and attributed the success mainly to its neutrality and the armed forces. Despite international criticism of neutrality, the Federal Council, after 1945, held on to this proven foreign policy instrument. It even elevated neutrality to an identifying feature of Swiss uniqueness and made it the crux of its entire foreign policy.[10] As a consequence, Switzerland opted for a low profile, one-dimensional and rather isolationist foreign policy. Non-membership in the UN for half a century stands as a symbol of the exceptional route taken.

Besides neutrality, the maxim of solidarity was the second pillar of Swiss foreign policy.[11] Its emphasis on international solidarity was meant to compensate and legitimise the disadvantages of neutral abstinence and to counteract international isolation. In the Federal Council's reading, solidarity was non-political and contained a co-operative and humanitarian dimension. Based on its own distinction between 'technical' and 'political' internationalism, Switzerland emphasised the former. As part of its solidarity policy after 1945, Switzerland joined numerous special UN organisations dealing with economic, social and humanitarian issues.

Well before the Second World War, the concept of humanity helped to cast neutrality in an ethical and moral light. In the context of what was called 'humanitarian solidarity', Switzerland after the war continued its efforts to codify and implement international humanitarian law thereby supporting the work of the ICRC. As a country left unharmed by the war, it also felt a moral obligation to contribute to the reconstruction of a ravaged continent. Swiss assistance, first limited to European countries, later gave rise to development aid in the Third World. The Federal Council stressed the non-political, technical or humanitarian character of solidarity.[12] In contrast, politically defined solidarity would have been at odds with neutrality instead of legitimising it.

6.1.3 Lack of human rights policy

Human rights were not a component of Swiss humanitarian solidarity. For decades, Switzerland's position on the internationalisation of human rights was one of scepticism and reserve. It was not that the Swiss authorities rejected human rights as such. As a democratic state adhering to the rule of law, Switzerland declared support for human rights and in general respected the fundamental rights of its citizens, although – like other countries – it is at times criticised for various human rights practices, as in the case of its asylum policy.[13] It was internationalisation that caused difficulties, as did related tendencies such as the legalisation, multilateralisation and the 'politicisation' of human rights.

With its emphasis on classical neutrality, Swiss foreign policy was strongly determined by political realism after 1945. The idealist and co-operative tradition of the League of Nations era was not maintained. Switzerland's view emphasised the anarchic structure of international politics, where rival sovereign states struggled to maximise their power. The main task of its foreign policy was therefore to assure the independent survival of the state. Moral issues were difficult to be integrated into this one-dimensional foreign policy conception, for international politics was seen as an arena where unpredictability reigns and a normative authority is lacking. It was also widely held that human rights would unnecessarily restrict decision-makers' freedom of action. Finally, a more active human rights policy – especially in terms of public human rights interventions – would have conflicted with neutrality.[14]

Switzerland's understanding of sovereign independence was still shaped by classical international law. It took a sceptical view of the development of modern international law, evolving as it did from the law of co-existence to that of co-operation and integration. Obviously, the expanded conception of international law constrained Swiss sovereignty. This fear also affected human rights policy and helps to explain why, for decades, Switzerland distanced itself from global and European human rights agreements. It did not, however, prevent Switzerland from joining the International Court of Justice in 1948. Non-membership in the UN and the Council of Europe also had negative effects on human rights matters. By abstaining, Switzerland removed itself almost completely from the efforts of these two organisations to develop and codify human rights. In fact this was a paradoxical situation. On the one hand Switzerland was a traditional advocate of the ICRC and the humanitarian law, and on the other hand it abstained from the international efforts to promote human rights, although both follow the objective of protecting human dignity.[15]

6.2 Cautious first steps

In response to Détente and growing European integration, the Federal Council, in the early 1960s, modified its foreign policy and revised the restrictive interpretation of neutrality. The government stressed solidarity more strongly, increased its humanitarian engagement and expanded development co-operation. This cautious foreign policy opening occurred first at the European level. Switzerland joined the CoE in 1963 and, late in the decade, participated actively in the CSCE process. UN membership, although debated, was still not a realistic option, however. Joining the CoE and taking part in the CSCE process was part of an attempt to shape a more active foreign policy, yet membership was also significant with respect to human rights. The Council of Europe and the CSCE (renamed OSCE in 1994) were and still are the most important European, or Euro-Atlantic, forums for human rights issues.

6.2.1 The European convention on human rights

For many years, Switzerland remained outside the CoE, founded in 1949. The Federal Council saw entry as incompatible with neutrality. Moreover, the Federal government's evaluation of the Strasbourg organisation was mostly negative. In the late 1950s, however, Bern changed its stance abruptly. It supported CoE membership and declared it compatible with neutrality. After a debate that was brief by Swiss standards, Switzerland joined the Council in May 1963.[16] As a member, Switzerland was faced with the decision to ratify the European Convention on Human Rights and the European Social Charter, both of fundamental significance to the Council of Europe's work. The process turned out to be difficult.

The Federal Council was still sceptical of the internationalisation of human rights and was in no hurry to ratify the CoE human rights conventions. It did not recommend accession to the ECHR until 1968 – the CoE's 'year of human rights'. Ratification was delayed by a few more years, however, due to domestic resistance and some contradictions between Swiss law and the Convention. Once most legal impediments had been resolved – Switzerland introduced women's suffrage in 1971 and lifted some ordinances hostile to the Jesuits – the Council made another attempt to ratify the European

Human Rights Convention. This time, parliament voted relatively strongly for ratification, and on 28 November 1974 Switzerland joined the Convention. However, ratification was bought at a price: in order to assure passage, Protocols 1 and 4 – because hotly contested – were not presented to parliament.[17]

Adhesion to the European Social Charter was even more controversial. It is true that in the early 1970s the Federal Council was favourably disposed towards this charter and signed it in 1976 after internal clarification of its compatibility with Swiss law. Yet difficulties began when it came to ratification. Legal uncertainties, domestic political resistance and indecisiveness on the part of the Council stood in the way of ratification. However, this was just the beginning of a long and painful process. No one suspected that even by 2002, Switzerland would have still not ratified the Charter.[18]

All in all, there was considerable distrust of the CoE supervisory bodies and the various conventions, particularly on the part of the parliament. Opponents to ratification argued that the 'foreign judges' sitting in Strasbourg were infringing upon Swiss sovereignty. The Federal Council sought to eliminate the opposition by playing down the possibility of unfavourable judgements, but it was wrong. Over the years, the European Court of Human Rights (ECHR) repeatedly decided against Switzerland, which led to defensive reactions and to a flare-up of the 'foreign judges' debate in parliament. The Swiss had to recognise that from a human rights perspective, their legal system was not as perfect as assumed and that it had to be adapted to ECHR standards.[19] However, the experience with the convention helped Switzerland to overcome its deep scepticism regarding international human rights protection. Conquering that reticence, along with a willingness to limit national sovereignty, was a core factor in promoting Swiss human rights policy. By joining the European Convention on Human Rights Switzerland recognised these changes.

6.2.2 The importance of CSCE

The issue of human rights and fundamental freedoms became an important part of the CSCE process. With the inclusion of Principle Nr VII in the 1975 Helsinki Final Act, the Member States declared that human rights are an indispensable prerequisite to international peace and stability. The importance of human rights was further emphasised in the 'third basket' of the Final Act, which addressed humanitarian and human rights issues.[20]

In contrast to its long abstinence from the Council of Europe, Switzerland was engaged in the CSCE process from the start.[21] Switzerland participated actively in the human rights debates during the CSCE follow-up conferences, stressing that the upholding of human rights was an indispensable prerequisite to peace and security. It also made efforts to ensure that as many citizens as possible in the participating states would profit from the results of the CSCE process. Its efforts were focussed on human contacts, the reuniting of families, travel, visits and religious freedoms. As a result, Switzerland – like the other countries – came to recognise that human rights are a legitimate foreign policy concern. The same issues also began to influence Switzerland's bilateral relations with East bloc countries. The Federal Council intervened on a number of occasions for the promotion of human rights.

In the 1970s, Switzerland laid important foundations for its future human rights policy. CoE membership and CSCE participation allowed the country to take part in multilateral efforts to protect human rights. This was all the more important, given that non-membership in the UN restricted Swiss possibilities to make a contribution in this field. For many years the European Convention on Human Rights and the Helsinki Final Act formed the most important instruments permitting Switzerland to intervene in cases of human rights violations in other countries. These positive aspects could not disguise that Switzerland remained an outsider to the international human rights regime. Until the 1980s, Switzerland did not ratify any major UN human rights convention and observed UN efforts towards international human rights protection from a distance. Generally speaking at that time there was no Swiss human rights policy worth its name.

6.3 Activating human rights policy in the eighties

In part at least, 1978 saw the birth of a Swiss human rights policy worthy of its name. It was the year in which the new foreign minister, Pierre Aubert, put human rights on his foreign policy agenda. The issue was part of Aubert's ambition to activate Swiss foreign policy in general. However, his efforts encountered strong political resistance and, with the public rejection of UN membership in 1986, it experienced a severe setback. Nevertheless, human rights slowly became a policy area of its own.

6.3.1 The 1982 human rights report

Pierre Aubert succeeded Pierre Graber as Federal Councillor and Head of the Department of Foreign Affairs in February 1978. While for Graber human rights had not been a serious issue, it was one of Aubert's declared foreign policy priorities. Involvement in international human rights protection was an important component of Aubert's plan to 'energise' Swiss foreign policy.[22] On his very first day in office, Aubert instructed his department to prepare a report on the country's previous activities in the area of human rights and to suggest ways in which Switzerland could increase its engagement. A departmental working group was formed, which presented its findings in April 1978. The report concluded that rather than being a temporary fad, human rights policy was a firmly established part of the international agenda. It cited as examples the CSCE process and President Carter's activation of American human rights policy. Swiss human rights policy was found to be lacking, and the report proposed increased involvement.

In the second half of the 1970s, the Federal parliament also showed an increasing concern for human rights. It demanded information on Swiss human rights policy and made proposals for improvements. Gabrielle Nanchen, Social Democratic Member of the National Council requested the government in October 1978 to submit a report setting out the options for increased efforts. Pierre Aubert accepted the proposal since it accorded well with his own initiative. This gave the government an opportunity to outline its own human rights policy in a public report.

With the preparations for a vote on UN membership taking priority, it was unfortunately another four years before the Federal Council in 1982 responded to Nanchen's postulate and presented its human rights report.[23] The study traced the development of international human rights since the Second World War and stressed their increased importance. The Federal Council criticised its own former handling of human rights: while Switzerland had pioneered international humanitarian law, it was slow when it came to international human rights protection. The report mentioned the many non-ratified human rights conventions and non-membership in the UN as the crucial organisation for global human rights concerns. The report concluded that Switzerland could and should do more. The global promotion of human rights had to be part of a coherent foreign policy. The Federal Council based this conclusion explicitly on Switzerland's long humanitarian tradition and the maxim of solidarity. Moreover, the upholding of human rights was an indispensable prerequisite to global peace and security.

The report proposed increased activity at the bilateral, European and international levels and placed the Swiss human rights concept on three pillars: (1) ratification of regional and universal human rights conventions; (2) active participation in international organisations and conferences including the development of new instruments and the financing of international and non-governmental organisations in the field of human rights; (3) increased bilateral interventions against human rights violations.[24] The Federal Council had created a solid human rights conception whose main features are still valid today. However, in the 1980s human rights policy lacked an institutional and financial foundation. The issue was handled ad hoc by individuals in the International Law Division of the Federal Department of Foreign Affairs until finally, in 1986, a small office for human rights was set up. It took another three years for the Federal Council to appropriate funding for human rights, which in 1989 was limited to a budget of 500 000 Swiss francs.[25]

6.3.2 Ratification attempts and multilateral activities

For a long time, one of the greatest weaknesses of Swiss human rights policy was its narrow foundation in international law. Other than the European Human Rights Convention, Switzerland had ratified no relevant instruments. In the 1980s, therefore, the Federal Council made the ratification of conventions a priority. Uppermost on the agenda was the ratification of the two UN Human Rights Covenants of 1966[26] as well as adherence to the European Social Charter mentioned above.

The Swiss Federal Department of Foreign Affairs had dealt already in the early 1970s with the two UN Human Rights Covenants of 1966, and the Federal Council announced adherence to the Covenants in 1977. In subsequent years, the government repeated its intention to sign the two Covenants. In the 1980s, however, ratification proved to be impossible. In late 1984, preparations for the ratification of the Covenants were well advanced within the Department of Foreign Affairs. The matter was put off, however, because the referendum on UN membership was pending. For political reasons, there was no intention to push ratification of the UN conventions prior to the membership decision. When membership was turned down in 1986, the Federal Council announced that it would take an increasing part in UN legal activities, but the heavily negative vote meant that quick ratification of the UN Covenants was politically excluded.

Efforts towards ratification of the European Social Charter, which Switzerland had signed in 1976, were equally difficult. A rather positive review by cantons, parties and interested associations in 1978/79 was encouraging. In parliament, however, the Social Charter met resistance. Both chambers turned down ratification resoundingly: the Council of States in 1984 and the National Council in 1987. Plans to ratify other treaties also came to nothing, including the UN Convention on the Elimination of All Forms of Racial Discrimination (1965), the Convention on the Elimination of All Forms of Discrimination Against Women (1979) and Protocols No. 1 and 4 of the ECHR.

The reasons for the non-ratification were various. Cantonal reservations on specific points slowed down the process. Another impediment was the Swiss practice of revising domestic laws, not conforming to treaties, prior to ratification. But beyond these more legalistic causes, the main reasons were political. Throughout the 1980s, parliament became increasingly uncomfortable with Aubert's foreign policy opening in general and his human rights policy in particular. The non-ratification of the European Social Charter showed specific distrust in matters of social rights.[27] The high point resistance came in 1988, when Hans Danioth in the Council of States demanded that the Federal Council withdraw from the ECHR. The background of the demand was a judgement of the European Court of Human Rights unfavourable to Switzerland, in a case involving the right of public demonstration. The outrage was massive, and the Council of States turned down the demand by only one vote, thanks to a tie-breaking decision by its chairman.[28]

The government's efforts against torture were more successful. On 29 September 1988, only two days after the narrow rejection of the Danioth request, the same Council of States approved the 1987 European Convention for the Prevention of Torture. One year earlier, Switzerland had been one of the first states to ratify the UN Convention Against Torture and Other Cruel, Inhuman or Degrading Treatment of Punishment of 1984. It was the first important UN human rights treaty that Switzerland approved. Both torture conventions did not threaten Swiss sovereignty, which may explain why they passed so easily. Moreover, Switzerland had played an active role in launching them. The struggle against torture was one of the few areas of human rights in which Switzerland participated actively in the 1970s and 1980s. This was not at the initiative of the Swiss government, however, but of Jean-Jacques Gautier of Geneva, who founded the *Comité Suisse Contre la Torture*.[29] Gautier proposed a treaty with an effective control system committing all ratifying member states to allow international experts access to their penal institutions. After some initial hesitation, Switzerland actively promoted the concept. Within the Council of Europe, Switzerland took a leading role in developing the torture convention.[30]

At the universal level, things were more difficult because many non-European countries questioned the idea of an effective torture convention. For Switzerland, it was even harder to get through its initiatives for a torture convention on the global level, because of its non-membership in the UN. It is true that Swiss officials had participated in the drafting of the torture convention with a working group of the Human Rights Commission since 1979. However, their activities were restricted mainly to the lobbying with like-minded states and to promoting the convention behind the scenes. It was Costa Rica that in 1980 submitted the proposal formally to the United Nations, although it was primarily Switzerland that had worked out the draft.[31]

6.3.3 Bilateral human rights policy

Given Switzerland's limited options at the multilateral level, first of all non-membership in the UN, bilateral efforts to promote human rights were of particular importance. The basic instruments were public or discreet human rights interventions. Since the late 1960s, the Federal Council has made some public declarations on human rights issues, for instance in connection with the Soviet invasion of Hungary (1956) or the crushing of the reform movement in Czechoslovakia known as the 'Prague Spring' (1968). However, such declarations were exceptional because of reservations imposed by neutrality. A further difficulty was that the Federal Council could not base its interventions on human rights conventions, such as the 1966 UN Human Rights Covenants, because Switzerland had not ratified them. Political recognition of human rights in the Helsinki Final Act of 1975 improved the situation, and the Federal Council intervened – usually discreetly – on various occasions to support victims of human rights violations in East bloc countries.

Such interventions became an issue with the activation of Swiss human rights policy in the late 1970s. The question of whether and how Switzerland should support human rights in other states was a key concern of Aubert's human rights policy. The working group of the Federal Department of Foreign Affairs dealt intensively with the problem. The 1982 human rights report summed up the findings. Credibility and coherence were to be the foremost criteria. In order to fulfil this objective, interventions should first of all not be directed against any particular form of government. Second, they should rest upon accepted international law and the most comprehensive and objective information possible. Third, general Swiss interests, neutrality and sensitive public opinion at home should be taken into account. And finally, interventions should differentiate between various types of violations, especially between occasional and systematic practices. This last criterion led the Federal Council to conclude that only systematic violations warrant public interventions. As a general rule, discreet interventions were considered to be more effective. Public exposure of a country might entail counterproductive results and could be to the detriment of those affected by the violations.[32]

How did the Federal Council actually practise intervention? The bits of official information available on discreet diplomatic interventions make an assessment more or less impossible. However, we know that since the late 1970s, the government had made more frequent public condemnations of events abroad in general and of human rights violations in particular. The Swiss government found it increasingly difficult not to speak out on massive violations, especially since the signing of the CSCE Final Act of 1975. Human rights could no longer be viewed as a domestic matter. The pressure to take a stand stemmed mainly from within Switzerland itself, and it grew through the 1970s. Parliament, non-governmental organisations and citizens were now playing a part in areas of foreign policy that had once been the exclusive domain of the Federal Council.

The increasing number of government statements on human rights violations caused domestic controversy. The ideological trenches of the Cold War made themselves felt; right-wing politicians reproached the Federal Council when it spoke out on Apartheid or on South American dictators. Criticism of East bloc countries, on the other hand, found conservative support. Left-wing politicians, in contrast, demanded a clear condemnation of Apartheid politics and human rights violations in South America.[33] Apart from an ideologically motivated critique there was also a more general opposition coming from the centre and the right, or what in Switzerland is called the 'bourgeois majority'. The argument was that public condemnation of other governments did not accord with the restraint expected of a neutral state. Disagreement on human rights policy also reigned in the Department of

Foreign Affairs and was one of the unspoken reasons that led to the involuntary early retirement of State Secretary Albert Weitnauer in 1980.[34]

The Federal Council's official standpoint was to play down the tensions between active promotion of human rights and its traditional neutrality policy by emphasising the humanitarian and therefore non-political dimension of human rights. From a humanitarian point of view this might have been appropriate. However, because of the tensions between human rights and state sovereignty and in the context of the opposing ideological blocs, this position hardly accorded with the matter at hand. The artificial separation of non-political and political involvement could at best work when applied to international humanitarian law or good offices. It failed, however, with respect to human rights, because these are not only humanitarian but also political in nature.

6.3.4 Reluctance regarding human rights conditionality

Attempts to link human rights to other political issues began in the late 1970s and at times led to public and parliamentary debates. In parliament there were requests to create a link between human rights and development assistance. In the 1982 human rights report, the government addressed the problem. It emphasised the similar objectives pursued by development and human rights and argued that the upholding of human rights was an important precondition to economic development. The two should consequently be combined, and serious human rights violations could result in the termination of aid. Moreover, the Federal Council as early as 1984 made respect for human rights an explicit criterion for determining countries with which Switzerland would enter into development co-operation.[35]

However, despite these conceptual guidelines, human rights concerns were of little practical importance in development assistance. Consequently, the list of main recipients of development assistance hardly changed over the years. The argument was that development co-operation should not be used to exert pressure. For humanitarian reasons, development co-operation projects should be maintained even in countries where human rights were seriously violated, as long as the projects continued to help people in need. Co-operation should be interrupted or terminated only where severe and systematic human rights violations made the attainment of development goals impossible. This position reflects Switzerland's understanding of development co-operation as something that is non-political and technical. Its responses to political problems in recipient countries were highly pragmatic.[36]

With regard to foreign economic policy, the government was emphatically opposed to using economic sanctions as an instrument to enforce human rights. The reasons given were the universal nature of international business and the preservation of jobs at home. This separation of human rights from foreign economics was part of a more comprehensive attempt to isolate foreign trade from the rest of foreign policy. However, the separation was difficult to maintain during the Cold War: Switzerland, by quietly co-operating with Cocom (Coordinating Committee for Multilateral Export Controls), joined NATO countries in sanctioning the Soviet bloc economically and, in fact, supported some UN sanctions against Rhodesia.[37]

The Federal Council's separation of human rights and foreign economic policy was criticised by the parties on the left as well as by non-governmental organisations (NGO). Armaments exports and the governmental Export Risk Guarantee (ERG) came under special attack.[38] The protest against the export of arms had shown results in the early 1970s. In response to a public initiative asking for a complete prohibition of the export of arms, parliament passed a law on war material in 1972. In the future no export licences would be issued for exports to zones of war and conflict. Moreover, the law contains a clause on human rights and development. It stipulates that the export of war material must not be to the detriment of human dignity and efforts in the area of humanitarian and development assistance.

In practice, this clause was more or less insignificant. Arms could be exported to countries violating human rights but not at war, a practice criticised sharply over the years by both parliament and human rights organisations. There was also a demand for a stricter implementation of the law. At the beginning of the 1990s, the law on war material was submitted to a total revision. Among other things, the government proposed the adoption of rather broad definition of war material and linked export authorisations more explicit to the human rights situation in the country of destination. On both the issues the Federal Council was defeated by parliament, which decided on a narrower definition of war material and an elimination of the reference to human rights. However, the Federal Council reintroduced the human rights criterion in its regulation on armaments exports. Under these circumstances these exports continued to be an issue where foreign trade, human rights and development policy conflicted.[39]

Efforts to introduce human rights and humanitarian criteria into the ERG legislation had little success. In fact, Aubert directed his department to analyse this question. Nanchen's parliamentary postulate to the Federal Council, mentioned above, had similar objectives. However, the 1982 report on human rights policy hardly dealt with the matter. It was confined to a presentation of legal regulations already in place. These stipulated only that exports to poorer developing countries should take the principles of Switzerland's foreign aid policy into account.[40]

To sum up, the attempt to bind development aid and foreign economic policy to human rights caused controversy in the 1980s. The Federal Council pleaded for separation of the various policy areas. Swiss development assistance was understood to be humanitarian and non-political. Only with respect to arms exports was there an explicit link between human rights and foreign economic policy. In all other areas, foreign policy was separated from human rights policy, most particularly in the general area of foreign economic policy.[41] The universality principle, inherent in free trade, took precedence over the equally propagated principle of the universality of human rights. From a human rights point of view, this policy was neither consistent nor credible.

6.4 Promotion of human rights as a foreign policy objective

With the redrawing of the world's political map in the early 1990s, Switzerland developed a new foreign policy orientation. The formerly dominant maxim of neutrality lost some of its weight and made way for a strategy of increased international co-operation. Human rights, too, gained importance. Switzerland began to catch up with the ratification of human rights conventions, and generally intensified its human rights involvement.

6.4.1 New foreign policy directions

The end of the Cold War effected a lasting change in international relations. The 1990s were characterised by the end of ideologically opposed blocs, far-reaching political, social and economic revolutions in Central and Eastern Europe, advancing European integration, globalisation of the economy and – not least – a UN with a greater ability to act. The end of the Cold War also had a positive effect on international human rights protection. The ideological dispute over human rights receded into the background. Human rights gained a firm place on the international agenda and – despite a number of enforcement problems – have become a widely accepted normative principle guiding international relations.

These developments constituted a challenge to Swiss foreign policy. The Federal Council responded relatively quickly to the changed international parameters and in 1993 presented a new foreign policy report.[42] The document signalled a conceptual break with the past. Instead of emphasising neutral abstinence, it was oriented towards co-operation and participation. The new conception was based on trust in international law and multilateral institutions. This stands in marked contrast to Switzerland's previous view of the international environment as an anarchic system characterised by a security dilemma. Also, the Federal Council explicitly gave up the distinction between foreign and domestic politics typical of the realist worldview, and it stressed that in an interdependent world the two were increasingly becoming one. Generally speaking, the 1993 foreign policy conception represents a departure from the realist worldview and signals a shift to a more idealist perspective.

For human rights, the foreign policy reorientation was highly significant. The Federal Council raised the promotion of human rights, democracy and the rule of law to one of five foreign policy objectives.[43] Now a foreign policy priority, human rights also became an explicit part of the new 1999 Federal Constitution. This document contains the five foreign policy objectives of the 1993 report and defines the goals of Swiss foreign policy in Article 54 Par. 2 as follows:

> The Confederation strives to preserve Swiss independence and welfare; it helps to alleviate suffering and poverty in the world, to promote respect for human rights, democracy, the peaceful coexistence of nations, and the preservation of natural resources.

Furthermore, in October 2002, the Federal Council put forward a federal law of peace promotion and human rights. This new law will become effective in 2004, provided that it is adopted by the parliament.[44] The explicit reference to human rights in the constitution as well as in the new federal law provides a solid legal basis for their promotion in foreign policy, which had been lacking so far. In addition, the mention of human rights as a foreign policy objective is a commitment to a foreign policy guided by ethical principles. It is an important departure from Switzerland's long disinclination to restrain the Federal Council's freedom of action by legally binding norms.[45]

The upgrading of human rights was accompanied by the Federal Council's admission that conflicts can arise between human rights and other foreign policy goals. Previously, such conflicts had been negated or played down. With the introduction of a multidimensional goal agenda this was no longer possible. The Federal Council declared its intention to make goal conflicts visible and to strive towards a more coherent foreign policy. The search for coherence, an important topic throughout the 1990s, implied the linking of policy areas and the explicit integration of human rights into other fields of foreign affairs.[46]

At first glance this looks like a break with the past, but a closer look reveals that the human rights objective did not emerge out of void. It had its roots in the solidarity maxim and the human rights foundations laid down in the 1980s. Seen historically, the embedding of human rights in a general foreign policy framework and in constitutional law is the culminating point of a development that had began in the 1960s and led to an increasing recognition of the importance of human rights for foreign policy.[47]

It also affected institutional arrangements. In 1995 the Human Rights Section in the Department of Foreign Affairs was divided into two parts, one responsible for legal, another for political questions. Later on, the latter was upgraded to become the Section for Human Rights and Humanitarian Policy. However, the funding and personnel resources currently appropriated are very limited, thereby restricting human rights activities.[48] A planned credit for the years 2004–07 for international peace and human rights promotion will hopefully improve the current situation and strengthen the financial basis for such activities.

6.4.2 The human rights conception 2000

In spring 2000 the Federal Council prepared a new report on human rights policy. It gave an account of human rights practice in the 1990s and adjusted some of the objectives of the 1993 foreign policy report.[49] It reiterated the fundamentals of the 1982 human rights concept and mentioned new elements that had developed in the 1990s. The new concept distinguishes various human rights instruments. It includes the classical legal and diplomatic means already mentioned in the 1982 report. These comprise the ratification of conventions, the participation in multilateral organisations as well as bilateral and multilateral interventions in cases of human rights violations. These classical mechanisms are accompanied by new instruments such as the so-called 'human rights dialogues' with selected countries as well as missions by teams of human rights experts.[50] In addition, the expanded concept encompasses a set of means ranging from foreign economic policy and development assistance to the co-operation with Eastern European countries.

The government distinguishes between positive and negative instruments to implement human rights. For states that do not protect human rights sufficiently, the Council recommends constructive measures. These include support for specific projects to promote human rights, development co-operation aimed at supporting human rights and political dialogue on human rights conceptions. In the case of serious and systematic human rights violations, the Council foresees the employment of negative measures, such as economic sanctions within the UN framework, reduction or termination of development aid, rejection of export and investment risk guarantees or declining permits for the export of war material.[51]

This recognition of human rights conditionality in the early 1990s took on a concrete form towards the end of the decade. With the aim to increase coherency, the Federal Council decided on 20 September 1999 to generalise political conditionality in certain cases. Only humanitarian aid was to be excluded. Accordingly, the respect for human rights is one of several criteria determining relations with another state.[52] As a completely new development, the Federal Council also decided to integrate human rights clauses in state treaties.

If the conditionality criteria are not upheld, development co-operation is to be either reduced or terminated. The cessation of relations, however, is to serve as an absolute *ultima ratio*. Constructive measures are to be preferred. Moreover, the government emphasised that conditionality should not be applied automatically. It reserves the right to decide each case individually and under consideration of all relevant factors. In the 1980s the government had rejected human rights conditionality, but in the 1990s it became a guiding principle. This was – at least at the conceptual level – a break with the past and the attempt to separate the various foreign policy areas. Switzerland finally followed the international trend in the area of human rights.

6.4.3 Catching up on ratifications

As shown, plans to sign human rights agreements in the 1980s were not fulfilled. By European standards, Switzerland lagged far behind and needed to catch up. Closing the ratification gap was therefore a priority for the Federal Council in the 1990s.[53] The efforts were now more successful than in the previous decade. Some important international and regional human rights conventions were ratified. Of particular importance was the ratification of the two 1966 UN Human Rights Covenants. The Federal Council had recommended ratification of these two covenants as early as the 1970s; they were finally ratified in 1992.[54] It is noteworthy that parliament passed ratification with an overwhelming majority. However, Switzerland is still not a party to the first Optional Protocol to the Covenant on Civil and Political Rights, which guarantees the rights of individuals to address complaints to the UN Human Rights Committee, although the Federal Council announced its intention to accede to the Protocol already in its 1995–9 and 1999–2003 policy agendas. Swiss NGOs criticised the absence from the Optional Protocol, and the UN Human Rights Committee itself recommended more than once that Switzerland adhere to it.[55]

In 1994 Switzerland adhered also to the 1965 UN Convention on the Elimination of All Forms of Racial Discrimination. As early as 1971, foreign minister Graber wanted to sign the convention as soon as possible, based on reasons of international solidarity. However, it took 20 years for the discrimination issue to surface again, this time for domestic reasons. An increase in racist violence created a need for action. The Federal Council seized the opportunity and laid the ratification of the convention before parliament in 1992. While the legislature approved, right-wing conservative circles organised a referendum against the Swiss criminal law that needed adaptation. The results of the 1994 vote backed the Federal Council by only a slim margin of 55 per cent. This strong opposition to one of the most fundamental international human rights conventions reflects the prevailing mistrust of the UN and its conventions. The attitude is underlined by the fact that parliamentary opposition also arose against the government's intention to adopt the communications procedure according to Article 14 of the convention.[56]

Other global human rights conventions were ratified more easily. These included the 1979 Convention on the Elimination of All Forms of Discrimination Against Women (ratified in 1997), the 1989 Convention on the Rights of the Child (ratified in 1997) and the 1948 Convention on the Prevention and Punishment of the Crime of Genocide (ratified in 2000). Finally, Switzerland ratified the Rome Statute of the International Criminal Court (ICC) on 12 October 2001.

At the European level, Switzerland adhered to a number of CoE conventions,[57] but there are still some serious ratification gaps. To date, Switzerland has ratified neither the European Social Charter nor Protocols 1 and 4 to the

European Convention on Human Rights. The story of non-ratification of these instruments is an odyssey: on innumerable occasions the Federal Council placed a priority on these three instruments, announced soon-to-be ratification, and then proceeded to shelve the matter once again. Parliament showed similar ambivalence: while numerous demands for ratification of the conventions were submitted, it was the legislative branch that was often responsible for dragging out and rejecting ratification. Switzerland is practically the only Western European country that has not ratified the Social Charter and Protocols 1 and 4. Even some young democracies in Central and Eastern Europe – that joined the Council of Europe only in the 1990s – have done so.[58] Given the opposition, ratification of the Social Charter is unlikely in the next few years. Unfortunately, the same may be true for the Protocols 1 and 4. Because of parliamentary opposition, the government again lags behind its own timetable. The Federal Council had planned to ratify the two protocols by the end of 2003.[59]

6.4.4 Human rights activities

Subsequent to the negative outcome of the first UN membership referendum on 16 March 1986, the Federal Council decided to improve its relations with the UN through selective participation. Among other things, Switzerland focussed its activities on the United Nations Commission on Human Rights. As an observer, the country had followed the Commission's work since the 1970s, and on occasions it managed to take the floor. Starting in 1987, the Swiss Delegation participated more actively by supporting practically all resolutions that foresaw political control mechanisms for the safeguarding of human rights. Not least because of Switzerland's support, the Commission has in recent years given a number of UN Special Rapporteur mandates to Swiss citizens.[60]

In March 2002 Switzerland voted to enter the UN and thus ended an anomaly that had persisted since the Second World War. Since the formal disadvantages of non-membership are now a thing of the past, the decision should have a positive effect on Switzerland's human rights engagement. In fact, the government declared the strengthening of human rights a core element of its UN policy. Switzerland can now come forward with its own initiatives and can be voted to all UN bodies, including the Human Rights Commission.[61] As to the further development and codification of international law, Switzerland will now work on an equal footing with others. The importance of this cannot be underestimated, for the country's abstinence from the development of the human rights conventions was in part responsible for the scepticism exhibited vis-à-vis these conventions.

In the CSCE, now OSCE, Switzerland continued its previous efforts to promote human rights. As part of the organisation's 'human dimension' it aimed at the protection of minorities by actively backing the High Commissioner on National Minorities (HCNM). In 1996 Switzerland held the OSCE chairmanship. Its programme included the protection of minorities, the promotion of democratic values and the strengthening of civil society. The programme found its main application in the 1996 elections in Bosnia-Herzegovina.[62]

Switzerland intensified other related activities as well, and continued to build up the human rights instruments at its disposal. These include financial support for the activities of NGOs, the establishment of an Expert Pool for Civilian Peace Building and several projects in the field of 'human security'. Two further examples are worthy of mention. The first relates to the reform of the European Convention on Human Rights and the installation of a European Court of Human Rights, a process initiated in 1998 by Switzerland. The second example is Switzerland's support for the establishment of international criminal courts. Bern supports the work of the Ad Hoc Tribunal for former Yugoslavia and for Rwanda. Switzerland also played an active role in the working out of the Rome Statute of the International Criminal Court (ICC) in 1998. Despite massive obstruction, particularly by the United States, the establishment of a 'toothless' court was prevented. After the entry into force of the Statute on 1 July 2002, the United States in particular continued to put pressure on the ICC. Switzerland on its part pursued its policy to back the Court.[63]

Compared to the limited human rights involvement in the 1980s, Switzerland played an active role in the 1990s. The intensification went hand in hand with a greater willingness to take a political stand. It is true that Switzerland rarely came forward in the 1990s with its own initiatives or with critique of other nations. But in general, Switzerland joined the WEOG (Western European and Other States Group) in supporting a common position, as for example in the UN Human Rights Commission. Neutrality considerations were now less important than multilateral co-ordination with like-minded nations.

6.4.5 Human rights, development and foreign economic policy

As shown, the human rights policy as developed in the 1990s established a link with other issues. The objective was to increase coherency within and among the various policy areas. This goal was put into practice particularly in development assistance and in co-operation with Eastern Europe. At a time when international practice began to make economic aid dependent upon political conditions, and in accordance with the 1993 foreign policy report, the government declared that the guiding principles of Swiss development co-operation would be the promotion of good governance, human rights, the rule of law and democracy.[64]

Once again a dual strategy embracing positive and negative measures is envisaged. On the positive side, development co-operation should promote good governance, human rights and the rule of law. On the negative side, sanctions such as termination of co-operation can be employed in case of gross human rights violations. Co-operation with Eastern Europe is even more directly contingent upon such requirements. The promotion of human rights and the rule of law were anchored in law. Moreover, in relation to the first war in Chechnya (1994–6) parliament attached a special conditionality clause to the law, authorising the Federal Council to interrupt co-operation, in part or wholly, in case of gross human rights violations and discrimination of minorities.[65]

However, the government applied conditionality only in isolated cases. Constructive measures still dominate. Rwanda, for many years a priority recipient of Swiss development assistance, is a case in point. Switzerland attempted to maintain a dialogue with the regime until the very end, without interrupting development co-operation. Only with the outbreak of genocide and faced with a disaster did the Federal Council terminate co-operation in 1994.[66] Switzerland showed similar patience – as did other Western countries – in the case of Russia. Neither the first nor the second Chechen war (since September 1999) has led to an interruption of co-operation with Russia, although legally possible. The Federal Council countered domestic objections by mentioning commercial, foreign policy and security interests. When it comes to positive measures, it is noteworthy that human rights and good governance have been integrated into various development programmes, including those with Eastern European countries. However, this is still a step removed from systematic integration of human rights and good governance into such programmes. Only in recent years have the responsible federal authorities undertaken efforts in this direction.

Generally speaking, there has been much reluctance to implement the human rights guidelines. Even after the conceptual shift in the 1990s, the traditional humanitarian approach ignoring the political conditions prevailing in the recipient nation has the upper hand. Human rights and good governance considerations continued to play a minor role in development assistance, as evidenced by the nearly unchanged list of major recipients. The Chechen example illustrates the limits and problems of political conditionality. The Federal Council strained the credibility and coherence of its policy by maintaining co-operation with Russia, despite the clear breach of the co-operation criteria as laid down in the decree of 1995. Still, there are positive effects. Goal conflicts and coherency problems were addressed more openly than in the decades before. Moreover, there is a recognisable trend towards a heavier weighting of political conditions and human rights criteria in development co-operation.

In the 1990s, goal conflicts arose most noticeably between human rights and foreign economic policy. The Federal Council addressed such conflicts and admitted that there were problems with coherency. As shown, in the 1993 foreign policy report the government rejected its former separation between human rights and foreign economic policy and declared that in cases of gross human rights violations it would consider participating in UN sanctions and reject credit guarantees. In its North–South Guidelines, the Federal Council mentioned specifically that human rights would be taken into account when granting export risk guarantee for poorer developing countries.[67]

Interestingly enough, Switzerland's participation in UN economic sanctions since the 1990s did not give rise to domestic criticism, at least not at first, even though this policy was in contrast to its traditional course of neutrality. In addition to the longstanding issue of armaments exports, it was the granting of ERG that caused a stir. Business circles and bourgeois parties criticised what to them was a detrimental mixing of politics and economics. On the other side, development and human rights organisations, joined by the political left, demanded that foreign economic policy be guided by development and human rights principles.

The granting of export credit guarantees for two large dam projects in China (Three Gorges Dam) and in Turkey (Ilisu Dam) proved to be important test cases for the Federal Council's new policy. Both projects were and are extremely controversial. NGOs demanded that human rights and development concerns be incorporated, and even within the administration the projects were contested.[68] In the case of the Three Gorges Dam Project, a number of administrative offices apparently opposed export risk guarantees to Asea Brown Boveri (ABB) and Sulzer Hydro. Yet the Federal Council approved export credit guarantees to the two Swiss companies in 1996 and 1999 (Three Gorges) and in 1998 (Ilisu), and thereby gave priority to economic considerations over human rights and development concerns. The government felt that a refusal to grant credit guarantees would not stop the projects but merely give foreign exporters the advantage over Swiss firms. With a view to the human rights situation in China, the Federal Council argued that intensifying economic relations would better serve the realisation of human rights than an economic boycott against China. Against the background of a worsening Chinese human rights record in the last ten years and the relatively poor results of the 'human rights dialogues' with China, this policy is far from credible and effective.

All told, it is clear that in recent years there has been intensive discussion on the integration of human rights issues in foreign economic policy. Non-governmental organisations have made a contribution by highlighting goal conflicts and by pushing the debate forward. Government agencies have increasingly had to face human rights issues and coherency problems and can no longer base their arguments upon the separation of economics and politics. But in general, human rights were and are still subordinated to security and to economic interests. This is especially true of highly contested and sensitive issues like ERG and armaments exports. In part, this is due to the fact that human rights are insufficiently anchored in political concepts and in the law. In particular, human rights are not firmly included in foreign economic policy decision-making. As long as this remains the case, it will hardly be possible to meet the challenge of developing a coherent human rights policy.[69]

Conclusions

Like that of other countries, Swiss foreign policy is marked by both a realist and an idealist tradition. The relative weighting of idealist openness and realist closure has shifted over the years. During the time of the League of Nations idealism was the driving force in Swiss foreign policy, but a realist perspective dominated for many years after the end of the Second World War. It implied Swiss abstinence from the UN, which had a negative effect on human rights policy. The country's participation in the development and codification of human rights was necessarily restricted. Furthermore, Switzerland refused to promote human rights, because the issue conflicted with neutrality and an outdated conception of national sovereignty. Rather than to venture into the politically difficult field of human rights, Switzerland limited its activities to the promotion of humanitarian law and to development assistance. These did not endanger sovereignty and neutrality.

This unusually sceptical posture began to change in the late 1960s. In cautiously opening up its foreign policy, Switzerland gradually became involved in international human rights protection. Joining the European Convention on Human Rights and the corresponding willingness to submit to international jurisdiction was an important step. Switzerland gradually overcame its classical understanding of national sovereignty, according to which human rights was a domestic matter. Just a few years later, during the CSCE process, Switzerland joined other Western nations in emphasising the importance of human rights as an element in international politics.

Switzerland undertook its first efforts to link human rights to foreign policy only in the late 1970s. During Pierre Aubert's time of office, important human rights principles were established. However, Aubert's idealist and outward-looking foreign policy was hotly disputed, which hindered the activation of human rights policy. Still, human rights became firmly established on the foreign policy agenda. Although important steps were undertaken, the move towards normalisation came only in the 1990s. Given the end of the Cold War, Switzerland was forced to rethink and redesign its foreign policy. Since then, Switzerland is trying to overcome its passive and inward-looking foreign policy and to give more weight to international co-operation. Human rights policy is a part of the new strategy. Within just a few years, Switzerland ratified a series of important human rights conventions and stepped up its engagement for human rights. Switzerland is on the way to a comprehensive human rights policy, although there are of course still various shortcomings.

Objectives and concepts are one thing; implementation is another. In Switzerland there is often a long delay before foreign policy objectives are implemented. Observe the two attempts that were required for UN membership. Further steps towards normalisation are needed, particularly with respect to the European Union. Fortunately, human rights policy is further along. In this field, Switzerland is no longer a special case. At long last it practises a human rights policy comparable to that of other Western countries, with all its strengths and weaknesses. This means that human rights have gained a firm place in Swiss foreign policy although, unfortunately, they are usually subordinate to other foreign policy interests. This, however, should not disguise the fact that human rights policy has worked its way up the Swiss foreign policy agenda and is likely to gain additional weight, particularly thanks to UN membership.

Acknowledgement

The author would like to thank Jürg Martin Gabriel, Daniel Möckli, Sascha Hardegger, Thomas Fischer and Andrea Heinzer for helpful comments on earlier versions of this article.

Notes

1 On the role of human rights in international relations, compare the newer literature: David P. Forsythe, *Human Rights in International Relations* (Cambridge: Cambridge University Press, 2000); Richard A. Falk, *Human Rights Horizons: The Pursuit of Justice in a Globalizing World* (New York/London: Routledge, 2000); Tim Dunne and Nicholas J. Wheeler (eds), *Human Rights in Global Politics* (Cambridge: Cambridge University Press, 1999); Jack Donnelly, *International Human Rights*, 2nd edn (Boulder: Westview Press, 1998). On integrating human right goals into foreign policy, see David P. Forsythe (ed.), *Human Rights and Comparative Foreign Policy* (Tokyo/New York/Paris: United Nations University Press, 2000); Jan Egeland, *Impotent Superpower – Potent Small State: Potentials and Limitations of Human Rights Objectives in the Foreign Policies of the United States and Norway* (London/New York/Toronto: Norwegian University Press, 1988); R. J. Vincent (ed.), *Foreign Policy and Human Rights* (Cambridge: Cambridge University Press, 1986); Stanley Hoffmann, 'Reaching for the Most Difficult: Human Rights as Foreign Policy Goal', *Daedalus: Journal of the American Academy of Arts and Sciences*, 4 (1983), pp. 19–49.

2 For this perspective, which is sceptical of or rejects the integration of human rights in foreign policy, see George F. Kennan, 'Morality and Foreign Affairs', *Foreign Affairs*, Vol. 64, No. 2 (Winter 1985/86), pp. 205–18; Henry Kissinger, *Diplomacy* (New York: Simon & Schuster, 1994); Stephen D. Krasner, *Sovereignty: Organized Hypocrisy* (Princeton: Princeton University Press, 1999).

3 For the idealist perspective, which approves explicitly of a foreign policy oriented to norms, see Chris Brown, *International Relations Theory: New Normative Approaches* (Hemel Hempstead: Harvester Wheatsheaf, 1992); Mervyn Frost, *Ethics in International Relations: A Constitutive Theory* (Cambridge: Cambridge University Press,

1996); Karen E. Smith and Margot Light (eds), *Ethics and Foreign Policy* (Cambridge: Cambridge University Press, 2001).

4 Daniel Frei, 'Sendungsgedanken in der Schweizerischen Aussenpolitik', in *Schweizerisches Jahrbuch für Politische Wissenschaft*, Vol. 6 (1966), pp. 98–113; Daniel Frei, *Neutralität – Ideal oder Kalkül? Zweihundert Jahre außenpolitisches Denken in der Schweiz* (Frauenfeld/Stuttgart: Huber, 1967).

5 Herbert Lüthy, *Die Schweiz als Antithese* (Zürich: Arche, 1969).

6 Madeleine Herren, *Hintertüren zur Macht: Internationalismus und modernisierungsorientierte Aussenpolitik in Belgien, der Schweiz und den USA, 1865–1914* (München: Oldenburg Verlag, 2000), pp. 215–370.

7 For an overview of Swiss efforts to promote humanitarian law, compare Marco Sassòli, 'La Suisse et le droit international humanitaire – une relation privilégiée?', in *Schweizerisches Jahrbuch für internationales Recht* (Jubiläumsband, 1989), pp. 47–71; Hans-Peter Gasser, 'Humanitäres Völkerrecht: Probleme – Perspektiven', in *Schweizerisches Jahrbuch für Politische Wissenschaft*, Vol. 28 (1988), pp. 209–20; Daniel Thürer, 'Humanität und Neutralität – zum politischen und völkerrechtlichen Spannungsverhältnis zweier Grundprinzipien der schweizerischen Aussenpolitik', in Yvo Hangartner and Stefan Trechsel (eds), *Völkerrecht im Dienste des Menschen: Festschrift für Hans Haug* (Bern/Stuttgart: Paul Haupt, 1986), pp. 279–308. On the history of the ICRC, compare Hans Haug, *Humanity for All: The International Red Cross and Red Crescent Movement* (Berne/Stuttgart/Vienna: Paul Haupt, 1993).

8 For a comparison of the Swiss attitude to the League of Nations and to the United Nations respectively, see Carlo Moos, *Ja zum Völkerbund – Nein zur UNO: Die Volksabstimmungen von 1920 und 1986 in der Schweiz* (Zürich: Chronos, 2001).

9 Compare the Preamble and Article 1 Par. 3, Article 55 and 56 of the UN Charter.

10 On Swiss neutrality, see from the newer literature: Andreas Suter, 'Neutralität: Prinzip, Praxis und Geschichte', in Manfred Hettling *et al.*, *Eine kleine Geschichte der Schweiz: Der Bundesstaat und seine Traditionen* (Frankfurt a. M.: Suhrkamp, 1998), pp. 133–88; Jürg Martin Gabriel, *Sackgasse Neutralität* (Zürich: vdf Hochschulverlag, 1997); Alois Riklin, 'Die Neutralität der Schweiz', in Alois Riklin, Hans Haug and Raymond Probst (eds), *Neues Handbuch der schweizerischen Aussenpolitik* (Bern/Stuttgart/Wien: Paul Haupt, 1992), pp. 191–209; Hans-Peter Brunner, *Neutralität und Unabhängigkeit der Schweiz im ausgehenden 20. Jahrhundert – Bestandesaufnahme und Ausblick: Die Fragen der europäischen Integration und die Sicherheits- und Friedenspolitik als Fallbeispiele*, Schweizer Studien zum Internationalen Recht 58 (Zürich: Schulthess, 1989).

11 For an overview of Swiss foreign policy maxims, see Walter Kälin and Alois Riklin, 'Ziele, Mittel und Strategien der schweizerischen Aussenpolitik', in Riklin, *Neues Handbuch der schweizerischen Aussenpolitik*, pp. 167–89. For the formulation of Swiss foreign policy guidelines in the 1940s, see Daniel Möckli, *Neutralität, Solidarität, Sonderfall: Die Konzeptionierung der schweizerischen Aussenpolitik der Nachkriegszeit, 1943–1947*, Zürcher Beiträge zur Sicherheitspolitik und Konfliktforschung 55 (Zürich: Forschungsstelle für Sicherheitspolitik und Konfliktanalyse der ETH Zürich, 2000).

12 For an analysis of Swiss 'solidarity policy', ranging from development assistance and good offices to the support of peace-keeping activities, compare Jon A. Fanzun and Patrick Lehmann, *Die Schweiz und die Welt: Aussen- und sicherheitspolitische Beiträge der Schweiz zu Frieden, Sicherheit und Stabilität, 1945–2000*, Zürcher Beiträge zur Sicherheitspolitik und Konfliktforschung 57 (Zürich: Forschungsstelle für Sicherheitspolitik und Konfliktanalyse der ETH Zürich, 2000).

13 For an in-depth analysis of the place of human rights in Swiss legislation and jurisdiction, see Jörg Paul Müller, *Grundrechte in der Schweiz: im Rahmen der Bundesverfassung von 1999, der Uno-Pakte und der EMRK* (Bern: Stämpfli, 1999); Peter Saladin, *Grundrechte im Wandel*, 3rd edn (Bern: Stämpfli, 1982). For a short overview see Claude Rouiller, 'Human Rights in Switzerland', *International Affairs*, Vol. 42, No. 4 (1996), pp. 106–15; Giorgio Malinverni, 'La Suisse et les droits de l'homme', in *Schweizerisches Jahrbuch für Internationales Recht* (Jubiläumsband 1989), pp. 153–92.

14 The writings of Rudolf Bindschedler, legal adviser to the Swiss Federal Department of Foreign Affairs from 1961 to 1980, are typical of such a worldview, inspired by political realism. See, for example, Rudolf L. Bindschedler, 'Zum Primat der Aussenpolitik', in Urs Altermatt and Judit Garamvölgyi (eds), *Innen- und Aussenpolitik: Primat oder Interdependenz? Festschrift zum 60. Geburtstag von Walther Hofer* (Bern/Stuttgart: Paul Haupt, 1980), pp. 27–36. Other authors expressed similar opinions and argued that it is not suitable and not possible to regulate foreign policy with legal norms because of the anarchical an unpredictable character of international relations. See Thomas G. Borer, *Das Legalitätsprinzip und die auswärtigen Angelegenheiten* (Basel/Frankfurt a. M.: Helbing & Lichtenhahn, 1986); Luzius Wildhaber, 'Legalitätsprinzip und Aussenpolitik – eine Problemskizze', in Edouard Brunner *et al.* (eds), *Einblicke in die schweizerische Aussenpolitik: Zum 65. Geburtstag von Staatssekretär Raymond Probst* (Zürich: Verlag Neue Zürcher Zeitung, 1984), pp. 443–60. For the opposite view stressing the importance of the rule of law in foreign policy and the feasibility of legal regulation of international politics, see Walter Kälin, 'Verfassungsgrundsätze der schweizerischen Aussenpolitik', *Zeitschrift für Schweizerisches Recht*, 105 II (1986), pp. 251–383; Josef Hofstetter, *Die Bedeutung rechtlicher Normen in der Aussenpolitik: Eine Darstellung anhand der schweizerischen Nord-Süd-Politik* (Basel/Frankfurt a. M.: Helbing & Lichtenhahn, 1990).

15 This attitude of the Swiss government towards international protection of human rights was criticised among scholars. See Alois Riklin, *Grundlegung der schweizerischen Aussenpolitik*, St. Galler Studien zur Politikwissenschaft 1 (Bern/Stuttgart: Paul Haupt, 1975), pp. 41–5; Peter Saladin and Hans Walder, 'Der Beitrag der Schweiz zum Kampf gegen die Folter', in Ulrich Häfelin, Walter Haller and Dietrich Schindler (eds), *Menschenrechte, Föderalismus, Demokratie: Festschrift zum 70. Geburtstag von Werner Kägi* (Zürich: Schulthess, 1979), pp. 267–99; Hans Haug, 'Die Schweiz, das humanitäre Kriegsvölkerrecht und die Konventionen über Menschenrechte', in *Recht als Prozess und Gefüge: Festschrift für Hans Huber zum 80. Geburtstag* (Bern: Stämpfli, 1981), pp. 577–93.

16 For an overview of the relations between Switzerland and the Council of Europe, see Rudolf Wyder, *Die Schweiz und der Europarat 1949–1971: Annäherung und zehn Jahre Mitarbeit in der parlamentarischen Versammlung* (Bern: Paul Haupt, 1984).

17 The ECHR Protocol guarantees property rights, the right to education and the right to free elections. Protocol 4 guarantees among other things free movement and the prohibition of collective expulsion of aliens. Some of these rights were at odds with Swiss law at the federal and cantonal levels. For an overview of the parliamentary debates concerning ECHR ratification, see Claudia Weiss, *Die Schweiz und die Europäische Menschenrechtskonvention*, Basler Schriften zur europäischen Integration 20 (Basel: Europainstitut an der Universität Basel, 1996).

18 For Switzerland's attitude towards the Social Charter in the 1970s, see Jörg Paul Müller, 'Die Schweiz und die Europäische Sozialcharta', in Alois Riklin, Hans Haug and Hans Christoph Binswanger (eds), *Handbuch der schweizerischen*

Aussenpolitik (Bern/Stuttgart: Paul Haupt, 1975), pp. 389–95; Bernardo Zanetti, 'Die Schweiz und die Ratifizierung der Europäischen Sozialcharta', *Schweizer Rundschau*, Nr. 1 (1978), pp. 13–7.

19 Therefore, the ECHR had a far-reaching positive effect on Swiss legislation from a human rights point of view. For an analysis of the ECHR on Switzerland's legislative and legal practice, see Arthur Häfliger and Frank Schürmann, *Die Europäische Menschenrechtskonvention und die Schweiz*, 2nd edn (Bern: Stämpfli, 1999).

20 An excellent analysis of the role and the effects of human rights in the Helsinki Process is found in Daniel C. Thomas, *The Helsinki Effect: International Norms, Human Rights, and the Demise of Communism* (Princeton/Oxford: Princeton University Press, 2001).

21 Christoph Breitenmoser, *Sicherheit für Europa: Die KSZE-Politik der Schweiz bis zur Unterzeichnung der Helsinki-Schlussakte zwischen Skepsis und aktivem Engagement*, Zürcher Beiträge zur Sicherheitspolitik und Konfliktforschung 40 (Zürich: Forschungsstelle für Sicherheitspolitik und Konfliktanalyse der ETH Zürich, 1996); Hans-Jörg Renk, *Der Weg der Schweiz nach Helsinki: Der Beitrag der schweizerischen Diplomatie zum Zustandekommen der Konferenz über Sicherheit und Zusammenarbeit in Europa (KSZE), 1972–1975* (Bern/Stuttgart/Wien: Paul Haupt, 1996).

22 Pierre Aubert, 'Pour une politique étrangère plus active', in Amnesty International, Swiss Section (ed.), *Menschenrechte im Spannungsfeld: Eine Herausforderung für die Schweiz* (Bern/Stuttgart: Paul Haupt, 1978), pp. 15–24.

23 *Bericht über die schweizerische Menschenrechtspolitik vom 2. Juni 1982*, in BBl 1982 II 729–90. For an account of Swiss human rights policy in the late 1970s and in the 1980s, consult Walter Kälin, 'Die Menschenrechtspolitik der Schweiz', in *Schweizerisches Jahrbuch für Politische Wissenschaft*, Vol. 28 (1988), pp. 185–207; Amnesty International, *Menschenrechte im Spannungsfeld*; Mathias Krafft and Jean-Daniel Vigny, 'La politique suisse à l'égard des droits de l'homme', in Riklin, *Neues Handbuch der schweizerischen Aussenpolitik*, pp. 223–45; Erwin H. Hofer, 'Menschenrechte und schweizerische Aussenpolitik', *Schweizer Monatshefte*, No. 11 (1982), pp. 931–43.

24 *Bericht über die Menschenrechtspolitik vom 2. Juni 1982*, in BBl 1982 II 740–43 and 788–90.

25 In October 2002 the Federal Council proposed a global credit for measures in the field of peace promotion and strengthening human rights. The credit line is 240 million Swiss francs for the years 2004–07. If the credit passes parliament this will improve the current situation and provide human rights activities with a solid financial basis. However, Switzerland still lags significantly behind the spending of comparable states such as Norway or Finland. See *Botschaft über einen Rahmenkredit für Massnahmen zur zivilen Konfliktbearbeitung und Menschenrechtsförderung vom 23. Oktober 2002*, in BBl 2002 7975–8058 (http://www.admin.ch/ch/d/ff/2002/7975.pdf).

26 International Covenant on Economic, Social, and Cultural Rights and International Covenant on Civil and Political Rights. These two treaties, together with the Universal Declaration of Human Rights, make up the 'International Bill of Human Rights'.

27 For an account of the Swiss attitude towards social rights, see Walter Kälin, 'Soziale Menschenrechte ernst genommen', in Caritas Schweiz (ed.), *Sozialalmanach 2000* (Luzern: Caritas-Verlag, 2000), pp. 69–82; Luzius Wildhaber, 'Soziale Grundrechte', in Peter Saladin and Luzius Wildhaber (eds), *Der Staat als Aufgabe: Gedenkschrift für Max Huber* (Basel/Stuttgart: Helbing & Lichtenhahn, 1972), pp. 371–91.

28 See on this issue Weiss, *Europäische Menschenrechtskonvention*, pp. 13–37.
29 See Claudine Haenni (ed.), *20 ans consacrés a la réalisation d' une idée: Recueil d'articles en l'honneur de Jean-Jacques Gautier* (Geneva: Association for the Prevention of Torture, 1997); see also Walter Kälin, 'The Struggle against Torture', *International Review of the Red Cross*, No. 324 (1998), pp. 433–44; Hans Haug, 'Efforts to Eliminate Torture through International Law', *International Review of the Red Cross*, No. 775 (1989), pp. 9–27.
30 For an overview of the Swiss efforts, consult Jean-Daniel Vigny, 'La Convention européenne de 1987 pour la prévention de la torture et des peines ou traitements inhumains ou dégradants', in *Schweizerisches Jahrbuch für internationales Recht* (1987), pp. 62–78.
31 An overview of the Swiss efforts is given by Jean-Daniel Vigny, 'L'action de la Suisse contre la torture', in Haenni, *20 ans consacrés a la réalisation d' une idée*, pp. 69–76.
32 *Bericht über die Menschenrechtspolitik vom 2. Juni 1982*, in BBl 1982 II 740–3. For a discussion of this topic, see the various contributions in Schweizerische Gesellschaft für Aussenpolitik (ed.), *Möglichkeiten und Grenzen der schweizerischen Aussenpolitik* (Bern/Lenzburg: 1985).
33 The Swiss government did intervene publicly on several occasions involving human rights violations, for example in 1977, 1979 and 1985, when the Federal Council condemned Apartheid in South Africa or in 1981 when the government denounced human rights violations in connection with the proclamation of martial law in Poland. For a brief analysis of the intervention practice, see Kälin, 'Die Menschenrechtspolitik der Schweiz', pp. 199–202.
34 While foreign minister Pierre Aubert was – as described above – in favour of an active human rights policy, State Secretary Albert Weitnauer was opposed, especially to public human rights interventions. Weitnauer spoke out for a low-profile foreign policy centred on traditional neutrality. For some hints on the controversy in the Department of Foreign Affairs, consult Edouard Brunner, *Lambris dorés et coulisses: Souvenirs d' un diplomate* (Genève: Georg, 2001), pp. 34–7. On Weitnauer's foreign policy thinking, see his autobiography: Albert Weitnauer, *Rechenschaft: Vierzig Jahre im Dienst des schweizerischen Staates* (Zürich: Artemis, 1982). For the standpoint stressing the dangers of an active human rights policy with respect to the credibility neutrality policy, see Luzius Wildhaber, 'Neutralität, Aussenpolitik und internationale Organisationen aus Schweizer Sicht', in Friedrich Koja and Gerald Stourzh (eds), *Schweiz – Österreich: Ähnlichkeiten und Kontraste* (Wien/Köln/Graz: Hermann Böhlau, 1986), pp. 209–27.
35 *Bericht über die Menschenrechtspolitik vom 2. Juni 1982*, in BBl 1982 II 772–4; *Botschaft über die Weiterführung der technischen Zusammenarbeit und der Finanzhilfe zugunsten von Entwicklungsländern vom 19. März 1984*, in BBl 1984 II 52 and 57.
36 Switzerland stopped co-operation with Vietnam (1979), Bolivia (1980) and Haiti and Myanmar (1988), but not with Turkey (after the 1980 military coup). For a short overview of the main features of Swiss development assistance and for the role of political conditionality, compare Jacques Forster, 'Conditionality in Swiss Development Assistance', in Olav Stokke (ed.), *Aid and Political Conditionality*, (Geneva/London: Frank Cass, 1995), pp. 201–24.
37 For an overview of the Swiss attitude towards economic sanctions, see Jürg Martin Gabriel, 'Switzerland and Economic Sanctions – The Dilemma of a Neutral', in Marko Milivojevic and Pierre Maurer (eds), *Swiss Neutrality and Security, Armed Forces, National Defense and Foreign Policy* (Oxford: Berg, 1990), pp. 232–45. For a discussion of the Swiss co-operation with Cocom, see André Schaller, *Schweizer Neutralität im West-Ost-Handel: das Hotz-Linder-Agreement vom 23. Juli 1951*

(Bern/Stuttgart: Paul Haupt, 1987). For the Swiss policy towards Rhodesia, see Rudolf Letsch, *Rhodesien, die Vereinten Nationen und die Schweiz: Konzepte und Inkonsistenzen der Rhodesienpolitik* (Universität St. Gallen: Dissertation, 1983).

38 The ERG was founded in 1934 as an instrument to fight unemployment in the export-oriented machine industry. The guarantee has a double purpose: it aims to maintain jobs in Switzerland and to promote exports. The ERG insures exporters against certain risks that can arise with countries where political or economic conditions are uncertain (non-payment due to political problems, foreign exchange restrictions, inability or unwillingness to pay on the part of public or public guaranteed debtors, and so on).

39 For an overview and a critical analysis of Switzerland's legislation concerning military export controls, compare Urs Cipolat, *Nonproliferation and Switzerland: a Critical Analysis of Switzerland's Legislation concerning Military Export Controls*, NFP 42 Synthesis, No. 39 (Bern: 2001). (http://www.snf.ch/NFP/nfp42/synthese/39Cipolatsynthesis42.pdf). For a critical analysis of the topic with regard to human rights policy, see Amnesty International, Swiss Section (ed.), *Menschenrechte und Waffenausfuhr: Eine Darstellung der Zusammenhänge, Gesetzgebung und Praxis in der Schweiz* (Bern: 1988); Walther L. Bernecker and Thomas Fischer (eds), *Unheimliche Geschäfte: Schweizer Rüstungsexporte nach Lateinamerika im 20. Jahrhundert* (Zürich: Chronos, 1991).

40 *Bericht über die Menschenrechtspolitik vom 2. Juni 1982*, in BBl 1982 II 772.

41 For the official viewpoint, see Franz Blankart, *Handel und Menschenrechte*, Basler Schriften zur europäischen Integration 25 (Basel: Europainstitut an der Universität Basel, 1997). For an analysis and a critic of Federal Council's policy, compare Erika Schläppi and Walter Kälin, *Schweizerische Aussenwirtschaftshilfe und Menschenrechtspolitik: Konflikte und Konvergenzen* (Chur/Zürich: Rüegger, 2001).

42 *Bericht über die Aussenpolitik der Schweiz in den 90er Jahren vom 29. November 1993.* In the year 2000, the Federal Council issued a new report, Foreign Policy Report 2000. The report confirms the 1993 conceptual framework. It describes European and world-wide changes that took place in the 1990s, draws conclusions about Swiss foreign policy activities in that decade and sets out some accents for future objectives and priorities. Compare here Federal Council, *Foreign Policy Report 2000, Presence and Cooperation: Safeguarding Switzerland's interests in an integrating world from November 15, 2000* (unofficial English translation). (http://www.eda.admin.ch/eda/e/home/recent/rep/forpol.Par.0003.UpFile.pdf/rp_001113_foreignpol_e). An analysis of the 1993 report can be found in Jürg Martin Gabriel, 'Neutralität für den Notfall: Der Bericht des Bundesrats zur Aussenpolitik der Schweiz in den 90er Jahren', in Jürg Martin Gabriel, *Sackgasse Neutralität*, pp. 129–58; Fanzun and Lehmann, *Die Schweiz und die Welt*, pp. 77–86.

43 The five objectives outlined in the foreign policy report of 1993 are (1) preservation and promotion of peace and security, (2) promotion of human rights, democracy, and the rule of law, (3) promotion of prosperity, (4) alleviation of poverty and inequality and (5) protection of the ecological bases of life. See *Bericht über die Aussenpolitik der Schweiz in den 90er Jahren vom 29. November 1993*, in BBl 1994 I 159.

44 *Botschaft zum Bundesgesetz über Massnahmen zur zivilen Friedensförderung und Stärkung der Menschenrechte vom 23. Oktober 2002*, in BBl 2002 7611–21 (http://www.admin.ch/ch/d/ff/2002/7611.pdf).

45 Compare on this issue Schläppi and Kälin, *Schweizerische Aussenwirtschaftshilfe und Menschenrechtspolitik*, pp. 24–40.

46 On the problem of goal conflicts in Swiss foreign policy, see Jürg Martin Gabriel, 'Zielkonflikte in der schweizerischen Aussenpolitik', in *Schweizerisches Jahrbuch für Politische Wissenschaft*, Vol. 28 (1988), pp. 17–31. On coherence in Swiss foreign policy from the viewpoint of development assistance, see Jacques Forster, 'The Coherence of Policies Towards Developing Countries: The Case of Switzerland', in Jacques Forster and Olav Stokke (ed.), *Policy Coherence in Development Co-operation* (London: Frank Cass, 1999), pp. 295–322.

47 Kälin, 'Verfassungsgrundsätze der schweizerischen Aussenpolitik', pp. 298–312.

48 At the start of 2002, six persons made up the staff of the Human Rights Section of Political Affairs Division IV of the Federal Department of Foreign Affairs (DFA). They follow the human rights situation in all countries of the world and, should the need arise, take the measures required by Swiss foreign policy. The DFA Section for Human Rights and Humanitarian Law deals with legal questions relating to human rights and international humanitarian law. It is to this Section that all relevant requests for legal information are passed. For up to date information on this topic, see the DFA Web page at http://www.eda.admin.ch.

49 *Bericht über die Menschenrechtspolitik der Schweiz vom 16. Februar 2000*, in BBl 2000 2586–609 (http://www.admin.ch/ch/d/ff/2000/2586.pdf).

50 In 1990, the DFA launched its first bilateral human rights dialogue with China. This also led to the opening up of a dialogue with Morocco, Pakistan, Vietnam and Cuba, the contents of which remain confidential. An evaluation of the efforts led the Federal Department of Foreign Affairs in autumn 2000 to concentrate on the dialogue with China and to terminate those with the other countries.

51 *Bericht über die Aussenpolitik der Schweiz in den 90er Jahren vom 29. November 1993*, in BBl 1994 I 181–3; *Bericht über die Menschenrechtspolitik der Schweiz vom 16. Februar 2000*, in BBl 2000 2590–7.

52 In cases of serious violations of peace and security or infringements of fundamental principles by individual countries the Federal Council conducts an in-depth review and decides on the basis of different criteria to stop co-operation either in part or totally. The criteria applied are: (1) grave violations of peace and security, (2) serious infringements of human rights, especially grave discrimination against minorities, (3) absence of efforts to achieve good governance, (4) interruption or reversal of democratisation processes, (5) lack of willingness on the part of a state to accept the return of its own nationals. See *Foreign Policy Report 2000*, p. 26.

53 For up-to-date information on human rights treaties ratified (or not) and for an analysis of the implementation of these treaties in Switzerland, compare the information provided on the official Web page of the Swiss Federal Department of Foreign Affairs at http://www.eda.admin.ch. For the standpoint of Swiss human rights NGOs, see the comprehensive information provided on the electronic human rights platform at http://www.humanrights.ch. Of particular interest are the Swiss reports on specific treaties (for example, the UN Human Rights Covenants), the 'shadow reports' by Swiss human rights organisations, and the decisions, observations and comments by the responsible international bodies (for example, the UN Human Rights Committee, the Council of Europe Anti-Torture Committee or the European Court of Human Rights).

54 For an in-depth analysis of the two Covenants from a Swiss perspective, see Walter Kälin, Giorgio Malinverni and Manfred Nowak, *Die Schweiz und die UNO-Menschenrechtspakte*, 2nd edn (Basel/Frankfurt a. M.: Helbing & Lichtenhahn, 1997).

55 By the end of 2002, Switzerland had presented two reports (in 1995 and 1998) under Article 40 of the Covenant. The Human Rights Committee treated the reports in 1996 and 2001. The related documents can be found on the Internet at http://www.eda.admin.ch and http://www.humanrights.ch.

56 By adopting this procedure a state recognises the competence of the Committee on the Elimination of Racial Discrimination to receive and consider communications from individuals or groups of individuals within its jurisdiction claiming to be victims of a violation by that State Party of any of the rights set forth in the convention. In August 2001 the government proposed the acceptance of the named procedure. While the National Council adopted this decision in December 2001, the Council of States rejected the government's proposal in June 2002 upon recommendation of its Foreign Affairs Committee. In November 2002 this Committee reconsidered the matter and proposed to adopt the communications procedure according to Article 14 of the convention. For details of the implementation of the convention in Switzerland, especially the periodic reports by the Swiss government and the according observations of the UN Committee against Torture, see information provided on the Internet at http://www.eda.admin.ch and http://www.humanrights.ch. For an overview of the parliamentary debates, compare the Swiss Parliaments Web page at http://www.parlament.ch.

57 Most particularly the European Charter for Regional or Minority Languages (ratification 1997), the Framework Convention for the Protection of National Minorities (ratification 1998) and Protocol Nr 11 to the European Convention on Human Rights concerning reorganisation of the control mechanisms (ratification 1998).

58 Up-to-date information on the status of ratification of CoE conventions can be found on the Internet at http://conventions.coe.int/Treaty/EN/CadreListeTraites.htm.

59 See the Legislative Planning Report by the Federal Council (1999–2003), the reports on the objectives of the Federal Council (2000, 2001 and 2002) and the annual reports of the Federal Council (2000 and 2001). The reports are available on the Internet in full-text (German/French/Italian) at http://www.admin.ch/ch/d/cf/rg/index.html#lp.

60 The UN entrusted the following Swiss citizens with UN Special Rapporteur mandates: Joseph Voyame on the situation in Rumania (1990); Walter Kälin on Kuwait (1992); René Felber on the Israeli-occupied territories (1993–4); Michel Moussali on Rwanda (since 1997). For an overview of the Swiss participation in UN human rights activities, see Jean-Daniel Vigny, 'La Suisse et la politique des Nations Unies à l'égard des droits de l'homme', in Riklin, *Neues Handbuch der schweizerischen Aussenpolitik*, pp. 265–75.

61 The election of Switzerland to the Economic and Social Council (ECOSOC) and to the Human Rights Commission are declared priorities of the Swiss government. See *First session of the United Nations General Assembly with Switzerland as a member: Background and Swiss priorities and perspectives*, 2002 (http://www.eda.admin.ch/sub_uno/e/uno/publi/doc/pdf.Par.0011.UpFile.pdf/dc_020729_goverdoc_e). There is a first Swiss success worth mentioning. On 9 September 2002 Walter Kälin, professor of international law at the University of Bern, was elected a member of the UN Human Rights Committee. It was established to monitor the implementation of the Covenant and the protocols to the Covenant on Civil and Political Rights in the territory of States parties. The Committee is composed of 18 independent experts of high moral character and having demonstrated competence in the field of human rights.

62 In terms of personnel resources, Switzerland made available to the OSCE 160 experts in connection with the 1996 elections. Human rights observers, elections experts, financial administrators and logistics specialists were in action in Bosnia. Switzerland's Gret Haller was appointed by the OSCE as ombudswoman for human rights in Bosnia-Herzegovina and served from 1995 to 2000. Furthermore, Gérard Stoudmann, a Swiss diplomat, served as Director of the Office for Democratic Institutions and Human Rights (ODIHR) from 1997 to 2002. For an overview of the Swiss contributions to OSCE, and especially of the 1996 chairmanship, see Laurent Goetschel (ed.), *Vom Statisten zum Hauptdarsteller: Die Schweiz und ihre OSZE-Präsidentschaft* (Bern/Stuttgart/Wien: Paul Haupt, 1997).

63 Comprehensive up to date information on the ICC can be found on the official Web page of the ICC at http://www.icc.int and on the Web page of the Coalition of the ICC, a network of over 1000 NGOs at http://www.iccnow.org.

64 Federal Council, *'North–South Guidelines', Report on Switzerland's North–South Relations in the 1990s*, 7 March 1994 (http://www.deza.ch/ressources/deza_product_e_21.pdf). Swiss Agency for Development and Cooperation (SDC), *Promoting Human Rights in Development Cooperation*, Guidelines approved on 24 February 1997. For an overview of Swiss development assistance in the 1990s, see Forster, *Coherence*; Fanzun and Lehmann, *Die Schweiz und die Welt*, pp. 271–305.

65 Compare Articles 2 and 4 of the Federal decree on co-operation with countries of Eastern Europe, 24 March 1995.

66 For a discussion of Swiss development assistance to Rwanda, see Joseph Voyame, Richard Friedli, Jean-Pierre Gern and Anton Keller, *La cooperation Suisse au Rwanda*, Rapport du Groupe d'Étude par le Département fédéral des affaires étrangères, 1996.

67 *Bericht über die Aussenpolitik der Schweiz in den 90er Jahren vom 29. November 1993*, in BBl 1994 I 182–3; Federal Council, *North–South Guidelines*, pp. 15–6; *Bericht über die Menschenrechtspolitik vom 16. Februar 2000*, in BBl 2000, here 2595.

68 Forster, *Coherence*, pp. 313–5. See the Berne Declaration's (BD) – a Swiss NGO – comprehensive dossier on the dam projects and on the export risk guarantee, available on the Internet at http://www.evb.ch.

69 For proposals to include human rights concerns in foreign economic decision-making, see Schläppi and Kälin, *Schweizerische Aussenwirtschaftshilfe und Menschenrechtspolitik*, pp. 261–75. Incoherence and goal conflicts are, of course, not a specific problem of Swiss foreign policy. Compared to other states, Switzerland received good marks from the Development Assistance Committee (DAC) of the OECD. In its 2000 review the DAC came to the conclusion that Switzerland has one of the most coherent policies regarding development co-operation of all OECD Member States. See Development Assistance Committee (DAC), Development Co-operation Review Switzerland, *DAC Journal*, Vol. 1, No. 4 (2000). A summary of the review can be found on the Internet at http://www.oecd.org/EN/document/0, EN-document-67-2-no-3-1894-67,FF.html.

7
Swiss Arms Control Policy: From Abstention to Participation

Andrea E. Heinzer

Introduction

In the area of arms control and disarmament, Swiss policy has undergone a significant shift since the Second World War. In the first few years after the war, the issue did not feature on the Swiss foreign policy agenda. The advent of the Nuclear Non-Proliferation Treaty (NPT) in the 1960s, however, triggered a lengthy discussion. It challenged Switzerland to weigh a number of different and conflicting interests – mainly military and economic – and to come to a decision for or against the treaty. In contrast, agreements like the Biological Weapons Convention (BWC) and the Limited Test Ban Treaty (LTBT) were signed and ratified quickly and without much controversy and debate. Those treaties did not entail practical obligations for the country. It must also be added that as a non-member of the United Nations (UN) and the Geneva Conference on Disarmament (CD),[1] Switzerland's participation in the Conference on Security and Co-operation in Europe (CSCE, later OSCE) was its only opportunity during the Cold War to engage in multinational arms control negotiations as an equal partner.

When the Cold War ended, Switzerland's passive and sceptical posture towards arms control changed. It adapted quickly to the new situation and began to participate in multilateral arms control initiatives. Switzerland was actively involved in the creation of the Chemical Weapons Convention (CWC), the Additional Protocol to the Biological Weapons Convention, the Comprehensive Nuclear Test Ban Treaty, and the Anti-Personnel Mines Treaty as well as in the various negotiating forums for small arms and light weapons control and other international negotiations. Arms control and disarmament became a cornerstone of Swiss foreign and security policy. In the 1990s the country also became a member of all informal export control regimes.

International efforts towards non-proliferation affect Switzerland significantly, both with respect to imports and exports. For this reason, the issue of export controls will also be addressed in this article. As a highly industrialized country, Switzerland had at its disposal a vast array of strategic sensitive commodities and technologies. If it wanted to ensure that such items would not be used for the production of weapons of mass destruction, it was necessary to place their export under control. On the import side, Switzerland has been and is still highly dependent upon import of high technology dual-use goods from other countries. By abiding the provisions of all informal export control regimes Switzerland is able to secure its own access to high-tech goods.

This essay sketches out the development of Swiss arms control and disarmament policy since 1945. In the first part, Switzerland's posture towards global arms control processes during the Cold War is examined. The second part deals with the period following the Cold War. Each of the two parts is organized according to the weapons systems involved.

7.1 Arms control policy during the Cold War

In the period between the two world wars the Swiss government had actively promoted disarmament and arms control initiatives. Within the framework of the League of Nations, Switzerland had played an active part in enacting the Protocol for the Prohibition of the Use in War of Asphyxiating, Poisonous or Other Gases and of Bacteriological Methods of Warfare in 1925. At the League's Geneva Disarmament Conference, which began in 1932, Switzerland submitted a number of proposals on arms control and disarmament. In addition to the prohibition of chemical and biological warfare, the Conference focused on 'qualitative disarmament' (reduction of offensive arms like tanks and heavy moveable artillery). Furthermore, Switzerland was promoting the control of so-called dual-use goods, or goods that can be utilized for both military and civilian purposes. These early initiatives came to an end in 1933, however, with Germany's withdrawal from the League and the resulting crisis at the Disarmament Conference.[2]

In the wake of the Second World War, and as a non-member of the United Nations, Switzerland saw no need to take the initiative in disarmament and arms control. Furthermore, most arms control agreements enacted during the Cold War were bilateral and limited to the two superpowers. There was little chance for states like Switzerland to participate in such a setting, with the exception of some technical issues that provided a niche for active Swiss involvement.

7.1.1 Nuclear weapons

Switzerland began to focus attention on arms control only in the 1960s, for it became evident at that time that the country would be affected by the Nuclear Non Proliferation Treaty. Limited Test Ban Treaty[3] negotiations were concluded successfully at the same time. While Switzerland ratified the LTBT without hesitation as early as 1964, the NPT triggered a domestic debate that raged for years. The treaty affected Swiss interests in two ways. In the civilian realm, Switzerland relied upon the import of fissionable material and nuclear technology for the peaceful use of nuclear energy. In the military realm, the procurement of tactical nuclear weapons was under consideration at that time.

It was the limited nature of the LTBT that permitted its quick ratification. The treaty banned nuclear weapons tests in the atmosphere, in outer space, and under water, but not underground. No verification measures were foreseen. The agreement had no practical consequences for Switzerland. In particular it had no bearing on the issue of equipping the Swiss Armed Forces with nuclear weapons. Only the underground tests that were still permitted were of any possible relevance. Switzerland's quick ratification rested mainly on considerations of potential damage to the environment through nuclear weapons tests, together with the fact that Switzerland would not lose its nuclear option through entering the LTBT.[4]

In contrast, NPT ratification entailed a long and tedious process of weighing diverging interests. Since the end of the Second World War, Switzerland's commitment to nuclear technology had continued to grow. The main problem, both for peaceful and eventual military uses of nuclear technology, remained the procurement of fissionable material. From 1947 on, there were intensive efforts to acquire uranium on the world market, a very difficult undertaking given its military importance. As early as 1946, the US Congress passed the Mac-Mahon Act,[5] which banned any uranium export and was meant to prevent nuclear proliferation. Not until the early 1950s, through co-operation agreements with various nuclear supplier countries,[6] did Switzerland manage to assure a certain supply of uranium.

The co-operation agreements were contingent upon the fulfilment of conditions. Nuclear materials were to be used exclusively for peaceful purposes and Switzerland had to accept that plants running on the supplied uranium would be subjected to foreign inspections. Nearly all of the Swiss nuclear installations came under foreign monitoring. From the very start, then, there was a conflict between the economy's interest in the peaceful uses of nuclear energy and the military's interest in the possible acquisition of nuclear weapons. While the control regime restricted the military's options, it represented the only way for Switzerland to procure the required fissionable material. This conflict played a central role in the debate on the Non-Proliferation Treaty.[7]

Public debate over the procurement of nuclear weapons for the Swiss Armed Forces intensified in the mid 1950s. In 1958 the Federal Council released a public statement that caused quite a stir both at home and abroad. In it the government indicated that should neighbouring countries acquire nuclear weapons, it would be necessary for Switzerland to follow suit. However, the government went on to say that a world free of nuclear weapons would best serve Swiss security interests and would make the decision on acquisition of costly nuclear weapons unnecessary.

Against this background two popular initiatives were launched in the late 1950s. The first demanded comprehensive prohibition of the production, import, transit, stockpiling and use of nuclear weapons. The other initiative aimed only to ensure that any decision to equip the Swiss Armed Forces with nuclear weapons would be put to a popular vote. Both initiatives were turned down in the early 1960s.[8]

Despite some reservations within business and military circles, the Swiss government signed the NPT on 27 November 1969. At the same time, however, it stressed that ratification would take place only when a sufficient number of countries had done the same. A further condition for Swiss ratification was the clarification of the still unresolved control issue. The relevant NPT articles were formulated so vaguely that the implementation of controls remained unclear.

The International Atomic Energy Agency (IAEA) was established as an autonomous UN organisation in 1957. It was to make sure that all nuclear research and production in states which were party to the NPT was only conducted for civil use of nuclear energy. Its Safeguards Committee was to work out the control agreements for the implementation of the treaty provisions. It began its work, with Swiss participation, in Vienna in 1970. Switzerland demanded effective and efficient controls[9] and was very concerned that there be no negative consequences on the exchange of equipment, fissionable material and scientific and technical information for peaceful purposes of nuclear energy. Together with other states, the country succeeded in having most of their misgivings met.

Although the question of the controls had been settled to Switzerland's satisfaction, the internal tug of war over NPT ratification continued. In the early 1970s, agreement was reached within the Federal Department of Foreign Affairs (FDFA) that the ratification process should be initiated. The first Review Conference, in which Switzerland wanted to participate as a full member, was scheduled for 1975. Furthermore, nuclear energy was becoming ever more important for the country's electrical supply. Switzerland grew quite dependent upon the import of fissionable material and nuclear equipment.

The FDFA ratification plans met with considerable resistance on the part of the Federal Department of Defence (FDoD). It feared that the loss of strategic options and the possible renunciation of nuclear arms might put Switzerland at a military disadvantage, especially in the absence of balanced compensation. The opponents of ratification argued that the NPT did not lessen the threat to small and medium states, because they lacked security guarantees coupled with concrete measures towards comprehensive disarmament. As the nuclear tests conducted by India showed, the NPT was unable to prevent proliferation. Finally, the number of member states was still too small for Swiss ratification.[10] Another underlying reason for FDoD resistance was the fact that the studies it had commissioned on the possible arming of the Swiss Armed Forces with atomic weapons had not been completed. The way the study had been delayed caused frustration among military circles.

The arguments of the NPT proponents carried more weight, however. Only the signing of the treaty would guarantee Switzerland's access to fissionable material, technology and equipment for nuclear power plants. They pointed out the growing difficulties Switzerland was experiencing in importing components for nuclear plants, for a number of supplier countries had already begun to put stricter export control regulations into effect. As a consequence, there were threatened delays to the building of reactors for Swiss nuclear power installations.

Once the military was given assurances that the studies it had demanded could be still carried out following NPT ratification, the Defence Department supported the treaty. In October 1974 the government finally took the decision to back ratification.

In 1976 both houses of parliament ratified the treaty. The process was helped along by a number of developments. All major nuclear supplier countries were now part of the NPT, and the final document of the First Review Conference of 1975 made clear that with common export requirements and comprehensive safeguards in importing non-nuclear-weapon states, non-member states would have little latitude for procuring fissionable material and equipment.[11] At this stage the Swiss industry still did not reach an agreement to support the treaty. The electricity companies demanded vehemently that Switzerland sign the NPT, while parts of the machine-producing industry and some of the export-oriented sectors expressed certain reservations.

On 9 March 1977 Switzerland filed the instrument of ratification in London, Moscow and Washington, adding a few reservations[12] taking into account the concerns voiced by the business community. After more than ten years, the struggle over the NPT finally came to an end.[13]

7.1.2 Biological and chemical weapons

Once negotiations in the Eighteen-Nation Committee on Disarmament had been concluded, disarmament efforts turned in 1968 towards biological and chemical weapons. For this area the FDFA requested an advisory opinion from the FDoD. The military concluded that the prohibition of biological and chemical weapons was in the Swiss interest, because the country had no such arms. Taking up the FDFA's proposal, in 1970 the government set up an interdepartmental working group that included representatives from the chemical industry. The group was mandated to prepare a study on the issue of biological and chemical weapons as a basis for the upcoming disarmament negotiations. The study group was not meant to consider a comprehensive and effective disarmament agreement. Its mandate was limited to studying Swiss options and to prevent international isolation.[14]

The working group's 1972 final report identified conditions to be fulfilled by any future biological and chemical weapons agreement. A treaty would be acceptable only if all parties had the same rights and obligations, in contrast to the NPT, which had created two classes of membership. In addition, the treaty would have to gain a certain degree of universality prior to the accession of Switzerland.[15] Third, Switzerland accepted prohibitions of the development, production and stockpiling of biological weapons even if the treaty did not contain verification measures. The Swiss position with respect to a chemical treaty had been different. Without verification and options for sanctions, so the reasoning went, it would worsen the situation for the parties that complied with the chemical treaty provisions.[16]

Switzerland was not represented on the Committee on Disarmament, and with its observer status in the UN General Assembly there was no real opportunity to influence the negotiations on the Convention on the Prohibition of the Development, Production and Stockpiling of Bacteriological and Toxin Weapons and on their Destruction (BTWC). Even without active participation in the negotiations, Switzerland did, however, sign the BWC as early as April 1972.

The parliamentary BTWC debate focused mainly on military considerations. For a small and neutral state with an army dedicated exclusively to defence, the threat of use of biological weapons would not be credible and the risk of self-damage was too great. In short, it would make little sense to equip the Swiss Armed Forces with biological weapons.[17] For security reasons, a prohibition of biological weapons governed by international law lay in Switzerland's interest and it was viewed as an important and significant step. The BWC was held to go beyond previous arms control agreement, because for the first time an entire category of weapons of mass destruction had been banned. This was a true step towards disarmament.[18]

For the business and science community the convention also presented no difficulties, as the treaty put no restrictions on the civil industry, and there were no provisions prohibiting university research. Switzerland ratified the Biological and Toxin Weapons Convention in 1976, although it did submit three reservations.[19]

7.1.3 CSCE involvement

The Conference on Security and Cooperation in Europe (CSCE) got started in the 1970s. The forum offered a platform where small, neutral and non-aligned states could participate actively in regional arms control and disarmament. The Helsinki Process, which established the first confidence-building measures in Europe with the Helsinki Final Act of 1975, gave Switzerland its first opportunity to participate in arms control negotiations as an equal partner. It did not participate as an individual nation but coordinated its policies with the other neutral and non-aligned states (N + N group).[20] In the early years, from 1973 to 1975, Switzerland took over leadership of the group, whose compromise proposals at times succeeded in overcoming stalemates between Western and Eastern countries.[21] Until Switzerland was granted observer status at the Geneva Conference on Disarmament, the CSCE was the most important forum for Swiss involvement in arms control and security issues.

At the CSCE follow-up meeting in Madrid (1980–3), agreement was reached to continue the negotiations on expanding confidence- and security-building measures (CSBMs). This led to the Stockholm Conference on Confidence- and Security-Building Measures and Disarmament in Europe (CDE). Switzerland's position at the CDE,[22] which after two years culminated in the historic September 1986 Stockholm Document, was based on its defensive strategy. The government instructed its delegates to prevent any conflicts with the defensive nature of Swiss security policy and the principle of permanent and armed neutrality.[23] This left little room for initiatives. Yet, the Swiss participated actively in the process and promoted the idea of a system for advanced notification of military activities. This measure, in the form of detailed data exchanges on military exercises and troop deployments according to specified information categories and contents, was approved by the conference and included in the Stockholm Document.

Switzerland vehemently resisted the idea of a fusion between the CDE and the discussions on Conventional Armed Forces in Europe (CFE), and it prevailed against other N + N states such as Sweden and Yugoslavia. After the Stockholm Conference, the 1986–9 CSCE follow-up conference in Vienna thus took place independently of the talks on conventional armed forces in Europe, and the two were linked only through a formal exchange of information. Non-aligned states therefore had little room for manoeuvre. By participating actively in the negotiations on the Stockholm Document and promoting transparency in military activities, however, Switzerland was able to make a contribution towards stability and confidence-building in Europe. During the Cold War, the CSCE process was the only forum in which Switzerland could fully participate in arms control negotiations.

7.1.4 Learning about export controls

Switzerland's earliest efforts in the area of export controls goes back to the turn of the twentieth century when, in accordance with its neutrality, it regulated the export of military equipment to states engaged in war on a case-by-case basis. The Swiss constitution allowed the Federal Government to control the export of war material. With the start of the Cold War, pressure to do more than this increased. Under US leadership, the Cocom states threatened trade restrictions if Switzerland did not conform to Cocom regulations. The pressures led Switzerland to sign a Gentlemen's Agreement negotiated with the United States, the so-called Hotz–Linder Agreement.[24] The country declared its willingness to restrict exports of strategic goods to the Soviet bloc. In return, the United States lifted trade restrictions and, in principle, permitted the export of strategic goods to Switzerland. Despite neutrality concerns and although never fully integrated into the Cocom export control regime, Switzerland abided by the pertinent regulations.[25]

Export controls in the area of nuclear goods also became a problem for Switzerland. As an early and active participant in the nuclear regime, however, it successfully achieved a formulation of export control measures favourable to its interests. Although the NPT places all exports of fissionable material and nuclear equipment under control, the treaty does not provide specific definitions. It was Switzerland that pointed this out to the Safeguard Committee in the early 1970s. Once an agreement to address this problem was reached Switzerland, as originator of the proposal, was given the chairmanship of the so-called Zangger Committee, a body created specifically for this purpose.[26] This occurred regardless of the fact that the NPT ratification of Switzerland was still outstanding.

In 1974 the Zangger Committee published a control list. Nuclear items on this list were exported to countries not party to the NPT only if these states accepted the submission of their nuclear installations, installation components and the fissionable material produced to complete IAEA controls. A further condition was a non-explosive use assurance and a re-transfer provision that required the receiving state to apply the same conditions when re-exporting these items. From the Swiss perspective, the work of the Zangger Committee was very positive. Here Switzerland was involved in an issue important to the country, the export control issue, and it could contribute significantly to an effective solution that did not run counter to its own economic interests.

Following the 'peaceful' Indian nuclear explosion of 1974, the United States tightened its own non-proliferation policy and launched an initiative for the creation of the Nuclear Suppliers Group (NSG), formerly known as the 'London Club'. Its aim was to co-ordinate and harmonize the export control policies of the most important nuclear supplier countries.[27] The NSG began negotiations on export controls directly affecting Switzerland. For this reason, and based on the positive experiences in the Zangger Committee, Switzerland requested NSG observer status even prior to ratifying the NPT. After ratification in the spring of 1977, it quickly sought full membership.

There were three main reasons for the Swiss interest in membership. First of all, in order to avoid market distortions, Switzerland wanted to see export controls for nuclear goods regulated consistently worldwide. Second, the country wanted to participate in the formulating of the definitive NSG Guidelines. And third, by participating, Switzerland expected that pressures exerted by the most important nuclear supplier countries would not escalate. As a consequence of NSG membership, Switzerland had to institute its own export controls for nuclear goods. Until now it had argued that only nuclear raw materials and specially processed fissionable material – which it did not produce – would fall under export restrictions.

NSG membership marked the hesitant beginning of a Swiss non-proliferation policy. The first years were difficult, as evidenced by a number of contested nuclear export cases in the late 1970s and early 1980s. Switzerland came under strong pressure, mainly from the United States, a development that negatively affected Swiss nuclear imports. Due to the pressure and in order to fully implement the NSG Guidelines, Switzerland had to change its Nuclear Energy Act accordingly.

7.1.5 Waiting and seeing

During the Cold War, Switzerland had no arms control and disarmament policy in the strict sense of the word. For a long time, the government had no interest to participate in arms control negotiations. The argument was that the Swiss would be willing to disarm only when the two military blocs took significant steps towards reduction of their own armed forces and arsenals. The justification lay in the fact that the Swiss Armed Forces were a purely defensive militia. The government also mentioned the country's status as a permanent neutral. A further factor standing in the way of active Swiss participation was that the country was a member of neither the UN nor the Eighteen-Nation Committee on Disarmament (later the Conference on Disarmament). The Swiss often found themselves in the self-chosen role of the passive and tolerated observer.

Moreover, arms control was then mainly a bilateral matter between the two superpowers, the United States and the Soviet Union. They dictated the arms control and disarmament agenda. But as Switzerland's initiatives in the early 1970s in the context of the Safeguard Committee and the Zangger Committee show, bipolarity left even small players with some room for realizing their own interests. It demanded a readiness for active participation, however, which in the case of Switzerland was not always forthcoming.

Basically the Swiss position was reactive and defensive. Only when forced by external developments did the Federal Government deal with arms control. Switzerland's motivation to become active was not based on an interest in effective and comprehensive arms control or disarmament agreements. Swiss reactions were meant to keep open as many options as possible without, at the same time, isolating the country internationally. Security benefits were often less important or simply not understood.

This defensive 'wait and see' attitude is reflected in the way that the federal administration responded and organized its efforts. From the start the Department of Foreign Affairs assumed leadership in the area of arms control, and it was characteristic of the initial phase that the government was largely unprepared. Before it could react, ad hoc organisation was necessary. Switzerland had no experts on arms control and disarmament at the time. Lacking special and often highly technical know-how, Swiss diplomacy quickly reached its limits. Fortunately, the government could draw on its expertise in civil nuclear technology. When the diplomats required support on technical issues, they could turn to members of the Federal Department of Transport and Energy, the Federal Office of Science and Research and other related institutes.

Given these unsatisfactory conditions, it is hardly surprising that Switzerland's contributions to the negotiations were often limited to general statements of policy. Staff members were overtaxed and had no opportunity to acquire the necessary expertise. It was mainly due to the initiative of individual members of the federal administration that Switzerland at crucial moments succeeded in defending its positions. Things did not change until the end of the Cold War, when for the first time arms control policy was defined as an instrument of security policy. Up to that time there had been no document situating arms control firmly within Switzerland's security policy.[28]

7.2 Arms control policy after the Cold War

The changes in world politics accompanying the end of the Cold War activated disarmament and arms control. The Soviet Union gave up its resistance to verification measures bringing new vitality to stagnating negotiations. At the same time, a process of multilaterialization set in that changed the bipolar system dominated by the United States and the Soviet Union. Non-governmental and transnational actors took on a more significant role leading to new negotiating forums and new forms of co-operation. States were no longer the sole actors in international relations, and the new participants brought new issues to the arms control agenda. While most of the arms control treaties negotiated during the Cold War focused on weapons of mass destruction and their delivery systems, attention was now also given to human security. Anti-personnel mines, small arms and light weapons were added to the arms control agenda.

For Switzerland the new realities presented both challenges and opportunities. On the one hand the multilateralization of world politics opened up new possibilities for participation, on the other hand the Swiss also had to learn to more effectively define and promote their specific interests in the ensuing negotiations. The government reacted positively and began to increase its involvement thereby signalling a move away from its passive and defensive Cold War policy in the area of arms control and disarmament.

7.2.1 Nuclear disarmament and non-proliferation

When in 1995 the NPT parties met for their Fifth Review Conference, the indefinite extension of the treaty was on the agenda. Switzerland's official statement expressed support for indefinite extension, which was a change from its former position on NPT duration. In the late 1960s, during the treaty negotiations, Switzerland had strongly supported a time limit. It objected mainly to the idea of firmly establishing the timeless monopoly of the five nuclear powers, which it saw as a form of discrimination and as an incentive for nuclear weapons countries not to reduce their stockpiles. At the Review and Extension Conference in 1995, Switzerland demanded that the nuclear weapons states begin to take determined steps towards disarmament with the goal to eliminate all nuclear weapons. With an eye on North Korea and Iraq, Switzerland also favoured a strengthening of the IAEA inspection system.[29]

Switzerland's disappointment was great when, in the same year, China and France resumed nuclear testing, thus endangering the success of the ongoing negotiations on a Comprehensive Test Ban Treaty (CTBT) in Geneva. The government criticised the tests scheduled by France.[30] Again in 1998, in response to tests by India and Pakistan, the Federal Council expressed regret and called on the two states to ratify both the NPT and the CTBT.

Switzerland's position on the CTBT was clear. From the start the country had called for a comprehensive, worldwide ban on all nuclear weapons tests also prohibiting hydronuclear experiments and security tests of existing nuclear weapons. In addition, the government called for a firm and efficient verification regime. When the UN General Assembly opened the CTBT for signature on 24 September 1996, Switzerland was among the 71 states signing the treaty on the very same day. Ratification was deposited at the UN in October 1999. The Swiss authorities saw the treaty's main contribution in its signalling effect. It contributed to international security by restricting both horizontal and, in part, vertical proliferation. Furthermore, in Swiss eyes the CTBT represented an important step towards environmental protection. A nuclear test ban eliminated a significant source of radioactive contamination.

Since 1996 Switzerland has participated in the Preparatory Commission for the Comprehensive Nuclear Test Ban Treaty Organization, which is preparing for the treaty's entry into force and establishing a global verification regime to monitor compliance with the comprehensive ban on explosive nuclear testing. Switzerland also participates in the International Monitoring System of the CTBT by operating a seismic auxiliary station.

After the completion of the CTBT, the Conference on Disarmament could not agree on future proceedings. In February 1998 Switzerland, as chairman of the conference, succeeded in bringing the members to agree to a programme of work. One of the points was a multilateral agreement banning the production of fissile material for military purposes. The Fissile Material Production Ban (FISSBAN) is seen as an instrument against further proliferation of nuclear weapons. It could also – if previous production of fissile material were also to be included in the ban – represent a first step towards the elimination of nuclear weapons.[31] However, negotiations on the FISSBAN, which Switzerland propagated, remain stalled, and there is no likelihood that the situation will change anytime soon.

7.2.2 The protocol to strengthen the Biological and Toxins Weapons Convention

Immediately after the end of the Cold War, confidence in the BTWC dropped markedly – particularly after the discovery of biological weapons programs in the former Soviet Union and in Iraq. At the same time, the process of strengthening the BTWC through confidence-building measures in the framework of the BTWC Review Conferences produced few results. It was against this background that a Special Review Conference was convened in 1994. Along with other states, Switzerland proposed a strengthening of the voluntary confidence-building measures by creating a legally binding instrument and establishing an inspection regime. An Ad Hoc Group[32] was mandated to improve the convention's effectiveness by developing an international legally binding protocol to the BTWC that would provide verification measures, including a system of declarations and inspections to deter non-compliance.

Switzerland welcomed the initiation of a multilateral Ad Hoc Group process. On its own it could do little against the increasing threat of biological weapons. In contrast to the way that non-compliance was being handled in the UN – by creating commissions like the UNSCOM[33] – the Ad Hoc Group allowed UN non-members like Switzerland to participate as an equal partner in the negotiations on the protocol.

From the start the Swiss participated actively in the negotiations, which took place from January 1995 to August 2001 in Geneva. It quickly became apparent that the future verification regime would affect Switzerland's own rapidly developing biotechnology industry, and it was for this reason that the Swiss delegation tried to negotiate for a verification regime also acceptable to the industry. While industrial concerns entered into the negotiating process, security interests were given clear priority over economic interests. Switzerland worked towards a strict verification regime in the hope for security gains.

Switzerland also sought greater transparency and lobbied for the introduction of a comprehensive declaration obligation covering biotechnology plants and facilities, activities with certain microbiological organisms and defensive biological weapons research programs allowed under the BWC. In a number of technical working papers, the Swiss attempted to develop precise criteria for the declaration obligation. They welcomed a provision for routine inspections in randomly selected plants and facilities declared by States Parties. The inspections were to serve as incentives for comprehensive and precise declarations, while at the same time they offered a way to keep a team of experienced professional inspectors ready for action in the case of suspected non-compliance. Routine inspections would also contribute significantly to confidence-building and transparency among states which were party to the BTWC.

The Swiss also proposed the creation of mediation procedures to settle disagreements over the protocol's implementation and interpretation. The establishment of a specific mediation mechanism would obligate states to conduct bilateral consultations and negotiations and reach a common position within a specified time limit. The proposal was included into the draft of the protocol, but many of the proposed mechanisms for regulating the process of bilateral consultations had been watered down.

Toward the end of the Ad Hoc Group negotiations, Switzerland and the Netherlands competed over the seat of the future Organization for the Prohibition of Biological Weapons (OPBW). Since the negotiations failed in August 2001, there was no decision on the issue. Switzerland expressed sincere regrets that despite several years of intensive negotiations, the verification protocol to the BTWC had not been concluded.

7.2.3 The Chemical Weapons Convention

In the late 1980s, the Conference on Disarmament stepped up negotiations on chemical weapons. At the close of the Cold War the two superpowers accepted the concept of a Chemical Weapons Convention prohibiting the development, production, stockpiling and use of chemical weapons. It also included a requirement for the destruction of all existing weapons. In contrast to the BTWC, the CWC was to contain a verification system of unparalleled dimensions.[34] Switzerland responded positively. It wanted to protect the interests of its own highly developed chemical industry, which would be affected by the verification regime. It also wanted to contribute towards a comprehensive ban of chemical weapons that served Switzerland's security interests.

As the negotiations began to look successful in 1990, the Swiss government decided to commission a specialized branch of the Spiez Laboratory[35] to provide technical support to the Swiss observer delegation to the Conference on Disarmament. The expertise developed at Spiez allowed Switzerland to contribute with technical working papers in a constructive way to the ongoing negotiations. In 1991, an expert of the chemical industry joined the Swiss, thereby including the private sector in the negotiation process at an early point in time.

Switzerland attached great importance to the verification regime. The government argued that only with strong and reliable verification measures would the CWC bring the necessary level of security. In order to test the verification procedures discussed, Switzerland conducted two national trial inspections in 1989 and 1990. In 1992 experts at the Spiez Laboratory began to develop a training program for future chemical weapons inspectors in which the Swiss chemical industry also participated. Several firms placed their facilities at the disposal of the training programme. The Swiss government and the industry took on a large part of the programme's costs.

Less successful was Switzerland's bid for the seat of the Organization for the Prohibition of Chemical Weapons (OPCW) in Geneva. Its 1991 proposal came after that of the Netherlands, Belgium and Austria. The Dutch were lobbying intensively for the new seat and they won by a narrow margin.

Switzerland's bid failed probably due to hesitation and delayed submission. Moreover, the Netherland's candidacy was supported by the EU members.

Following ratification of the CWC in 1995, Switzerland worked towards quick and pragmatic implementation within the newly created OPCW. As the country has no chemical weapons, its work focused mainly on verification in the chemical industry and on protection measures. Switzerland worked actively on unresolved issues of industrial verification and, to this day, has led and co-ordinated various activities. Due to the highly technical nature of the issues, the OPCW values the expertise of the Spiez Laboratory. The CWC requires each state party to contribute to the OPCW's programme regarding protective measures against chemical weapons. So far Switzerland has made a financial contribution to the respective fund and provided protection masks for 10 000 civilians. Since 1999, Switzerland has conducted regular training courses on protecting the civilian population. Most of the expenses for these courses are carried by the Federal Department of Defence.

The CWC offered Switzerland its first opportunity to participate actively in a specific arms control and disarmament process. It profited from this new opportunity made possible by the end of the Cold War and was able to influence the negotiations in areas that were important to Switzerland. It remained active in the ensuing implementation phase by making practical contributions towards the full and even implementation of the CWC. In recent years, the Swiss have tried to resist efforts towards watering down treaty provisions. They want to ensure that the CWC remains an effective and credible means of countering the threat of chemical weapons.

7.2.4 Anti-personnel mines and small arms

In the framework of the 1995 Review Conference on the Convention on Prohibitions or Restrictions on the Use of Certain Conventional Weapons Which May be Deemed to be Excessively Injurious or to Have Indiscriminate Effects (1980), the 1981 landmines protocol (Protocol II) was amended. It strengthened the treaty's original restrictions on the use, stockpiling, production and transfer of anti-personnel landmines.[36] Although the amended protocol also dealt with domestic conflicts, Switzerland, along with other countries, was not satisfied with the results of the revision that restricted only the use of landmines instead of demanding an outright ban. As a consequence, the Swiss government decided to ban anti-personnel mines unilaterally and to destroy its own existing stocks.

In May 1996 – following the Review Conference – the Ottawa Process initiated by Canada started with the aim to establish a comprehensive ban on anti-personnel mines. The Canadian Minister of Foreign Affairs, with the participation of interested non-governmental organisations, invited all governments to a first anti-personnel landmine conference in October 1996. The conference passed an action plan for a future ban on anti-personnel landmines, which Switzerland supported. A further meeting in Vienna was called in February 1997. At Switzerland's initiative, a core group[37] was formed of the states that expressed unconditional support for a total ban of anti-personnel landmines. This core group provided an important impetus to the Ottawa Process by presenting initial drafts of the treaty under Austrian direction.

After a second meeting in Brussels in June 1997, the draft treaty reached its final form in September of the same year in Oslo. As its most urgent goal, the Swiss negotiating delegation in Oslo wanted to prevent agreement over the final draft at the expense of its original strength. It would be unacceptable if extensive exceptions and reservations were to be written into the treaty.[38] Another Swiss concern was a legally binding obligation for demining. After the ten-year period granted for the removal of all mines, prolongations should only be granted by a conference involving all treaty states. With this approach, Switzerland wanted to oblige the affected states to conduct demining as agreed and as rapidly as possible.[39]

The Ottawa Process came to a close with the signing of the Convention on the Prohibition of the Use, Stockpiling, Production and Transfer of Anti-Personnel Mines and on Their Destruction. More than 120 countries gave their signature in December 1997.[40] The convention entered into force on 1 March 1999 after 40 countries, including Switzerland, had deposited their instruments of ratification. It was an important success, but major powers such as the United States, China and Russia have not joined the treaty.

In spring 1998 Switzerland founded the Geneva International Centre for Humanitarian Demining. By funding this institution the Swiss government wanted to contribute to the implementation of the Ottawa process as well as to the promotion of peace and security. The Centre's main activities – namely the establishment of an expert group and a data base on demining and the training of leaders for demining teams – meet mainly the needs of the United Nations Mine Action Services.

Following the campaign to ban anti-personnel landmines, in which non-governmental organisations (NGOs) played a key role, Switzerland maintained its contacts to NGOs and in 1998 set up a working group composed of federal authorities and interested NGOs. The working group met for a discussion of the Swiss initiative in the area of small arms and light weapons. The government was, and still is, actively engaged in the area of small arms and light weapons in the framework of several negotiation processes. Switzerland participated actively in preparations for the UN Small Arms Conference, in the negotiations in Vienna on the Firearms Protocol[41] and in the drafting of the OSCE policy statement on small arms issues.[42]

At the end of February 1999, the FDFA invited the UN Group of Governmental Experts on Small Arms and other international experts to a workshop on small arms monitoring and control in Geneva. The meeting focused specifically on the marking and tracing of small arms, for in this area Switzerland belongs worldwide to the leading countries. Through marking, the route of a weapon can be traced from production to use. This serves transparency, which contributes to confidence building. Switzerland also organized further workshops[43] dedicated to dealing with different aspects of the small arms problem. At the workshops, for the first time government representatives and arms experts from private industry came together to discuss practical and technical possibilities of preventing the illicit trafficking of small arms. The results were summed up in a Chairman's Report[44] and made available to the UN Preparatory Committee for the United Nations Conference on the Illicit Trade in Small Arms and Light Weapons in All Its Aspects. Prior to the UN Conference of 2001, Switzerland met informally for an exchange of views with other states interested in small arms.

Although Switzerland had invited the UN to hold the global conference on illicit trade in small arms in Switzerland, it took place in July 2001 in New York. The main reason is that the Swiss government and the UN had not been able to reach agreement on dividing the costs. At the conference, and together with France, Switzerland presented a proposal on the marking and tracing of small arms and light weapons. The initiative aimed to anchor in the final document of the conference a concrete mandate for the drafting of a convention that would establish legally binding measures for the marking of small arms. To the disappointment of the Swiss, the initiative was watered down by the United States. The final document contains only a vague formulation to the effect that the convention will attempt to establish measures for marking and tracing.[45]

7.2.5 From CSCE to OSCE

After the end of the Cold War, the CSCE confidence- and security-building measures were expanded with the Vienna Documents of 1990[46] and 1992.[47] Switzerland demanded repeatedly that the negotiations on the level of conventional armed forces in Europe take into consideration the Swiss militia system. Having no standing army, the country is entirely dependent upon mobilizing its militia. Switzerland's position on arms control measures was therefore very cautious. Together with other N + N states, it expressed clearly that it would wait for the implementation of the first Treaty on Conventional Armed Forces in Europe (CFE) before it would be willing to enter into discussions that went beyond confidence-building measures in a narrow sense.[48]

After 1992, negotiations on further confidence and security building measures took place on a regular basis within the Forum for Security Cooperation (FSC).[49] The Swiss government saw its participation as an opportunity to design stable security arrangements in Europe. In particular, Switzerland promoted the democratic control of armed forces[50] and continued the development of confidence- and security-building measures. The 1994 Vienna Document expanded and deepened the provisions of the 1990 and 1992 documents. As a country with limited military means, Switzerland attempted to promote transparency, predictability and equal rights of all states through co-operation.

In 1996 Switzerland held the OSCE (formerly CSCE) chairmanship.[51] Switzerland saw this as an opportunity to show to the international community that it was ready to depart from its self-chosen position of isolation. It also gained experience in a multilateral organisation and practised new forms of its traditional good offices.[52] It became clear, however, that non-membership in the UN, NATO and the EU represented a considerable handicap, for one of the tasks of the OSCE chairmanship was to exchange and co-ordinate information with other international and regional organisations.[53]

As a part of its policy to reform the armed forces, Switzerland unilaterally cut the size of its militia into half, and at the 1994 OSCE Review Conference in Budapest it declared its readiness to establish upper limits for personnel and for certain weapons systems. With this, it gave up its fundamental reservations to the CFE treaty and the Vienna Document of 1992 in which it had declared that Switzerland, because of its defensive strategy, would not reduce militia forces and weapons systems.

At the 1999 OSCE Summit Conference in Istanbul, 30 states signed the Agreement on the Adaptation of the Treaty on Conventional Armed Forces in Europe, which took account of the new security environment (for example, end of the Cold War, eastward expansion of NATO) and jettisoned the bloc-to-bloc and zonal limits of the original treaty and replaced them with a system of national and territorial ceilings. A new element of the CFE treaty is the Accession Clause allowing the admission of all OSCE member states with territory in the area of application.

With the Accession Clause, the question of Swiss membership arose once again. However, the CFE treaty continues to be directed towards states with mobile armed forces that stand in active service during peacetime. This could present problems with regard to the verification obligations that Switzerland would have to fulfil.[54] The national ceilings foreseen by the treaty could also be a problem: in comparison to similar states in size and population, Switzerland maintains very high equipment levels in conventional armaments. However, the latest defence reform programme envisages additional reductions. Given the changing European security setting, Switzerland is now re-evaluating CFE membership.[55]

7.2.6 Tightening export controls

Switzerland is a participant of all four informal export control regimes – the Nuclear Suppliers Group, the Australia Group, the Missile Technology Control Regime and the Wassenaar Arrangement. Members pursue the aims of these regimes through the following means: information exchange on programmes and activities in countries of concern, common lists of relevant materials and technologies that need to be controlled and guidelines governing the conduct of export controls. Decisions are adopted through consensus.

It is a principle of the Swiss government's export control policy that all internationally agreed measures should enhance security while not producing market distortions or hindering normal trade of materials and equipment. Only those goods and technologies should be controlled that are indispensable for the production of weapons of mass destruction and that are not generally available outside the regime. Switzerland is decidedly against any attempts to practice trade protectionism under the guise of non-proliferation. When implementing internationally negotiated export control measures, the Swiss authorities place a high priority on efficient and strict adherence within the country.

Since Swiss industry is highly dependent upon exports, it has a tendency to view export controls as harmful to free trade. On the other side, Switzerland has a strong security interest in preventing sensitive goods and technologies from getting into the wrong hands and being misused to produce weapons of mass destruction or delivery systems. The balancing of these two interests has not always been easy. Also, the Swiss authorities have at times come under foreign pressure, not infrequently exerted by the United States. Sometimes domestic pressure is also exerted by a critical Swiss public. Given these tensions, the Swiss government tries to work towards clearly defined export control measures that are executed consistently by all participating states.

For export controls to be implemented effectively, the authorities seek co-operation with industry. In the past it often proved useful to consult the industries affected by specific export control measures for new proposals that emerged in the regimes. The Swiss delegation has profited regularly from the technical expertise at the disposal of industry and has brought this input into the negotiating process. In that way, solutions have been found that the industry can bear. Some of the technical proposals that Switzerland introduced in export control regimes were worked out in co-operation and consultation with industry.

The decreasing quality of the information exchange in export control regimes represents a problem and appears to be a consequence of sharp rise in the number of member states in recent years. Important members have become much less willing to share intelligence information within this larger circle. Since the Swiss authorities have only limited intelligence resources available for the purpose of evaluating export license, they are interested in obtaining reliable information from their export control regime partners.

7.2.7 Participating in the export control regimes

The year 1991 saw a reactivation of the London Club under the new name of the Nuclear Suppliers Group (NSG).[56] Iraq had been discovered to pursue a clandestine nuclear weapons program through acquisition of significant dual-use items. This gave major impetus to the NSG's development of its controls of nuclear related dual-use items. Switzerland participated in these activities from the start, for control measures in dual-use goods affect the country considerably. In recent years, the Swiss promoted the increased exchange of information among the NSG states and the creation of more transparency regarding exported dual-use items. Unfortunately, these initiatives produced no visible results. Following the nuclear tests by India and Pakistan, the sobering reality of export control effectiveness was once more visible after 1998. It appears to many that the effectiveness of nuclear export controls cannot be improved so long as the NSG member states show little readiness to exchange intelligence information openly.

The Australia Group was called into existence in the 1980s upon the initiative of Australia. The member states agreed on controls of chemical weapons precursors, dual-use chemical manufacturing equipment that could be misused to produce chemical weapons. Since 1993 the participating countries also required licenses for the export of biological agents and toxins as well as dual-use biological equipment with a potential to be diverted to the production of biological weapons. Switzerland has been a member of the Australia Group since 1987.

In recent years there has been increasing criticism of the Australia Group. States such as Iran, India and Pakistan have accused the Australia Group of barring their access to Western technology under the guise of non-proliferation, thereby impeding development. A whole group of non-aligned states demands the abolition of the Australia Group. They want to see export control mechanisms established within the Chemical Weapons Convention and the Biological Weapons Convention, which would then be applied only against non-member states to these conventions. The Australia Group opposes this idea and is led by the United States, which ratified the CWC under the reservation that the Australia Group would remain in place.

Switzerland accords legally binding arms control agreements a higher priority than mere political arrangements. It therefore views the Australia Group as a complementary measure, the necessity for which must be re-evaluated periodically. However, since the negotiations on the BTWC protocol have failed, the export control measures of the Australia Group regarding biological agents, equipment and technologies continue to be highly relevant. Yet Switzerland comes to a somewhat different conclusion with respect to chemical agents: here there is considerable double tracking with respect to the chemicals controlled by the Australia Group and the CWC. Swiss efforts towards eliminating the double track in the Australia Group had no success. As a consequence Switzerland began to plead for a harmonization of export control parameters in the Australia Group and the CWC wherever there is an overlap. For some of the technical issues, this effort finally bore fruit. If the CWC verification regime proves to be stable and reliable, Switzerland may be willing to consider the relaxing or lifting of certain export control measures concerning dual-use chemicals on the Australia Group's control list.

The Missile Technology Control Regime (MTCR) is another informal export control arrangement. It co-ordinates export controls for ballistic missiles and missile-related materials and equipment. The MTCR was founded in 1987 by the Group of Seven industrialized countries. Switzerland has been a member since 1992.

In May 1998 Switzerland launched an initiative to improve transparency within the MTCR. The MTCR requires notification of export license denials as well as notification of exports in the field of highly sensitive missile equipment and technologies. Switzerland maintained that notification should be mandatory for all approved exports of materials controlled under MTCR Guidelines and its Annex. Transfer notifications would provide useful information. However, a number of states, with the United States at the lead, were opposed to this proposal. They did not wish to disclose information on their exports of sensitive materials to specific countries.

In 1997 and 1998 Switzerland organized two MTCR workshops, one on transshipments[57] and another on risk assessment.[58] In addition to MTCR countries, the workshops were also attended by selected non-participating states. Switzerland used the opportunity for bilateral consultations with non-participating states. These contacts yield information on the export control systems of states outside the MTCR of importance for the implementation of Switzerland's own export controls. The talks gave Switzerland an opportunity to explain the philosophy and goals of the MTCR and sensitize non-participating states to existing export control problems.

At the end of the Cold War the Cocom regime became obsolete. In 1993 the 17 Cocom members agreed to terminate the informal regime and to establish a new multilateral arrangement, temporarily known as the 'New Forum'. Switzerland was eager to see the successor regime succeed, for it would provide an international basis for its own rather restrictive export policy on war material. Agreement to establish the Wassenaar Arrangement on export controls was reached in 1995 at a meeting held at the Dutch city of Wassenaar. Its purpose is to prevent the export of conventional arms and dual-use goods and technologies to states whose behaviour threatens regional or international security and stability. The arrangement has two control lists: the Munitions List, which contains weapons and other military items, and the Dual-Use Goods and Technologies List.

Participating states exchange information on deliveries of conventional arms on the Wassenaar Munitions List and submit extensive notification of licenses denied and approved for goods on both lists. Together with other states, Switzerland pleaded for a more equal handling of the two lists. The stricter controls for goods on the Dual-Use List result from the policies of some of the big powers, which seek to conduct certain deliveries of conventional weapons without causing a stir. Weapons exports in support of friendly states were and still are important to these powers not only for economic reasons, but also because they are used as an important foreign and security policy instrument.

Another problem with the Wassenaar Agreement for Switzerland was the control of machinery tool exports. Only high precision machinery is contained on the Dual-Use Goods and Technologies List. This affects Swiss producers and puts them at a disadvantage relative to foreign competition. For this reason the Swiss demanded that controls be placed on either none, all or only those machine tools that are built specifically for the production of weapons. After a long struggle, a solution acceptable to Switzerland was reached in 2002.

Switzerland continues to support export controls, but the relevant authorities feel that it would make sense to conduct a comprehensive review of the various lists involved in the four export control arrangements. The lists were created more than a decade ago, and an increasing number of controlled items are available outside the participating states. Foreign availability in particular should be given greater importance. Export control lists should not expand indiscriminately and randomly, placing an increased burden on both the authorities and the industries affected. Instead, the focus should be placed on key goods and technologies that are indispensable to the development and production of weapons of mass destruction. Export control regimes should be improved in terms of quality rather than quantity.

7.2.8 Shaping an arms control policy

Switzerland gradually developed an arms control policy only after the end of the Cold War. Disarmament and non-proliferation policy became an important instrument of Swiss foreign policy and a cornerstone of its commitment to security and peace. The shift can in the main be attributed to a change in the government's concept of security. The new threat analysis, along with the cost factor and limited technical and financial resources, led to a growing recognition that one nation alone cannot counter the new risks and dangers. Facing new security threats successfully demands international co-operation.[59] For a small state like Switzerland it is important that international policy rests upon reliable and predictable procedures and regulations and that the rights of the mighty be qualified by international obligations.[60] It is therefore the goal of Swiss arms control policy to promote international security and stability at the lowest possible level of armament.

In response to a request by the Swiss parliament, the government in the mid 1990s for the first time defined principles to guide arms control and disarmament policy.[61] Three areas of emphasis were defined: (1) implementation and further development of international legal norms; (2) improvement of export controls in the area of sensitive goods and technologies; and (3) measures towards eliminating the sources of conflict that can lead to the proliferation of weapons of mass destruction.

The establishment of arms control as an instrument of foreign and security policy triggered a process of institution building on the part of the Swiss administration. Appropriate divisions and offices were created within the Department of Foreign Affairs and the Department of Defence. Through the new structuring, responsibilities were assigned to specific authorities, and the necessary specialized competency was built up, allowing Switzerland to engage actively and successfully in international arms control processes. With the implementation of the Chemical Weapons Convention and export controls in the mid 1990s, the administration faced new tasks calling for additional human resources. Export controls are now mainly the task of the Ministry of Economics, which means that an additional department is involved.

Successful implementation of international commitments and obligations and continued active participation in ongoing arms control processes requires considerable interdepartmental co-operation. Co-ordination is assumed by various offices depending on the specific issue at hand. This means that the shaping of policy takes place in an interdepartmental negotiation process. Not infrequently diverging foreign trade and security interests have to be integrated into a comprehensive policy. This is the reason why Swiss arms control and disarmament policy at times suffers from a certain degree of incoherence.

Conclusions

As has been pointed out, the end of the Cold War marks a break in Swiss arms control and disarmament policy. Since the 1980s Switzerland, once an observer adhering strictly to a defensive posture, has become an active and reliable partner in multilateral efforts towards arms control. This development was triggered essentially by foreign developments, but domestic factors were also relevant.

With the end of the East–West confrontation, a multitude of new opportunities for co-operation arose in the area of arms control and disarmament. The multilateralisation of international relations opened up opportunities for participation that Switzerland had lacked during the Cold War. As a state party to the Biological and Toxins Weapons Convention, for example, Switzerland could participate as an equal partner in the meetings of the Ad Hoc Group to draft the BTWC protocol. For the negotiations leading the ban on anti-personnel landmines, a process outside established arms control channels was initiated that Switzerland was free to join, even though it was a member of neither the United Nations nor the Conference on Disarmament.

At the domestic level, arms control and disarmament was no longer seen as a cosmetic measure having no practical benefit or, as in the case of the NPT, as a treaty limiting the country's freedom of action. Instead, efforts in this area were seen to contribute to Switzerland's own security. Accordingly, Switzerland began to work actively towards the shaping of arms control treaties stipulating equal rights and obligations for all and containing effective verification mechanisms. Economic and security interests were weighed carefully. During the Cold War the main objective had been to keep all possible options open – including, for instance, procurement of nuclear weapons for the Swiss Armed Forces. It was from this defensive position that Switzerland had often, and in most cases unsuccessfully, attempted to influence ongoing negotiation processes at the last moment.

In the area of export controls, Switzerland went through a long learning process. In the Cold War years, importing fissionable material for peaceful as well as military purposes proved to be arduous. As a non-member of the NTP, it became more and more difficult to assure the civilian demand for fissionable material and equipment necessary to operate nuclear power plants. A real solution to the problem came only with NPT ratification. But Switzerland also encountered problems in its role as an exporting state. The adaptation of domestic laws to conform to international commitments and obligations occurred only gradually. In the 1980s and 1990s, Switzerland came under considerable international pressure regarding problematic exports of dual-use goods, which in some cases led to actual or threatened sanctions against Swiss companies.

Since the mid 1990s the development of multilateral arms controls has stagnated. The CTBT, which opened for signature in 1996, has still not entered into force, because a number of countries have yet to ratify it. For years, the Conference on Disarmament has not made progress; the negotiations on the protocol to strengthen the Biological Weapons Convention failed. Moreover, the United States' tendency towards unilateralism has increased recently. In the present environment, it will be more and more difficult for Switzerland to continue to play an active role.

As long as there is a lack of political will in key states to negotiate further arms control agreements, there will be little opportunity to overcome the present stagnation. In the current setting, Switzerland will have to work to defend existing arms control treaties against tendencies towards their weakening. At home, it will have to continue to maintain its own expertise. Should the current stagnation in arms control and disarmament be overcome, Switzerland should be ready to support multilateral arms control in order to further its own interests. This it can do with success, if it is able to discover and occupy niches where it possesses specialized expertise. For the moment, however, Swiss arms control policy is left with the mere hope of better times.

Acknowledgements

The author would like to thank Jon A. Fanzun, Jürg Martin Gabriel and Jonathan Murphy for their comments on and help with the manuscript.

Notes

1 Switzerland acceded to the UN only in 2002. In the Geneva Conference on Disarmament Switzerland obtained observer status in 1980 and became a full member in 1996.

2 Peter Hug, *Biologische und chemische Waffen in der Schweiz zwischen Aussen-, Wissenschafts- und Militärpolitik*, Studien und Quellen 23 (Bern: Schweizerisches Bundesarchiv, 1997), pp. 24–34.

3 This treaty bans nuclear weapons tests in the atmosphere, in outerspace and under water.

4 *Botschaft des Bundesrates an die Bundesversammlung betreffend die Genehmigung des in Moskau geschlossenen Abkommens über das Verbot von Kernwaffenversuchen in der Luft, im Weltraum und unter Wasser vom 13. September 1963*, p. 620; see also *Vorarbeiten zum Bericht über die Abrüstungs- und Rüstungskontrollpolitik der Schweiz vom September 1995*, p. 10. This preliminary report reflects the view of the administration it was never formally adopted by the Federal Council.

5 Gary T. Gardner, *Nuclear Nonproliferation: A Primer* (Boulder/London: Lynne Rienner Publishers, 1994), pp. 38–9.

6 Bilateral co-operation agreements were concluded with France, Canada, United Kingdom, Brazil, Sweden and the United States.

7 Nicolas Michel, *La prolifération nucléaire: Le régime de non-prolifération des armes nucléaires et la Suisse* (Fribourg: Editions Universitaires Fribourg, 1990), p. 265; Theodor H. Winkler, *Kernenergie und Aussenpolitik: Die internationalen Bemühungen um eine Nichtweiterverbreitung von Kernwaffen und die friedliche Nutzung von Kernenergie in der Schweiz* (Berlin: Berlin Verlag, 1981), pp. 53–60.

8 Winkler, *Kernenergie und Aussenpolitik*, pp. 152–61 and Michel, *La prolifération nucléaire*, pp. 43–53.

9 Winkler, *Kernenergie und Aussenpolitik*, pp. 221–2.

10 Winkler, *Kernenergie und Aussenpolitik*, pp. 252–7.

11 On the occasion of the Review Conference in 1975 the States Parties worked towards tightening the treaty provisions in the area of nuclear activities against non-member states in order to create a negative incentive for the outsiders to enter the treaty. See also Winkler, *Kernenergie und Aussenpolitik*, p. 288.

12 The Swiss reservation contained three aspects as follows: (1) The use of nuclear energy for peaceful purposes is exempted from the prohibitions contained in the Articles I and II of the NPT; (2) It is Switzerland's understanding that the definition of 'source or special fissionable material' (Article III, 2 NPT) corresponds with the respective Article in the IAEA statute and each new interpretation requires Switzerland's consent; (3) The implementation of the Treaty on the Non-Proliferation of Nuclear Weapons, especially its control measures, does not discriminate Swiss industry in international trade.

13 Winkler, *Kernenergie und Aussenpolitik*, pp. 315–6. Almost simultaneously Switzerland ratified the Treaty on the Prohibition of the Emplacement of Nuclear Weapons and Other Weapons of Mass Destruction on the Seabed and the Ocean Floor and in the Subsoil Thereof.

14 Hug, *Biologische und chemische Waffen*, pp. 102–3.

15 The degree of universality was defined as follows: the superpowers, if possible all countries in Europe, especially the neighbouring countries of Switzerland and the countries having a well developed chemical and/or biological industry. See *Botschaft betreffend das Übereinkommen über das Verbot der Entwicklung, Herstellung,*

Lagerung und des Einsatzes chemischer Waffen und über die Vernichtung solcher Waffen vom 20. April 1994, p. 16.

16 Thus based on the erroneous assumption that there were no significant offensive biological weapons programmes existent and therefore no verification measures needed. The situation was different in the area of chemical weapons. Several states were already known to possess chemical weapons, and this constituted a need for verification and control.

17 Hug, *Biologische und chemische Waffen*, p. 105.

18 *Botschaft des Bundesrates an die Bundesversammlung betreffend zwei Abkommen gegen Massenvernichtungswaffen auf und unter dem Meeresgrund und biologische und Toxinwaffen vom 17. Januar 1973*, p. 303.

19 First, Switzerland reserved the right to define what weapons, equipments and means of delivery would be subject to the BTWC's prohibition for operating resources of biological weapons. Second, for neutrality reasons the Swiss wanted to keep the option of not obeying a possible request of the UN Security Council to support states parties that suffered from an attack with biological weapons.

20 Neutral countries: Austria, Finland, Sweden, and Switzerland; non-aligned countries: Cyprus, Liechtenstein, Malta, San Marino and Yugoslavia.

21 On the early phase of Swiss CSCE commitment, see: Christoph Breitenmoser, *Sicherheit für Europa: Die KSZE-Politik der Schweiz bis zur Unterzeichnung der Helsinki-Schlussakte zwischen Skepsis und aktiven Engagement*, Zürcher Beiträge zur Sicherheitspolitik und Konfliktforschung 40 (Zürich: Forschungsstelle für Sicherheitspolitik und Konfliktanalyse der ETH Zürich, 1996); Hans-Jörg Renk, *Der Weg der Schweiz nach Helsinki: Der Beitrag der schweizerischen Diplomatie zum Zustandekommen der Konferenz über Sicherheit und Zusammenarbeit in Europa (KSZE), 1972–1975* (Bern/Stuttgart/Wien: Paul Haupt, 1996).

22 Fred Tanner, *Die Schweiz und Rüstungskontrolle: Grenzen und Möglichkeiten eines Kleinstaates*, Zürcher Beiträge zur Sicherheitspolitik und Konfliktforschung 14 (Zürich: Forschungsstelle für Sicherheitspolitik und Konfliktanalyse der ETH Zürich, 1990), pp. 4–7.

23 Tanner, *Die Schweiz und Rüstungskontrolle*, p. 5.

24 André Schaller, *Schweizer Neutralität im West-Ost-Handel: Das Hotz-Linder-Agreement vom 23. Juli 1951* (Bern/Stuttgart: Verlag Paul Haupt, 1987).

25 Jürg Martin Gabriel, *The American Conception of Neutrality after 1941* (New York: Macmillan, 1988), pp. 116–22.

26 The committee was given the name of Prof. Dr Claude Zangger. As a member of Swiss delegation he contributed significantly to the resolution of a variety of export control questions.

27 Canada, France, Germany, Japan, the United Kingdom, United States and the Soviet Union participated in this process.

28 Tanner, *Die Schweiz und Rüstungskontrolle*, pp. 15–17.

29 'Für unbegrenzte Verlängerung des Atomsperrvertrages: Forderung der Schweiz nach fortgesetzter nuklearer Abrüstung', *NZZ*, 21 April 1995, p. 13.

30 'Die Schweiz bedauert', *NZZ*, 15 June 1995, p. 13; 'Protest gegen Frankreichs Atomtestpläne', *NZZ*, 23 June 1995, p. 18; 'Der Bundesrat bedauert französische Atomtests', *NZZ*, 6 September 1995, p. 13.

31 *Vorarbeiten zum Bericht über die Abrüstungs- und Rüstungskontrollpolitik der Schweiz vom September 1995*, p. 11.

32 Ad Hoc Group of the State Parties to the Convention on the Prohibition of the Development, Production and Stockpiling of Bacteriological (Biological) and Toxin Weapons and their Destruction: henceforth Ad Hoc Group.

33 United Nations Special Commission (on Iraq).

34 For a survey of the CWC negotiations, see: Perry J. P. Robinson, Thomas Stock and Ronald G. Sutherland, 'The Chemical Weapons Convention: the Success of Chemical Disarmament Negotiations', in *SIPRI Yearbook 1993 on World Armaments and Disarmament* (Oxford: Oxford University Press, 1993), pp. 705–34.

35 The Spiez Laboratory is part of the Federal Department of Defence. On the one hand, the Lab is involved in research in the area of protection against NBC weapons, and on the other hand, its experts have since 1990 also been involved in providing technical support to the Swiss delegations in various ongoing arms control negotiations.

36 Marcel Gerber, 'Schweizerische Rüstungskontrollpolitik in einem neuen internationalen Umfeld: Das innovative Engagement für ein Personenminen-Verbot als Modell für die Zukunft?', in Kurt R. Spillmann and Andreas Wenger (ed.), *Bulletin 1999 zur schweizerischen Sicherheitspolitik* (Zürich: Forschungsstelle für Sicherheitspolitik und Konfliktanalyse der ETH Zürich, 1999), p. 84.

37 The members of the core group were: Belgium, Canada, Germany, Mexico, Norway, Philippines and South Africa.

38 Lucius Caflisch, 'Ist ein Totalverbot von Personenminen in Sicht? Vor der nächsten Runde im Ottawa-Prozess', *NZZ*, 21 August 1997, p. 7.

39 *Botschaft betreffend das Übereinkommen über das Verbot des Einsatzes, der Lagerung, der Herstellung und der Weitergabe von Anti-Personenminen und über deren Vernichtung vom 19. Januar 1998*, BBl 1998 IV 10.

40 David C. Atwood, *Tackling the Problem of Anti-Personnel Landmines: Issues and Developments*, Zürcher Beiträge zur Sicherheitspolitik und Konfliktforschung 51 (Zürich: Forschungsstelle für Sicherheitspolitik und Konfliktanalyse der ETH Zürich, 1999).

41 Protocol Against the Illicit Manufacturing of and Trafficking in Firearms, Their Parts and Components and Ammunition.

42 OSCE Document on Small Arms and Light Weapons, adopted by the 308th Plenary Meeting of the OSCE Forum for Security Cooperation (FSC) on 24 November 2000.

43 Federal Department of Defence, Civil Protection and Sports: Press release from 24 June 1999: Begrenzung von Kleinwaffen – Internationales Treffen mit Vertretern der Rüstungsindustrie.

44 Swiss Federal Department of Foreign Affairs: *Chairman's Report on the Workshop on small arms monitoring and control 22/23 November 1999, Geneva.*

45 From January 1999 to March 2001 at the UN Centre for International Crime Prevention in Vienna, Switzerland took an active part in the negotiations on a firearms protocol, formally titled the Protocol Against the Illicit Manufacturing of and Trafficking in Firearms, Their Parts and Components and Ammunition to the UN Convention Against Transnational Organized Crime. Switzerland worked towards the marking of weapons that would make them traceable.

46 The Vienna Document of 1990 contained primarily an expansion of the information exchange, of the verification system and a new form of communication and consultation mechanisms. At the same time annual meetings of all CSCE countries were insititutionalized in order to discuss the implementation of the current and future confidence building measures.

47 With this Document the information exchange was again expanded, which constituted above all an improvement of the 1990 Vienna Document.

48 Tanner, *Die Schweiz und Rüstungskontrolle*, p. 6f.

49 The Forum for Security Co-operation is about a permanent institution dealing with questions of arms control, disarmament, confidence and security building

and conflict prevention. There are weekly meetings of the Forum in Vienna. Its work, taking place under alternating chairmanship, aims at enhancing the security co-operation among member states.

50 Based on a Swiss initiative, 23 countries founded in October 2000 the Geneva Centre for the Democratic Control of Armed Forces (GCDCAF). Switzerland aided the formation of the Centre with major financial contributions.

51 In 1994 the CSCE was renamed OSCE – Organisation for Security and Co-operation in Europe.

52 'OSZE-Präsidium: das Positive überwiegt', *NZZ*, 21 December 1996, p. 11.

53 On the Swiss chairmanship of the OSCE, compare Laurent Goetschel (ed.), *Vom Statisten zum Hauptdarsteller: Die Schweiz und ihre OSZE-Präsidentschaft* (Bern/Stuttgart/Wien: Paul Haupt, 1997).

54 To comply with the respective verification measures Switzerland would have to disclose all its national installations for defence, thus causing major concerns from a military point of view.

55 Sicherheits- und Verteidigungspolitik, Informationsabteilung: *Factsheet zur Rüstungskontroll- und Abrüstungspolitik der Schweiz vom Februar 2001.*

56 The important factors for the revival of the NSG were the detection of the secret Iraqi nuclear weapons program and the recommendations of the 1990 NPT Review Conference to reinforce the nuclear non-proliferation regime. The existence of the Iraqi nuclear weapons program revealed the limits and defects of the export control measures in place.

57 *Transshipment* means a transfer whereby an export from state A to state B goes through state C. This kind of transfer can be problematic if the export control measures of state C are either insufficient or non-existent and State B is a potential proliferator.

58 *Risk assessment* is about assessing the risk of the transfer of a specific good to a specific end-user in a given country.

59 *Swiss Security Policy in Times of Change: Report 90 of the Federal Council to the Federal Assembly on the security policy of Switzerland of October 1, 1990*, p. 10, 32, 38 (http://www.ssn.ethz.ch/ssnlinkslib/documents/report90.htm). And *Security through Cooperation: Report of the Federal Council to the Federal Assembly on the Security Policy of Switzerland (Report 2000)*, Released on 7 June 1999 (http://www.vbs.admin.ch/internet/SIPOL2000/E/index.htm).

60 Erwin Dahinden, 'Rüstungskontrolle und Kriegsvölkerrecht: schweizerische Sicherheitskooperation mit Leistungsausweis', in Hans Eberhart and Albert A. Stahel (ed.), *Schweizerische Militärpolitik der Zukunft. Sicherheitsgewinn durch stärkeres internationales Engagement* (Zürich: NZZ Verlag, 2000), p. 180.

61 (1) Armament is a consequence (and not a reason) of conflicts; (2) In the long run Switzerland strives for the complete and universal disarmament of all weapons of mass destruction; (3) In the field of conventional weapons and armed forces, Switzerland supports measures that contribute to transparency and predictability of military activities and troops and foster defensive structures while guaranteeing the security of all states; (4) Switzerland has a strong preference for multilateral, legally binding, balanced and verifiable treaties and co-operative approaches as compared to unilateral and only politically binding measures; (5) Switzerland takes account of its status of neutrality and the obligations resulting from this status. *Bericht des Bundesrates über die Rüstungskontroll- und Abrüstungspolitik der Schweiz vom 31. Januar 1996*, pp. 1–2. And *Bericht des Bundesrates über die Rüstungskontroll- und Abrüstungspolitik der Schweiz vom 30. August 2000.*

8
Swiss Foreign Trade Policy

Richard Senti

Introduction

A nation's foreign trade policy is the expression of the government's activity or inactivity. It consists of taking or avoiding certain measures. It is also a function of the political and economic circumstances prevailing both at home and abroad, and it is influenced by the constitution and a specific set of goals. In a market-oriented economy, the state intervenes only where actors encounter difficulties that they cannot handle alone. Among other things, the state may enter into international agreements to remove tariff and non-tariff trade barriers thereby supporting the private sector in a complementary way.[1]

In a planned economy, the state goes beyond supporting the trading partners of private industry. It takes decisions, such as fixing prices, that could be handled by private companies. Market conditions also determine international trade policy. A highly developed international market with many multinational corporations and a significant international capital market demand different policies than a market mainly oriented towards the inside.

As mentioned, international trade policy is also determined by a state's objectives, which in turn are defined by the prevailing legal framework and by the administration itself. The Swiss Federal Constitution requires the government to safeguard national independence, promote welfare, alleviate global suffering, work towards peaceful co-existence and safeguard natural resources for future generations.[2] Accordingly, the Federal Council has emphasised in some of its proclamations that the first and lasting goal of Swiss international trade policy is to promote the country's peaceful prosperity.[3]

The goals set forth in the constitution and in official announcements do not preclude administrators and politicians from pursuing their own objectives. Elected politicians and public officials make sure that international economic relations will secure their re-election or, where there are term limits, will maintain their party in power. Whatever goals politicians follow, they take care to hide their own political ambitions behind professions of altruism and go to great lengths to convince the public that measures taken serve solely the general welfare.[4]

My discussion of Swiss foreign trade policy is organised in four parts. The first part provides key data on *foreign trade* and a brief overview of the organisation of the administrative offices involved. The second part examines the agricultural sector, the third part the sector of *industrial* goods and the fourth part the *service* sector. I close with some remarks on the new orientation of foreign trade policy in recent years.

8.1 Basic data and organisation

Let me begin with some *basic data* on Swiss foreign trade and a few remarks about its administrative organisation. Although Switzerland is a comparatively small country both in population and geography, foreign trade is considerable. Switzerland comes after the European Union (EU), the United States, Japan and Canada as one of the world's ten most important trading partners, both in imports and exports. Switzerland's share in world trade in goods lies between 1.5 and 2 per cent, and in the services sector at about 2 per cent. Cross-border trade in services (tourism, finance, insurance and transportation) is particularly significant, with a share of 30 per cent of trade in goods. In comparison, the worldwide average is approximately 20 per cent.[5]

As early as the 1940s and 1950s, Switzerland showed a considerable volume of foreign trade. Many states damaged by the war were rebuilding their economies and showing, relative to the low reference values, high growth rates. Over the last decades, annual Swiss growth rates have reached world averages and stand for trade in goods at about 5 per cent and in services at about 6 per cent.

Moreover, the Swiss economy, like that of Canada and Norway, is internationally highly interdependent. For years, the export value of all the three countries has made up between 25 and 35 per cent of the gross domestic product (GDP). In Australia and New Zealand the export value lies between 15 and 20 per cent, while that of the EU, Japan and the United States stays between 8 and 10 per cent. The Organisation for Economic Cooperation and Development (OECD) assumes an average level of 13 per cent of foreign trade for industrial nations.

Table 8.1 shows that Switzerland has traditionally had a trade deficit. In recent years, the negative balance has decreased. In contrast, the service balance has been positive since the 1950s. The declining deficit in the area of goods, along with the simultaneous surplus in services, has in the last two decades resulted in a favourable contribution by external trade to the GDP.

Switzerland has also assumed multiple commitments by joining international organisations and signing agreements. The country has been a

Table 8.1 Foreign trade of Switzerland in billion Swiss francs (current prices)

Year	Goods			Services			Balance
	Export	Import	Balance	Export	Import	Balance	I + II
1950	3.9	4.5	−0.6	0.9	0.4	0.5	−0.1
1960	8.1	9.6	−1.5	2.3	0.9	1.4	−0.1
1970	22.1	27.9	−5.8	6.5	2.7	3.8	−2.0
1980	49.6	60.9	−11.3	12.0	6.6	5.4	−5.9
1990	88.3	96.6	−8.3	24.0	12.8	11.2	2.9
2000	126.5	128.6	−2.1	45.8	23.2	22.6	20.5

Source: Bundesamt für Statistik, *Statistisches Jahrbuch der Schweiz* (Zürich: NZZ Verlag, annual).

member of the OECD (formerly OEEC) since 1947 and signed the General Agreement on Tariffs and Trade (GATT) in 1958, which became the World Trade Organization (WTO) in 1995. Switzerland joined the European Free Trade Area (EFTA) in 1960 and in 1972 signed a Free Trade Agreement with the European Economic Community (EEC), which later became the European Community (EC).

In 1992, Switzerland joined the Bretton Woods Institutions (International Monetary Fund and the World Bank). It also signed many international agreements on raw materials (coffee, cacao) and the agreements on protection of intellectual property rights (Paris Convention, Berne Union, etc.). At the same time, as do other countries, Switzerland maintains a number of bilateral agreements with its trading partners.

Let me turn next to the *organisational* side of foreign trade. It is the Federal Government that has primary responsibility for Switzerland's international economic affairs. Paragraph 1 of Article 101 of the Constitution states that the Federal Government protects the interests of the Swiss economy abroad. Paragraph 2 gives power to the Confederation to decide on measures deviating from free trade, if necessary, in order to protect the domestic economy.

It is meaningless to separate general foreign policy from international trade policy. Foreign policy encompasses international trade just as much as international trade requires the backing of foreign policy. Their interaction explains why external trade issues have over time been assigned either to the Federal Department of Foreign Affairs or of Economic Affairs. The organisation has had less to do with the matter concerned than with the inclinations of the various ministers making up the Federal Council.[6]

In the 1920s, foreign trade was assigned to the Federal Department of Economic Affairs.[7] This is the case till today. In 1979, the Commerce Division was renamed the Federal Office for International Trade,[8] and on 1 July 1999, it became the State Secretariat for Economic Affairs (Seco). Seco is headed by a State Secretary and divided into five branches:[9]

- The Office of *World Trade* handling matters affecting WTO, OECD, EFTA and export controls;
- The *Integration Office*, to maintain EU relations; this office is also part of the Department of Foreign Affairs;
- The Office of *Development & Transition* dealing with the relations to developing and transition countries (Third World and Eastern Europe);
- The Office of *Promotion Activities* co-ordinating domestic and foreign trade promotion;
- The *Directorate of Labour* with two sub-departments, one on Working Conditions and another dealing with the Labour Market and Unemployment Insurance.

At present Seco has a staff of about 550 persons. It is not possible to compare foreign trade administration across countries due to the different forms of organisation of the departments.

8.2 Trade in agricultural products

8.2.1 Data and facts

When looking at the development of Swiss agricultural trade in the last half-century, it is useful to distinguish between the post-Second World War phase of protectionism and the gradual opening of the market starting in the 1980s. Furthermore, statistics for this period highlight three main agricultural features: a low level of self-sufficiency and the related deficit in the trade balance, a constant structural change in the products traded and a concentration on a few trading partners.[10]

For many years, the level of Swiss self-sufficiency remained at about 60 per cent, in contrast to 90 per cent and higher in other industrialised nations. Two-fifths of domestic foodstuff requirements are imported. Besides non-seasonal and exotic products, Switzerland imports staples like cereals, flour, sugar, animal products, vegetables and fruits like apples and pears. No OECD country has as high a per capita import of agricultural goods as Switzerland, while exports in the same field are modest. In the 1950s, ten times more agricultural products were imported (in value) than exported. Today the import/export ratio is five to one.

A second special feature of Swiss agricultural trade is its structural change. In 1950, the most important agricultural goods exported were hard cheese (71.5 per cent), flour for baby formulas (10.2 per cent), fruit (5.4 per cent), cattle (4.8 per cent), condensed milk (2.6 per cent) and other goods (5.5 per cent). In the late 1990s, these five products made up 42.7 per cent (of which 35.2 per cent was cheese), while 57.3 per cent of all exports were distributed among products such as canned vegetables and fruits, fruit juices, coffee products, fats and oils, meats and meat products, milling products and fresh vegetables.

Imports show a similar pattern of development. Just after the Second World War, animal products, cereals, vegetables and sugar made up about 80 per cent of imports. Today those products make up just 20 per cent. Instead, the main imports are processed foods like fresh fruit, canned fruit and vegetables, and a continuing rise in the import volume of cheese, seafood and wines.

A third feature of Swiss agricultural trade is its strong concentration on neighbouring countries, that is, the EU market. In the last five years, nearly 60 per cent of agricultural exports have gone to the 15 EU member states. At the same time, almost 80 per cent of all agricultural imports stem from EU countries. The remaining imports and exports are distributed about equally to Asia and North America, whereby trade relations with Asia have weakened recently while trade with North America has somewhat increased. Agricultural trade with Africa, Australia and New Zealand is modest.

8.2.2 Protectionist phase

Up to the 1930s, the legal basis of Swiss agricultural policy rested almost exclusively on decrees of a technical and public health nature regulating, for example, animal diseases and alcohol consumption. A constitutional re-orientation occurred following the Second World War when Art. 31bis authorised the Confederation to issue regulations deviating from the free market in order to maintain a healthy farming community and efficient agriculture.

The Agricultural Law of 1951 and its revision in 1998 rested on that constitutional basis. In the new constitution that is valid today the basis is Art. 104. It authorises the Federal Government to ensure that agriculture, through sustainable, market-oriented production, contributes to a secure food supply, to the conservation of natural resources and the environment and to specific forms of rural planning and settlement.

In the 1950s and 1960s, Switzerland's agricultural policy was the result of the emergency wartime situation. Highest priority was given to the securing of an optimal degree of self-sufficiency possible within the limits of Swiss natural resources. Following this objective, Art. 22 of the 1951 Agricultural Law authorised the Federal Council to (a) restrict the volume of imports of agro-food products, (b) increase tariffs on the non-quota volume of comparable products and (c) require importers to buy comparable domestic products. If an agricultural sector should be threatened by foreign competition in spite of these measures, the Federal Council had the authority to increase import prices and to levy compensation payments.

In the years following, the Federal Council set import quotas for slaughter animals, meat, wine, potatoes and flowers; it required the buying of domestic products when importing eggs, powdered whole milk and lactic acid casein; it instituted a so-called three-phase system for fresh fruit, vegetables and berries; it increased prices and taxes on animal feed, fats and oils, butter, cream, condensed milk and powdered skim milk; and it introduced monopolistic regulations for butter and alcohol. Complementary to the import regulations, Art. 23 contained regulations for agricultural exports. The Confederation was obligated to subsidise the exporting of cattle, animal and dairy products, and products from domestic fruit growers and wine producers.

The official justification for taking these measures was to keep Swiss agricultural self-sufficiency at the maximum. However, it is reasonable to assume that export subsidies for cattle and dairy products (cheese) mainly served the purpose of agricultural income maintenance and had little to do with self-sufficiency.

This situation explains Switzerland's agricultural policy in three instances: in the *integration negotiations* of the 1950s, in the *GATT negotiations* of the 1950s and 1960s and in negotiations on the *Free Trade Agreement* with the EEC in the 1960s and 1970s.

With respect to *European integration*, the Federal Council came to the conclusion that the EEC was incompatible with 'democratic traditions as anchored in the constitution' and would result in Switzerland losing its ability to shape its own foreign trade policy. In addition to the general EEC objections, agricultural policy also played an important role. Membership in the EEC, according to the Federal Council, would make Switzerland's agriculture subordinate to the EEC's common agricultural policy. This would prevent Swiss agriculture from fulfilling its obligation to feed the population in times of war. Moreover, EEC membership would restrict Switzerland's ability to influence prices on imported agricultural goods.[11]

In retrospect, the argumentation is hardly convincing. Agricultural production did not decline in any of the EEC founding member states. In addition, imports of cheap animal feed led to surplus production, which had to be sold abroad with subsidies. This hardly made economic sense. However, Swiss agricultural interest groups feared the EEC's low producer prices, particularly in the area of meat and milk, and they also dreaded the structural changes this would imply.

In the negotiations leading up to the creation of a European Free Trade Area (EFTA), Switzerland also made sure that the general removal of duties and non-tariff restrictions would not affect agriculture. The future EFTA partners therefore agreed upon Art. 21ff of the EFTA Convention that free trade conditions would not be applied to the agricultural sector. In its Third Report on the National Economy of 10 December 1965, the Federal Council was happy to announce that as part of the EFTA negotiations it had reached special bilateral trade agreements in agricultural products with Denmark and Portugal. Hence, agriculture would not be affected adversely permitting it 'to make the required adjustments in an orderly fashion and to continue to fulfil its obligation to secure national self-sufficiency'.[12]

The Swiss government defended the same position towards the GATT in the 1950s and 1960s and again in its dealings with the EEC in the 1960s and 1970s. When the GATT was founded in the 1940s, Switzerland had declined to join for two reasons: it feared restrictions in the area of exchange rates,[13] and it was unwilling to allow its agricultural policy to be determined by Art. XI of the GATT, that is, to link its import volume restrictions to GATT conditions.[14] During the 1950s negotiations on provisional GATT membership, Switzerland again succeeded in obtaining preferential treatment in agriculture. Switzerland reserved the right to levy price and tariff increases as well as other duties. These reservations are part of the 22 November 1958 protocol on the provisional GATT accession of Switzerland.[15]

Despite its provisional membership status, Switzerland participated in the Dillon Round (1961–2) and the Kennedy Round (1964–7). During these two rounds, Switzerland entered into negotiations with the EEC and the United States on agricultural trade.[16] The protocol on definitive Swiss accession to the GATT of 1 April 1966, shows that Switzerland had succeeded in upholding its protectionist position in agriculture. The Tokyo Round (1973–9) also resulted in no change to agricultural protection policy.[17]

Switzerland again defended its traditional agricultural protection during the negotiations with the EEC leading up to the 1972 Free Trade Agreement. Some EEC members wanted a balanced agreement including industrial and agricultural free trade. Switzerland, however, referred to its traditional high volume of imports from the EEC market and demanded reciprocity in the agricultural sector. It rejected a package that would make industrial free trade dependent upon agricultural concessions. Ultimately, the deal excluded agriculture – in analogy to the EFTA Convention. According to Art. 2 of the 1972 agreement it does not apply to tariff positions 1 through 24 (agricultural products). It was agreed that individual problems would be handled on a case-by-case basis, as had been done in the past. To this day there has been no change to these basic provisions.[18]

8.2.3 Steps towards market opening

The first significant shift in Swiss agricultural trade policy occurred in the 1980s in the context of creating the European Economic Area (EEA). In April 1984, EFTA and EC ministers signed an agreement to create a dynamic European Economic Area.[19] It was to extend beyond trade in industrial products and to encompass agricultural products and foodstuffs.

Proposed changes included reduction of tariffs on agro-foods from economically less developed EC states (sweet peppers and courgettes from the Mediterranean countries), mutual increases in cheese quotas (additional Swiss import quotas for Roquefort and Gorgonzola cheeses in exchange for higher EEA import quotas for Swiss Raclette and Tomme cheeses), a lowering of Swiss tariffs on potted plants and cut flowers and elimination of Swiss import duties on foreign alcoholic spirits (the discussion focused on *Kirsch*). An evolution clause stipulated that agricultural trade would be reassessed every two years, beginning in 1993.[20] However, the Swiss voters rejected the EEA agreement in December 1992, and the negotiated agricultural compromises were not implemented.

Following the rejection, Switzerland proposed *bilateral and sectoral negotiations* with the EU in the areas of scientific research, technical barriers to trade, government procurement, and air and road transport. The EU was willing to negotiate on condition that the free movement of labour and trade in agriculture would be included in the discussions. The Swiss government in December 1994 approved a mandate providing for graduated sector-by-sector process of liberalisation that would accord with Switzerland's WTO obligations and take full account of Swiss objectives of maintaining efficient agriculture and a healthy farming community.

The Federal Council rejected any farther-reaching opening of the agricultural market. Moreover, the liberalisation of agricultural trade had to be adapted to the realisation of the Agricultural Reform Programme 2002 ('AP 2002', maintenance of the production volume). The technical details of the agreement were settled in June 1998, and in December the treaty came into force. Parliament and the voters approved the bilateral treaties in October 1999 and May 2000, respectively.

The *Bilateral Agricultural Agreement* contains a framework agreement and 11 annexes. The framework agreement regulates certification of origin of goods and institutional issues. The annexes contain concessions for specific products. The central part of the agreement concerns cheese, which is of existential importance for Swiss agriculture and some EU member states. Bilateral trade in cheese is scheduled to be completely liberalised (no import duties, no quotas) five years after the agreement comes into force. The agreement on specialty meats (dried ham and beef) foresees a slightly modified continuation of existing agreements, where not affected by food safety regulations and border 'Mad Cow Desease' (BSE) controls in the individual countries.

Concessions concerning fruits and vegetables, in the form of duty-free tariff rate quotas and duty reductions, pertain to specific product areas where individual markets have export and protection interests. For the wine trade, there are guarantees for labels of origin. Further agreements concern protection of plants and controls on animal feed and seed. No matter how individual interest groups assess the results of the negotiations, there is no doubt that these agreements – for the first time – bring change into the previously closed agricultural market. There is a danger, however, that the more than 300 pages of detailed and complicated regulations will 'liberalise' agricultural market 'to death'.

At the same time that the EEA and EC negotiations were underway, there were efforts by the GATT to include an agreement on agriculture in its framework. This initiative was a reaction to some GATT contracting parties formerly exempting agriculture from world trade regulations (the United States insisted upon and received an open-ended waiver from its GATT obligations for quotas and other restrictions in 1955). This affected existing regulations, like the levy system of the EEA in 1958, or special arrangements such as Switzerland's 1958 protocol of accession.

The Punta del Este Ministerial Declaration on the Uruguay Round in 1986 declared that the 'contracting parties agree that there is an urgent need to bring more discipline and predictability to world agricultural trade by correcting and preventing restrictions and distortions'. The declaration also stated the following objectives: 'to achieve greater liberalisation of trade in agriculture...to improve the competitive environment...and to minimize the adverse effects that sanitary and phytosanitary regulations and barriers have on trade in agriculture.' [21]

The first half of the *Uruguay Round* (1986–8) set up a negotiating group having primary responsibility for all aspects of agriculture. It issued a text on agriculture with three main clauses during the mid-term review of the Round (1988–90): removal of technical barriers to trade; freeze on current levels of domestic support, export subsidies and border protections; and common agreement on application of sanitary and phytosanitary measures. During the attempt to revive the Uruguay Round (1990–3), the negotiations delegates agreed upon the Agriculture Agreement that is valid today.[22] The agreement planned to initiate a reform process in international agricultural trade leading to additional liberalisation measures within six years after entry into force of the agreement.

WTO membership forced Switzerland to recognise the Agriculture Agreement and to give up the exceptions that had been granted under the protocol for the accession of Switzerland to the GATT. Three core issues are involved: market access, domestic price supports and export subsidies.

As to *market access*, Switzerland opened its borders by instituting tariffs and non-tariff barriers (such as quotas) and by reducing duties by an average of 36 per cent (15 per cent minimum). However, in order to protect Swiss agriculture from overly harsh foreign competition, Switzerland, like many other governments, transformed previous restrictions on import volumes into tariff quotas. Tariff quotas exist to this day on live animals, meat, cereals, oil seeds, sugar, eggs, beverages and dairy products. Quota volumes can either be imported duty free or at a very low duty. In contrast, volumes exceeding certain quotas are often taxed prohibitively. For example, duties on a horse imported under the quota are SFr. 120.-, outside the quota the duties are SFr. 3834.-; for 100 kg of veal, the respective duties are SFr. 159.- versus 2212.-; and for 100 kg of carrots, SFr. 4.- versus SFr. 710.-.

The second core issue affects the lifting of *domestic support measures* affecting production and/or international trade. This includes product-specific price supports or sales supports, price schedules, price regulations, and price and acceptance guarantees. Exceptions include internal support measures and direct payments that do not or only little affect foreign trade, and the production of agricultural products.[23]

Agriculture lobbyists view today's direct payments to farmers as reimbursement for general economic services. The Swiss Federal Council was somewhat more frank in connection with the Uruguay Round by pointing out very clearly that the WTO Agriculture Agreement was a fundamental reorientation of agricultural protection at the borders, but that it effected only limited reduction of agricultural protection. The Swiss government stated its intention to gradually replace internal supports with product-specific direct payments.[24]

The third essential provision of the WTO Agriculture Agreement is a 21 per cent decrease in *export subsidies* in 36 per cent of export volume. No reduction in export volume is required for processed products such as cheese. Since about 80 per cent of cheese exports go to member states of the EU, this WTO regulation will cause no great changes. For these exports, the subsidies will end completely over the course of five years (following entry into force of the agreement) in accordance with the bilateral EU agreement.

In early 2000, the WTO members began talks to continue the agricultural trade reform process. In Phase 1 (2000–March 2001), WTO members, then numbering 140, submitted 125 reform suggestions for expansion of import quotas, decreasing agricultural duties and export subsidies, and food safety and health. The WTO Ministerial Conference on November 2001 accepted the reduction of export subsidies without, however, 'prejudging the outcome of the negotiations'.[25]

8.3 Trade in industrial goods

8.3.1 Data and facts

As I have pointed out, agricultural policy knew a protectionist phase following the war and, although hesitantly, began to open up in the 1980s. In contrast, the Swiss government has always attempted to follow the most liberal foreign trade policy possible in the sector of commercial and industrial commodities. Despite this basic position, there is a gap between rhetoric and reality. Switzerland, like other countries, strove to protect its own economy via tariffs and non-tariff barriers in the area of migrant labour, credit and foreign exchange.

The *structure* of exports in this area has not changed significantly over the last decades. Chemical goods and machinery as well as precision instruments each account for 30 per cent of total exports, while watches make up less than 10 per cent. Among chemical products, pharmaceuticals, vitamins, diagnostics and, more recently, agrochemical products and flavourings are in demand. Machinery exports concentrate mainly on special machines and precision instruments. Jewellery exporting has experienced strong fluctuations. Various products, such as textiles, clothing, paper and paper goods, leather, plastics and vehicles make up the remaining 30 per cent.

The composition of *imports* shows wider variation than do exports. Electrical and non-electrical machines and appliances stand in the first place with about 25 per cent of total imports, followed by chemical products with 15 per cent, vehicles with somewhat over 10 per cent and foodstuffs with 7–8 per cent.

Geographically, Swiss foreign trade is strongly focused on the EU market. At present, in terms of value, 60 per cent of Swiss exports go to the 15 EU member states. Nearly 80 per cent of imports to Switzerland come from the EU. Within the EU, Germany is Switzerland's most important trading partner, followed by France and Italy, each having about an equal share. The figures for industrialised countries outside the EU (United States, Canada, Australia, New Zealand, South Africa) are approximately 17 per cent of Swiss exports and 10 per cent of imports. With less than a half per cent of Swiss exports and imports, the EFTA states Norway and Iceland have little trade importance. The so-called threshold countries take about 10 per cent of Swiss exports, developing countries 6 per cent and transition countries about 4 per cent. Switzerland's imports from threshold, developing and transition countries are about 4 per cent in each case.

For the EU, Switzerland is a relatively important trading partner, although the difference in market size accounts for a smaller proportion of EU trade. Of total EU exports (excluding trade within the EU) 20 per cent (in value) go to the United States, its most important trading partner, while 6 per cent is exported to Switzerland and 4 per cent to Japan. Goods imported to the EU show the following make-up: 22 per cent from the United States, 10 per cent from Japan and 8 per cent from Switzerland. For the United States, trade with Switzerland is of only modest importance. About 1 per cent of US exports go to Switzerland; *Swiss imports* make up 1 per cent of the US imports.

8.3.2 General tariff policy

Switzerland uses tariffs as its main foreign trade instrument. Subsidies and quotas, in contrast to trade in agricultural products, find no direct application. With the adoption of the 1848 Federal Constitution, customs authority was transferred from the cantons to the Confederation. Recognising Switzerland's strong ties with foreign countries, Art. 25 of the constitution stipulated that duties on vital materials required by industry be kept low. The first duty was levied in 1850. The average duty was 2–3 per cent of the value of goods. Duties were also raised on foodstuffs as well as raw materials and finished products. The objective was to cover the administrative costs of the new federal institutions and to reimburse the cantons for lost revenue. These payments were terminated in 1874 when the Confederation took over military expenditures previously carried by the cantons. At this time transit duties and, with a few exceptions, export duties were also lifted.

The following decades saw a steady increase in the level of tariffs, partly as a consequence of the government's increased need for funding as it expanded its activities and partly in order to have a 'cushion' when entering into future trade negotiations. The increases were contained in the tariff revisions of 1884 and 1887, and in the General Tariff of 1902. At that time the Federal Council also issued a Federal decree authorising it to levy retaliatory duties on countries that excluded Switzerland from Most-Favoured-Nation treatment.

The precarious state of national finances after the First World War made another tariff revision necessary. As a result of monetary depreciation, the average level of pre-war duties sank from an average of 4–5 per cent to 2 per cent. In 1921, therefore, the duties were raised based on weight.[26] As fate would have it, as a result of deflation the average duty rate rose to over 20 per cent. Now out of control, the tariff became a truly protectionist trade instrument both in the area of agriculture and industry.

The 1921 Tariff was the basis for Swiss policy during the approaching Depression, the *Second World War*, and the beginning of the post-War period. In the 1930s, Switzerland moved away from its traditional tariff policy and, in response to growing protectionism and foreign exchange controls, it also initiated import and export restrictions. Imports were positioned to serve exports, which means that Switzerland favoured imports from countries that demanded its own products.[27] After the *Second World War*, retaliatory duties, compensation and quotas were suspended. In 1959, a new tariff policy came into force. The customs tariff today goes back to the year 1986. Switzerland has to this day retained weight duties.

Table 8.2 shows the customs duties levied in the WTO (or GATT) and in Switzerland from 1946 to the year 2000. After the end of the *Second World War*,

Table 8.2 Average tariffs of GATT/WTO and Switzerland (as a percentage of import value)

Year		**GATT/WTO Excluding oil**	**Switzerland**	
			Excluding oil tariff*	**Including oil tariff***
1946			7.5	8.4
1947	Foundation of the GATT	40		
1949	Annecy	30		
1950			8.7	10.3
1950/51	Torquay	25		
1956	Geneva	23		
1960			8.1	11.0
1960/62	Dillon Round	15		
1964/67	Kennedy Round	10		
1970			4.3	8.5
1973/79	Tokyo Round	6.4		
1980			1.6	5.2
1990			1.2	4.4
1986/93	Uruguay Round	4.0		
2000			0.9	5.0

* Fiscal tax.

Source: Bundesamt für Statistik, *Statistisches Jahrbuch der Schweiz* (Zürich: NZZ Verlag, annual); WTO, *News of the Uruguay Round* (Geneva: WTO publications services, 1994), p. 11; WTO, *Market Access: Unfinished Business*, Special Study 6 (Geneva: WTO publications services, 2001), p. 7ff.

the average tariff lay at about 40 per cent, and as a result of the eight rounds of negotiations it dropped to an average of 4 or 5 per cent. In Switzerland, the average duties were 7.5 per cent (excluding petrol tax) and 8.4 per cent (including petrol tax). This means that in the immediate post-War period, Switzerland was a low-tariff country compared to other industrial nations. Swiss tariffs increased lightly in the 1950s but dropped sharply in succeeding decades. Today, customs duties stand at 0.9 per cent (excluding petrol tax) and 5.0 per cent (including petrol tax).

The fact that Switzerland's tariffs were so much lower than EEC tariffs in the 1950s was one of the reasons why the Federal Council did not approve EEC membership. The higher tariff rates that Switzerland would have had to adopt might, according to the Federal Council, have endangered its economic position worldwide. Raw materials would have become more costly, and Switzerland would have been less competitive.[28]

In addition to import duties levied on weight rather than on value, there are three additional aspects of the Swiss tariff that are unique. *First*, Switzerland levies a uniform rate on certain imported products independent of their source. With this, Switzerland expands the reductions negotiated within WTO to include all countries, regardless of whether they are WTO members. The other industrial countries make a distinction between 'contractual' rates for products exported by WTO members or by countries to which the Most-Favoured-Nation principle is applied and 'autonomous' rates for products from other countries.

Second, Swiss import duties on leather, leather products, shoes, textiles and clothing – in comparison to duty rates of other industrialised countries – are higher than average to protect domestic industries from low-wage developing nations.[29]

And *third*, nearly half of the Swiss duties are under 1 per cent of the value of the imported goods. Such low duties make no fiscal sense, as the administrative costs probably exceed revenues. Moreover, duties this low do not allow any leeway for future negotiations with other countries. Finally, duties at a level of less than 1 per cent have no protective function. In fact, the only things that the import regulations protect are the jobs of administrators.

8.3.3 Preferential tariff policy

Nowhere did the North–South conflict become so apparent as in the GATT negotiations. Due to persistent pressure by non-industrialised nations (People's Republic of China, India and Lebanon), GATT Art. XVIII (Governmental Assistance to Economic Development) was revised in the late 1940s. Also the Haberler Report addressing the problems facing developing countries in their trade was published in 1958, and Part IV of the GATT treaty (on Trade and Development) was adopted in 1965. The Generalised System of Preferences (GSP) was introduced in 1971 to promote economic growth in developing countries. It was applied internationally by creating the so-called 'Enabling clause' in 1979.[30]

Official pronouncements show that for Switzerland, the North–South conflict did not constitute an issue right after the Second World War. At that time Switzerland was not a member of the GATT and therefore did not participate in the discussions on the reshaping of world trade. Also, Swiss duties on commodities originating in developing countries (made up of about 80 per cent raw materials and 20 per cent industrial goods) were very low in comparison to other countries. Textiles and agricultural products were the exception. In 1963 Switzerland lifted customs duties on tea, maté and tropical woods and, in 1970, on textiles made of silk and cotton. Moreover, outside the GATT, Switzerland extended the trade concessions negotiated in the Kennedy Round to developing countries.

Initially, together with the United States, Norway and Sweden, Switzerland rejected the GSP as laid down in the Haberler Report and during the UNCTAD conference of 1964, the objection being that preferences would weaken the GATT Most-Favoured-Nation principle.[31] When the United States changed its position with the Declaration of the Presidents of America in 1967 in Punta del Este, Uruguay, Switzerland announced that it would also apply special treatment to developing countries. It now argued that the Most-Favoured-Nation principle had not allowed these countries to increase their share of world trade sufficiently. For that reason, Switzerland would conform to preferential tariffs for developing nations.

The Federal Council was authorised to determine preferential goods, the countries to which preferences would be applied, the amount of tariff reductions and to revoke the concessions should economic circumstances dictate the necessity.[32] The Federal Council issued the preferential tariffs scheme in September 1971, to enter into force in March 1972 for a duration of ten years. This was followed by the decree of 1981, which has undergone numerous revisions and, in its present form, will remain effective until February 2007.

The Federal Council's message pertaining to preferential tariffs now in force explains that in total, preferential tariffs affected about 2 per cent of Swiss commodity imports. The preferential goods come mainly from threshold countries, foremost from India, Brazil, Argentina, Chile and South Korea.

Switzerland's preferential policy differs from that of the other industrialised countries, in that the same advantage is accorded to all developing countries. The United States and the EU, in contrast, base the generalized system of preferences on need and withdraw GSP benefits when a country no longer requires the benefit to maintain satisfactory export levels. For example, GSP benefits were withdrawn from Malaysia in 1997 given the country's economic growth.[33]

8.3.4 Export risk insurance

A further instrument of trade promotion is the Swiss Export Risk Insurance (Exportrisikogarantie, ERG). The ERG is a fund organised by the Federal Government, the revenue of which is financed by risk-related premiums paid by exporters. If the ERG's revenues are not sufficient to cover damages, necessary funds can be made available by the government, subject to interest charges and repayment.

Parliament approved a Federal Council ordinance in March 1934 that was intended to promote exports by means of a governmental risk insurance scheme.[34] The underlying reasons for the plan were the sharp decreases in exports at the time and the fact that the city and canton of Zurich, as well as all countries neighbouring Switzerland, already had similar export promotion instruments. The Council's ordinance foresaw the ERG as a scheme of the Federal Government to cover a certain percentage of export risks from exchange rate losses, monetary transfer problems (impossibility of payment due to government currency measures) as well as a foreign government's inability or refusal to make payment. The guarantee was originally extended to exporters free of charge. At the time, the guarantee was restricted to the machine industry whose association took on the programme's administration.

Initially the Federal Government participated with 10 million SFr., an amount that rose two years later to 30 million and four years later to 50 million. At the start, the ERG guaranteed 35 per cent of the losses incurred. This percentage was increased in the late 1930s to 50 per cent, and in some cases to 80 per cent. In the first five years, the ERG insured exports to the amount of 60 million SFr., which was equivalent to just under 5 per cent of total exports. Actual payments for losses made up just 1 per cent of the approved funding.

In 1939, the previously temporary measure was transformed into a permanent institution, and the guarantee was extended to cover goods and services outside the machine industry. In contrast to funds in other countries, Switzerland maintained a distinction between private and political risks: private risks were to be carried by the exporter, whereas political risks, which are harder to recognise and carry, were to be the subject of government insurance.[35]

During the *Second World War*, Swiss exporters made heavy use of the ERG. Nearly half of all exports were insured under the ERG. Loss payments made up about 1 per cent of the approved funds. By 1947, a sharp increase in payments and the government's shortage of funds made it necessary to introduce insurance premiums. With the premiums flowing in, wartime deficits of 8.5 million SFr. could be paid off by 1951. In the following 30 years, the ERG became a self-supporting fund.

Starting in 1982, ERG funds were no longer sufficient to cover damages. The reason was that foreign exchange risks had been included in the ERG following the collapse of the fixed exchange rate system in 1973. The ERG discontinued coverage of foreign exchange risks in 1985, and since the early 1990s, the ERG has been able to build up reserves covering possible liabilities.

The ERG today is based on the federal legislation enacted in 1958 and the relevant executive ordinance of 1998. Together the law and the ordinance issue guarantees in the following areas:[36]

- *Political risk* caused by events abroad such as war, revolution and civil unrest. Terrorist attacks are not mentioned specifically in the law or the ordinance and thus are not covered in all cases.
- *Transfer risk* making it impossible for customers to make payment due to currency measures implemented by governments. The customer has deposited the equivalent payment in local currency, but the central bank cannot make the necessary currency available.
- *Delcredere risk*, or risk of inability or unwillingness to pay by the customer. This risk is covered by the ERG – in contrast to funds in other countries – for public-law customers or so-called public utilities only and not for private customers unless a bank (national or private) accepted by the ERG is liable for the payments.
- *Manufacturing risk*, which occurs when goods cannot be shipped abroad due to political events or government measures in the country concerned.

Risks of private parties, costs resulting from deficiency claims and transport and foreign exchange risks are not insurable. As already mentioned, foreign exchange risks were covered between 1973 and 1985. Today such risks must be insured privately.

ERG insurance covers at most 95 per cent of the commodities' value as well as possible interest on credit loans. The insurance premium (in percentages of the export value covered) depends on the duration of the guarantee as well as the nature of the trading partner. The short-term is defined as less than two years, the medium-term lasts from two to ten years, OECD-guidelines permitting.

In recent years, the ERG covered 2 to 3 billion SFr., or 2 per cent of the value of total Swiss exports. Payments for losses currently range from 100 to 200 million SFr., which is about 2 per cent of the funding budgeted each year. At present, almost 5 billion SFr. of the approved 8 billion funding is budgeted for exports to Turkey, Mexico, China, Iran and Indonesia. For the ERG, the most important export branches are machinery and chemicals.[37]

In summary, thanks to its self-supporting funding, the ERG fits seamlessly into Swiss economic policy and accords with the WTO agreements (elimination of export subsidies for industrial products). While complaints that Switzerland was indirectly subsidising the secondary sector through the ERG may have been justified in the 1940s and 1970s, this is certainly not the case today. However, the beneficial effects of the ERG on foreign trade should not be overestimated. The new guarantees each year lie at approximately 2 per cent of the value of Swiss exports, and they are restricted mainly to a few product areas and to just a few countries.

8.3.5 Export promotion

A further instrument of Swiss foreign trade policy is export promotion, which in the past was achieved in co-operation with the Swiss Office for Trade Promotion (OSEC). In 1927, two private promoting institutions in Zurich and Lausanne joined to form the OSEC. Their objectives were to help and advise exporters, mainly small- and medium-sized enterprises. OSCE was meant to provide contacts to experts in the export markets, to organise or assist with trade fairs and special events and to undertake promotional information and media work to advertise Switzerland as an exporter in the importing countries.

The Federal Government supported the OSEC for decades with annual funding of about 10 million SFr., an amount not to exceed 45 per cent of OSEC's total expenditures. For the OSEC, this meant a constant struggle between maintaining its own economic efficiency and promoting exports. In addition, any marketable offers opened the office to the criticism that it was competing with the private sector. However, if it restricted its activities to unprofitable general services, it endangered its own financing.

In a survey of the food export industry in the first half of the 1980s, Swiss export firms across the board made an unfavourable assessment of the OSEC's export promotion activities. The companies surveyed reported in particular that the organisation lacked the required expert knowledge and, in addition, did not have the necessary authority and instruments.[38]

The Federal Law on the Promotion of Trade of 6 October 2000 established a new legal foundation for Swiss export promotion. The orientation now consists in authorising the Federal Government to commission one or more institutions to provide export promotion services for a period of not more than four years. The first mandate was awarded to the OSEC. Today, the government contributes annual funds of about 14 million SFr.

The law demands that the provider of export promotion focus particularly upon small- and medium-sized enterprises. As a complement to private initiatives, export promotion is to identify potential export market segments and business opportunities, to position Switzerland as an internationally competitive exporter and to aid Swiss exporters to tap into foreign markets. The mandated export promotion organisation, at present still the OSEC, informs and advises Swiss exporters, promotes Swiss-made goods and services abroad, and organises delegations of exporters to trade fairs. In the fall of 2001, the OSEC, now renamed *Business Network Switzerland*, began creating export promotion facilities called Swiss Business Hubs in Vienna, Milan, Stuttgart, Chicago and Bombay.[39]

should take special consideration of the economic circumstances of countries of the Third World. These priorities will continue to guide trade policy in the future and will, in view of the events of 11 September 2001, be given even more weight.

These concluding comments make it clear that Swiss foreign trade policy in the next 50 years will not resemble that of the last 50 years.

Notes

1 Hans Christoph Binswanger and Reinhardt Büchi, 'Aussenpolitik und Aussenwirtschaftspolitik', in Alois Riklin, Hans Haug and Hans Christoph Binswanger (eds), *Handbuch der schweizerischen Aussenpolitik* (Bern/Stuttgart: Paul Haupt, 1975), p. 696.
2 Art. 54 Swiss Constitution.
3 *Botschaft des Bundesrats an die Bundesversammlung betreffend ein Bundesgesetz über die internationale Entwicklungszusammenarbeit und humanitäre Hilfe vom 19. März 1973*, p. 21. See also Binswanger und Büchi, 'Aussenpolitik und Aussenwirtschaftspolitik', p. 693.
4 Compare works on political economy, such as Robert E. Baldwin, *Trade Policy in a Changing World Economy* (Chicago: University of Chicago Press, 1988).
5 For the statistical sources, see Bundesamt für Statistik, *Statistisches Jahrbuch der Schweiz* (Basel/Zürich: Verlag Neue Zürcher Zeitung, annual); GATT, *International Trade* (Geneva: annual 1952–94); Schweizerische Bankgesellschaft, *Die Schweizerische Wirtschaft 1946 bis 1986* (Zürich: 1986); Seco, *Die Volkswirtschaft, Aktuelle Wirtschaftsdaten* (Bern: monthly); WTO, *Annual Report* (Geneva: WTO publications services, annual since 1994).
6 Right after the foundation of the Confederation in 1848, international trade policy was part of Section II of the Department for Railroads and Trade. In 1882, the Section was turned into an office for 'Commerce' as part of the Department of Agriculture and Trade. One year later, the office was called 'Commerce, Industry and Trade'. In 1888, the same office was transferred to the Foreign Ministry and again called 'Commerce'. In 1896, the office was returned to the original department now called 'Department for Commerce and Industry'. In 1914, parliament decided to once again attach the office of 'Commerce' to the Foreign Ministry, but the solution lasted for only three years, because a newly elected member of the Federal Council demanded that the office be returned to the department handling economic matters. This was legally confirmed in 1923. For more details on the period between 1848 and 1975, see Binswanger and Büchi, 'Aussenpolitik und Aussenwirtschaftspolitik', p. 697f.
7 In German 'Volkswirtschaftsdepartment'.
8 In German 'Bundesamt für Aussenwirtschaft' (BAWI).
9 www.seco-admin.ch
10 Figures emanating from Schweizerischer Bauernverband (SBV), *Statistische Erhebungen und Schätzungen* (Brugg: annual), chapter on exports and imports; see also Bundsamt für Statistik, *Statistisches Jahrbuch der Schweiz*.
11 For a summary of the arguments raised against EEC membership, see BBl 1960 I 859f (EFTA-Botschaft).
12 BBl 1965 III 478f (Third Report on Agriculture.).

13 By signing the GATT as a non-member of the IMF, Switzerland would have assumed similar responsibilities as regular IMF members.

14 For a summary of the critcism raised, see Emil Küng, *Das Allgemeine Abkommen über Zölle und Handel* (Zürich: Polygraphischer Verlag, 1952), p. 83, 88ff.

15 'The Government of the Swiss Confederation reserves its position with regard to the application of the provisions of Art. XI of the General Agreement to the extent necessary to permit the Government...to apply import restrictions pursuant to...of the Federal Law of 3 October 1951 as well as to the legislation concerning the alcohol and wheat monopolies...' Protokoll Ziff. 1 lit. b, published in: GATT, *Basic Instruments and Selected Documents (BISD)*, 7th Supplement (Geneva: 1959), p. 20.

16 At issue were the easing of import restrictions favouring Swiss exports of various types of cheese, medicinal powdered milk and cattle in exchange for increased import quotas for wines, sausages, flower and canned ham, as well as tariff reductions, on flour for baby formula and sweetmeats or confectionery. Compare BBl 1967 II 623ff.

17 BBl 1979 III 284ff. The protectionist agricultural policy pursued by Switzerland, the EC and Japan was not affected by the multilateral agreements on cereals, dairy products and meat negotiated during the Tokyo Round.

18 BBl 1972 II 668.

19 Luxemburg Declaration of 9 April 1984, published in *EFTA-Bulletin*, Nr 2 (Geneva: 1984), p. 6ff.

20 BBl 1992 IV 740 and 1034.

21 GATT, 'Ministerial Declaration on the Uruguay Round of 20 September 1986', in GATT, *Basic Instruments and Selected Documents (BISD)*, 33rd Supplement (Geneva: 1987), p. 19ff.

22 For an account of the origins and contents of the agricultural agreements, see Richard Senti, *WTO, System und Funktionsweise der Welthandelsordnung* (Zürich: Schulthess, 2000), paragraphs 200, 216ff und 1001ff.

23 Exemption from the Reduction Commitments, Annex 2 of the Agreement on Agriculture, in WTO, *The Results of the Uruguay Round of Multilateral Trade Negotiations, The Legal Texts* (Geneva: WTO Secretariat, 1995), p. 56.

24 Eidgenössisches Volkswirtschaftsdepartement, *Die Uruguay-Runde des GATT*, Vernehmlassungsunterlagen vom 25. Mai 1994, Bern, p. 56.

25 *WTO*, Doc WT/MIN(01)/DEC/W/1 (Ministerial Declaration), 14 November 2001, Geneva, paragraph 13. The proviso was submitted by the EU as a complement to the draft declaration which mentioned 'reductions of, with a view to phasing out, all forms of export subsidies'.

26 In a system of weight tariffs, the depreciation of a currency affects a decrease in import duties, this in contrast to a tariff on value.

27 For a history on the Swiss tariff, see Alfred Bosshardt, 'Zollpolitik', in Schweizerische Gesellschaft für Statistik und Volkswirtschaft (ed.), *Handbuch der schweizerischen Volkswirtschaft*, Bd. II (Bern: Benteli, 1955), pp. 671–8; Eidgenössische Oberzolldirektion, *Das schweizerische Zollwesen* (Bern: 1948), pp. 9ff and 172ff.

28 BBl 1960 I 860 (EFTA-Botschaft).

29 Compare Sections VII, XI and XII of the Swiss Commodity Tariff.

30 For an account of the North–South conflict in the course of the GATT history, see Richard Senti, *WTO, System und Funktionsweise der Welthandelsordnung*, paragraphs 393ff and 590ff.

31 BBl 1971 I 701.

32 BBl 1971 I 703.

33 For a comment on the selectivity of preferences, see Richard Senti, *WTO, System und Funktionsweise der Welthandelsordung*, paragraphs 596ff.

34 For a history of ERG, see Silvio Arioli, '50 Jahre Risikogarantie (ERG)', *Die Volkswirtschaft* (Oktober 1984), pp. 727–31; ERG, *Die ERG im Überblick* (Zürich: April 1989); Rolf M. Jeker, 'Die schweizerische Exportförderung', in Alois Riklin, Hans Haug and Raymond Probst (eds), *Neues Handbuch der schweizerischen Aussenpolitik* (Bern/Stuttgart/Wien: Paul Haupt, 1992), pp. 889–904.

35 See *Botschaft zum Erlass des BG über die ERG*, in BBl 1939 I 189.

36 For details, see ERG, *Die ERG im Überblick*, p. 3ff; see also Jeker, 'Die schweizerische Exportförderung', p. 893f.

37 See ERG, *Jahresberichte* (Zürich: various annual reports).

38 Richard Senti, *Analyse des schweizerischen Nahrungsmittelexportes* (Grüsch: Rüegger, 1985), pp. 57ff and 75.

39 OSEC, *networknews*, Nr 1 (Oktober 2001), p. 1.

40 GATS Art. 1 Abs. 2. For a useful discussion of the services terminology, see Matthias Koehler, *Das Allgemeine Übereinkommen über den Handel mit Dienstleistungen (GATS)* (Berlin: Duncker & Humblot, 1999), p. 27ff.

41 Bundesamt für Statistik, *Statistisches Jahrbuch der Schweiz*, various years.

42 For a survey of the various agreements and decisions, see Kurt Schiltknecht, *Beurteilung der Gentlemen's Agreements und Konjunkturbeschlüsse der Jahre 1954–1966* (Zürich: Dissertation, 1969).

43 EG-Kommission, *Die Vollendung des Binnenmarkts* (Luxemburg: Amt für Amtliche Veröffentlichungen der Europäischen Gemeinschaften: 1986), paragraphs 95–132.

44 GATT, *Basic Instruments and Selected Documents (BISD)*, 33rd Supplement (Geneva: 1987), p. 28.

45 WTO, *The Results of the Uruguay Round of Multilateral Trade Negotiations, The Legal Texts*, p. 325ff. Exceptions are contained in lists called the negative and positive lists.

46 For details see Richard Senti, *WTO, System und Funktionsweise der Welthandelsordnung*, paragraphs 1266ff.

Index